The Syntax of American Sign Language

Language, Speech, and Communication

The Syntax of American Sign Language

Functional Categories and Hierarchical Structure

Carol Neidle
Judy Kegl
Dawn MacLaughlin
Benjamin Bahan
Robert G. Lee

The MIT Press
Cambridge, Massachusetts
London, England

Second printing, 2001

© 2000 Massachusetts Institute of Technology

This book was set in Times New Roman by Asco Typesetters, Hong Kong and was printed and bound in the United States of America.

Library of Congress Cataloging-in-Publication Data

The syntax of American Sign Language : functional categories and
  hierarchical structure / Carol Neidle ... [et al.].
    p. cm. — (Language, speech, and communication)
  Includes bibliographical references and index.
  ISBN 978-0-262-51221-3
  1. American Sign Language—Syntax. I. Neidle, Carol Jan.
II. Series.
HV2474.S994 2000
419—dc21   99-15444
                                                          CIP

Contents

Preface

The American Sign Language Linguistic Research Project (ASLLRP) has involved a number of researchers working together over several years to explore the structure of American Sign Language. We initially came together fortuitously, as fascination about the syntactic structure of ASL spread from one to another of us. We began by surveying the existing literature, and we quickly became convinced that, from both a theoretical and a data-oriented perspective, much work remained to be done. Although we did not realize it at the time, we now see that we were embarking on a major enterprise that was to be shaped by the different talents and viewpoints of the members of our group. Perhaps most important has been the direct involvement of a native Deaf signer as a full-fledged member of the research team. Our approach has emphasized the importance of careful data collection and analysis and also of providing public access to the critical data we discuss. This book does not just represent a summary of our major findings thus far; it also reflects an ongoing endeavor that seeks to build a coherent picture of the syntactic organization of ASL.

The research has benefited greatly from support provided by the National Science Foundation (grants SBR-9410562, SBR-9729010, SBR-9729065, SBR-9513762, EIA-9809340, EIA-9809209, and IIS-952898). Information about this project is available at http://www.bu.edu/asllrp/. This site also contains information about obtaining digitized video corresponding to key grammatical examples discussed here.

Some of the questions considered in this book are addressed in greater detail in other ASLLRP publications, many of which are also available over the Internet. (Information about downloading available publications and video examples can also be found at our Web site.) In this book, such publications are cited by the authors' initials. For example, Bahan, Kegl, MacLaughlin, and Neidle 1995 is cited as BKMN 1995.

We are grateful for help from many people. Special thanks go to Carol Padden, Marco Haverkort, and Tarald Taraldsen for offering detailed comments on earlier versions of this manuscript and for sharing their ideas. We would also like to thank Debra Aarons, who participated in some of the early ASLLRP research (and who is now investigating related issues in South African Sign Language); Debbie also provided helpful comments on a draft of this book. In addition, we are grateful to Arto Anttila, Tiffany Beechy, K. P. Mohanan, Tamara Rae Neuberger, Neil Smith, and Martha Tyrone for their comments. We would like to acknowledge the following people, who have contributed in various ways to the research reported on here: Kim Hand Arrigo, Luce Aubry, Norma Bowers, Annmarie Buraceski, Sue Burnes, Guglielmo Cinque, Dennis Cokely, Barbara Eger, Thorstein Fretheim, Jimmy Challis Gore, Ken Hale, Lars Hellan, Bob Hoffmeister, Jack Hoza, Riny Huybregts, Richard Kayne, Jaklin Kornfilt, Seth Minkoff, Marie Philip, Vieri Samek-Lodovici, Peggy Speas, Höski Thráinsson, Patty Trowbridge, Laurie Tuller, and Bencie Woll. Finally, we wish to offer special thanks to Anne Mark for her invaluable editorial assistance.

Chapter 1

Introduction

Recent research on the syntax of signed languages has revealed that, despite some interesting modality-specific differences, signed languages are organized according to the same fundamental principles as spoken languages. This book presents some of the major findings of the American Sign Language Linguistic Research Project (ASLLRP), which has sought to investigate the organization and distribution of functional categories in ASL.[1]

Signed languages provide a unique and illuminating type of evidence about functional projections of a kind not available in spoken languages. Simultaneously with manual signing, crucial syntactic information is expressed nonmanually, by specific movements of the face and upper body. We argue that, in many cases, such nonmanual marking is, in fact, a direct expression of abstract syntactic features. Moreover, the distribution and intensity characteristics of these markings provide information about the location of functional heads and the boundaries of functional projections. In this book, we focus on tense, agreement, and *wh*-constructions and discuss the relevance of the ASL data to general issues in syntactic theory.

As we will show, the evidence from ASL is useful for evaluating a number of recent theoretical proposals, concerning, among other things, the status of syntactic agreement projections and constraints on phrase structure and the directionality of movement. ASL has thus far not been among the languages that have received careful consideration in relation to such issues. Most of the data-oriented work on ASL sentence structure has been descriptive in nature. Theoretically oriented research has been much more limited and has been hindered by methodological complexities involved in the study of signed languages.

1.1 Organization of the Book

In chapter 2, we address important methodological considerations related to the sociolinguistic setting in which ASL is used. The context for ASL linguistic research is somewhat unusual, in that only about 5–10% of the users of this language have acquired it natively (from Deaf signing parents).[2] There are important issues surrounding the collection and interpretation of data from a language used by a linguistically oppressed minority, particularly in a situation where very few of the linguists who have studied the language are themselves native signers. In this chapter, we discuss such issues and describe the methodology used for the syntactic research reported in the rest of the book.

In chapter 3, we describe those aspects of ASL relevant to the material that follows, providing basic information about the organization of the language. In particular, we consider several ways in which space is used linguistically. We show that there is a systematic spatial instantiation of φ-features (i.e., agreement features) and that locations in space are used for expressing determiners, pronominals, possessives, and reflexives/ emphatics, as well as agreement inflections on lexical items. Another interesting and important feature of ASL is the use of nonmanual markings in parallel with manual signing.[3] Such markings are used for a variety of purposes—for example, to express syntactic features, such as +neg and +wh. In this chapter, we present the generalizations that govern the distribution of the nonmanual correlates of syntactic features, to be examined more closely in later chapters.

In chapter 4, we briefly address issues of word order. Although earlier claims about ASL suggested a great flexibility in word order, we show that much of this variation can be accounted for in terms of material occurring in CP-external positions, including topics, tags, and right-dislocated pronominals. It is essential to identify such clause-external elements before undertaking an analysis of the word order internal to CP. In the chapters to follow, we present arguments for different aspects of the tree illustrated in figure 1.1. This tree represents the basic clausal structure that has emerged from our research.[4]

In the next three chapters, we consider specific aspects of ASL structure. In chapter 5, we examine tense and agreement in the clause. We show that, despite the widespread belief that ASL lacks grammatical tense, ASL does, in fact, have lexical tense markers. Although many of

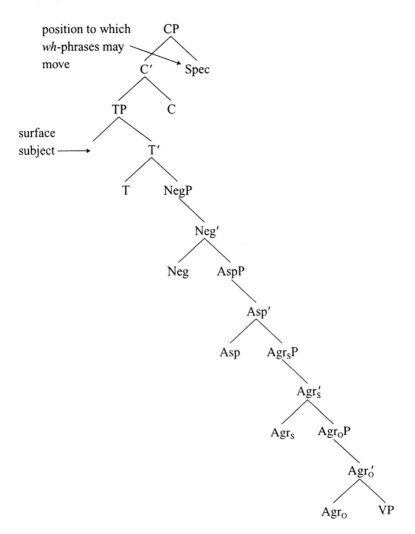

Figure 1.1
Skeletal structure of CP

these are related to adverbials, tense markers are distinct from adverbials; they differ in their articulatory and distributional properties. We argue that tense (T) heads the ASL clause. In this chapter, we also investigate agreement in transitive and intransitive clauses. We show that there are nonmanual correlates of subject and object agreement. By postulating distinct subject and object agreement projections (Agr$_S$P and Agr$_O$P), we can account for the distribution of these nonmanual markings of agreement in terms of the same generalizations established in chapter 3. Recognition of the existence of nonmanual instantiations of agreement allows for a better understanding of several related phenomena. For example, we show that null arguments are systematically licensed by an overt expression of syntactic agreement—either manual or nonmanual—and thus we provide a unified account of the distribution of null arguments in ASL.

In chapter 6, we turn to the structure of determiner phrases. First, we argue that (despite prior claims to the contrary) ASL has both definite and indefinite determiners, and that such determiners occur in initial position. We show that the nonmanual expression of agreement features within DP is comparable to what is found in the clause. Specifically, possessive constructions provide evidence for two distinct agreement projections, analogous to subject and object agreement projections in the clause. Nonpossessive DPs display patterns of agreement similar to those found in intransitive clauses. Such parallels lend support to a growing body of crosslinguistic evidence suggesting that noun phrases and clauses are quite similar in structure.

In chapter 7, we examine question constructions, focusing in particular on wh-questions. We show that when wh-movement occurs, the wh-phrase moves rightward to the specifier of CP ([Spec, CP]). Evidence for this analysis comes from both basic word order facts and the distribution of nonmanual syntactic markings associated with the +wh feature. We argue against several alternative proposals involving leftward wh-movement. Thus, we claim that Universal Grammar must allow for rightward movement.

In chapter 8, we discuss a number of interesting consequences of the analyses presented in earlier chapters. The evidence from ASL provides striking support for several aspects of linguistic theory that have been argued for on the basis of very different considerations.

• The presence of visually detectable syntactic markings over phrasal domains confirms the existence of a hierarchically organized phrase structure, and in particular, of the kind of clause structure proposed in Pollock 1989 and subsequent work.

• Such markings also support the fundamental distinction between lexical and functional projections (as nonmanual syntactic markings spreading over c-command domains are associated only with the latter).

• Careful study of nonmanual syntactic markings may be helpful in resolving uncertainties about the existence of particular projections. For example, there has been some controversy about the status of agreement, and whether agreement features are contained in independent functional projections. Evidence that φ-features have essentially the same status as other abstract syntactic features can be adduced from the fact that, like +neg and +wh, agreement features have nonmanual syntactic correlates that exhibit a comparable distribution. Furthermore, the distribution of nonmanual correlates of agreement in both IP and DP supports the postulation of agreement projections in both domains.

• Nonmanual syntactic markings provide evidence for the boundaries of specific functional projections. For example, there is overt evidence relevant to the ordering of functional categories such as Agr and T, independent of the presence of lexical (manual) material in functional heads.

• The evidence from ASL also supports a feature-checking approach, such as proposed in Chomsky 1993, whereby features are found both on lexical items and in functional heads. In ASL, both the abstract feature located in a functional head (such as +wh) and the matching feature located elsewhere (such as in a *wh*-phrase) are visibly detectable.

Thus, we show how the visible evidence of syntactic features available from nonmanual syntactic marking in ASL sheds new light on syntactic structure and current controversies.

1.2   Reporting of Data

The notational conventions used for glossing ASL examples are discussed briefly in chapter 2 and summarized in the appendix. As will be discussed, the gloss representations used to present ASL example sentences in written form omit important details about what was signed. This has made claims about data presented solely via glosses in the ASL literature difficult to evaluate. We are making digitized video corresponding to the key grammatical constructions discussed in this book accessible both over the Internet and on CD-ROM. Further details are available at http://www.bu.edu/asllrp/.

1.3 Theoretical Backdrop

We adopt many, but not all, of the theoretical assumptions of Chomsky's Minimalist Program (Chomsky 1995b). Readers unfamiliar with this framework are referred to other sources.[5] We suggest in subsequent chapters that the results from ASL provide evidence *against* a few specific proposals found within Chomsky 1995a.

It should be noted, however, that much of our work is not theory-dependent, in the sense that the essential findings could be restated within other frameworks. The theoretical ideas that are fundamental to our analysis include some that have been an integral part of generative grammar for decades, such as the structural relation of c-command[6] and syntactic movement processes like those that result in *wh*-phrases moving to [Spec, CP] (the canonical landing site for *wh*-phrases in, e.g., Chomsky 1986 and much recent work).

With respect to X-bar theory (Bresnan 1976, 1977; Chomsky 1970; Jackendoff 1977), we adopt the more traditional view of phrase structure (as in, e.g., Chomsky 1986) rather than the view whereby intermediate-level projections are eliminated (as in, e.g., Chomsky 1994, 1995a). We do rely on a distinction between lexical and functional projections, the latter housing syntactic features such as those that have been postulated in recent work, including +wh, +neg, and ϕ-features (see Rizzi 1991; Haegeman 1995; Chomsky 1993).[7]

We also argue, on the basis of language-internal evidence, for an articulated IP structure (as proposed by Pollock (1989), Chomsky (1991), and others). We suggest, moreover, that the nonmanual correlates of syntactic features in ASL support the existence of various specific functional projections as well as the general "feature-checking" approach taken in Chomsky 1993 and subsequent work, although again, the findings presented here are not inherently incompatible with other possible approaches to the same phenomena within competing syntactic frameworks. We do believe, in any event, that the data from signed languages provide important linguistic evidence that any theory of Universal Grammar must accommodate.[8]

Chapter 2
Methodological
Considerations

2.1 Introduction

Whereas ethnographies typically begin with a chapter devoted to methodological considerations, it is rare to see an entire chapter devoted to such concerns in a book on linguistic theory. However, this is especially warranted in relation to the study of ASL. We often stress the parallels between signed and spoken languages, but it is important to understand that unique demands are placed upon linguists studying signed languages. Users of signed languages represent a particularly unusual linguistic community, in that 90–95% (Schein and Delk 1974) of them do not share a primary language with their parents and siblings. For this and other reasons, one must pay special attention to sociolinguistic considerations and methodological details when engaging in linguistic research on signed languages.

In this chapter, we examine some of the factors that can complicate ASL research specifically and signed language research in general. We begin by discussing several aspects of the sociolinguistic setting in which signed languages are used that have implications for the conduct of linguistic research. In the rest of the chapter, we focus on the collection, analysis, and reporting of sign language data.

2.2 Sociolinguistic Context

Signed languages, such as ASL or LSF (*la langue des signes française*, French Sign Language), are natural languages. Such languages have developed as a natural way of communicating in Deaf communities and have evolved over generations. Contrary to one popular misconception, there is no single, universal signed language. As with spoken languages,

distinct signed languages are found in different parts of the world. Moreover, individual signed languages exhibit dialectal variation. For example,
there are regional variations in the use of ASL.[1]

In reality, the language used by the deaf population in the United
States is extremely heterogeneous, although ASL is the primary language
used within the Deaf community. In this section, we address some of the
factors that contribute to variations in language use, including the status
of ASL as a minority language and the family background, educational
experience, and cultural identification of individual signers.

2.2.1 ASL as a Minority Language

Like other minority languages, a signed language coexists with a dominant majority language.[2] An interesting situation results, however, when
the minority and majority languages are of different modalities (visual vs.
aural), particularly when the majority language is in a modality that is not
fully accessible to the minority language community.

One striking result of the contact between the signed and spoken language communities is that artificial sign systems have been created by (a
few) educators (and used by many others) in an attempt to manually code
the majority language and thereby represent that language in the visual-
spatial modality. These artificial sign systems are not natural languages;[3]
nonetheless, native signers are likely to have had varying degrees of exposure to such systems, as will be discussed in section 2.2.3. Thus, native
signers, in addition to their primary language, have command over other
communication systems that incorporate the majority language to some
extent. They also have some knowledge of the majority language itself, at
least in its written form. As a result of this language interaction, many
deaf people are bilingual to differing degrees.

Thus, like other minority speakers, signers engage in code-switching. In
this situation, "code-switching" refers to the use of a signed form of the
majority language in alternation with native sign language structures.[4]
Whenever multiple linguistic systems coexist in the repertoires of a language community, code-switching is a natural consequence. Speakers
evaluate each other's language use/competence and adjust their own communication accordingly. Native signers, consciously or unconsciously,
often engage in code-switching when interacting with nonnative signers or
when conversing about topics they typically discuss in English.[5]

Within communities that are, to some extent, bilingual, code-switching
occurs so naturally that attempts to artificially suppress it can cause

breakdown in communication.[6] Researchers must be keenly aware of code-switching because it may affect an informant's linguistic output. Ideally, circumstances should enable informants to keep code-switching to a minimum when the researcher is collecting ASL data (as will be discussed in section 2.3).

Another consequence of minority language status is that the language of Deaf people is often undervalued by the majority community. This attitude is reflected in policy decisions (particularly those related to education) and social arrangements that may lead Deaf people to internalize negative attitudes about their signed language, causing them to view it as inferior to the majority spoken language.[7]

Within this context, language choice by individuals is further influenced by family background, educational experience, and cultural identification. These factors will be addressed in turn.

2.2.2 Family Background

Deaf people are linguistically unique in that fewer than 5–10% are born into Deaf families that use a signed language and thus can acquire language naturally by exposure from infancy in the family setting. For those deaf children fortunate enough to be born to Deaf signing parents who provide native language input from birth, the acquisition of a signed language, such as ASL, parallels the acquisition of any other human language in a comparable environment (Hoffmeister 1982; Meier and Newport 1990; Newport and Meier 1985; Newport and Supalla 1980; Petitto 1983; Petitto and Marentette 1991).

However, even those children who are born into families that sign may not be receiving input from native signers. The educational experience of the parents (discussed in section 2.2.3), along with their attitudes about language, can influence the type of linguistic behaviors they use with their children. Nonetheless, as has been noted in the literature (e.g., Singleton 1989; Singleton and Newport 1987, 1994; see also Ross and Newport 1996), since innate language expectations drive acquisition and supplement inadequacies in external language input, native language acquisition often occurs even with impoverished input.

Whereas a deaf child from a Deaf, ASL-signing family will normally acquire native fluency in ASL, the deaf child of hearing, English-speaking parents has no guarantee of acquiring any native language at the usual age. Since the child does not have sufficient access to the spoken language input provided by the family to acquire that spoken language,[8] his or her access to language depends largely on circumstances of exposure to signed language in childhood, not only within the family, but also within an educational setting.[9]

2.2.3 Educational Experience

The environment in which deaf people are educated can have an enormous impact on their linguistic knowledge and attitudes. The settings in which deaf children are educated vary.[10] In the United States, for many years the primary locus of deaf education was residential schools. Deaf children attended classes and lived in dormitories, usually quite a distance away from their families.

ASL was generally not used in the classroom;[11] rather, instruction focused on teaching the majority spoken language. Much time was spent on amplification of the child's residual hearing, along with intensive speech therapy. This educational philosophy, known as the oral method, dominated deaf education in the United States from the early 1900s until the late 1970s.

By the mid 1980s, many schools had switched to using visual communication systems in the classroom, and this has remained the predominant methodology in deaf education. As mentioned earlier, many schools have relied on artificial signing systems, invented by educators in an attempt to teach deaf children the grammar of the majority language. Many school systems have required a coded form of the spoken language to be used in classrooms instead of a natural signed language.

Concurrently, since about 1985, there has been a slow movement toward a bilingual-bicultural approach to deaf education, teaching ASL as a first language and (written) English as a second language. Thus far, however, relatively few schools have adopted this approach.

In any case, even when there was no instruction in ASL, deaf children in residential settings were exposed to ASL through interaction with older Deaf children or peers who came from Deaf signing families. Since formal ASL instruction was not a part of the curriculum, it was *outside* the classroom that most of the sign language learning occurred.[12] As a consequence, for the many deaf children who were not exposed to ASL until later in childhood, language acquisition was delayed. In contrast, deaf children who were not exposed to sign language at home but who entered such schools at a sufficiently early age had a significant advantage with respect to language development.[13]

In the early 1970s, several laws were passed in the United States that affected the educational placement of deaf children. Since that time, there has been a trend toward mainstreaming (also called "inclusion")—that is, placing deaf children in a public school setting with hearing children, rather than in a residential school. Sometimes, the deaf child is placed with a sign interpreter or with other support staff.[14] Often, there are only one or two deaf children in such programs. The effect has been to isolate deaf children from appropriate sign language models (as well as Deaf adult role models in general), further inhibiting acquisition of ASL. Nonetheless, it should be noted that the majority of deaf people—even those educated in oral schools—eventually develop some competence in ASL (or a pidgin form of signing developed from contact between ASL and English (Lucas and Valli 1990b)) once they become members of the Deaf community, where ASL is clearly the primary language.

The lack of adult models can also lead to internalization of negative attitudes about the status of ASL. Given that the dominant language in a child's life may be some form of English, the child may grow to perceive any form of ASL as somehow inferior and therefore may reject such signing in favor of a more English-like form.

2.2.4 Cultural Identification

ASL exists as a minority language in the context of a dominant, English-speaking, American culture. Most signers do, however, share a minority Deaf culture (Charrow and Wilbur 1975; Cokely and Baker-Shenk 1980; Lane, Hoffmeister, and Bahan 1996; Padden and Humphries 1988); their cultural identification is intimately related to their attitudes about language and to their own language use (among other things).

In America, Deaf people often actively seek out Deaf peers in both personal and professional arenas. Deaf people have their own sports teams, social clubs, and political advocacy groups. Involvement in such organizations helps to strengthen the bonds in the community. In such settings, the language used is primarily ASL.[15] Thus, the use of ASL in one's personal and professional life serves as a marker of one's cultural identity.

2.2.5 Summary

Native signers of ASL are exposed to a variety of forms of signing on a daily basis. Since more than 90% of Deaf people are nonnative signers and have very different linguistic histories, native signers are accustomed to communicating with people whose signing departs, to differing degrees, from native ASL. Native signers are thus quite tolerant of varying forms of signing and have a great deal of experience in understanding signing somewhat different from their own. They also regularly engage in code-switching behaviors, adjusting their own signing in response to the language used by their interlocutors.

The language we seek to study in this book is the language that native ASL signers use naturally when signing with each other. It may already have become obvious that isolating this variety of language for linguistic study poses a challenge for researchers. In the next section, we discuss considerations relevant to collecting data on this language.

2.3   Data Collection

Both naturalistic data and elicited grammaticality judgments are of great use in formulating and testing linguistic hypotheses. Each has advantages and limitations.

2.3.1   Naturalistic Data

Naturalistic data, uninfluenced by the research questions under consideration, are likely to yield interesting grammatical forms not yet analyzed. In addition, a corpus of naturalistic data can serve as a database in which to test hypotheses about current analyses of specific grammatical constructions. It also allows researchers to examine the types of contexts in which particular constructions naturally occur, and to observe a variety of constructions that might not appear in more constrained settings.

A good source of naturalistic data is communication observed in everyday contexts. However, when such situations are videotaped, they tend to involve more formal or specialized registers. Even semicasual conversations staged in front of a camera will be influenced to some extent by the camera's presence.

Many commercially available tapes of ASL also exist. These videotapes include conversations, interviews, stories, narratives, and autobiographies, among other genres of communication. Many (but not all) of these tapes show native signers. Still, knowing that one's communication is being permanently documented affects one's production to some degree. The signer being videotaped may be more sensitive to word choice and grammar, so the language sample may represent a more monitored form of language than might be found in free conversation.

2.3.2   Elicited Data

As useful as naturalistic data may be, testing of linguistic hypotheses, including predictions of both grammaticality and ungrammaticality, requires use of elicitation. In the collection of sign language data, many variables need to be taken into account. Researchers must take great care in the selection of informants and the procedures used in data collection.[16]

2.3.2.1   Informants   Given the factors just discussed affecting language use and preference, it is essential for this kind of research to be conducted with the help of native signing informants—that is, Deaf people who grew up with Deaf signing parents and who identify with the Deaf community. However, native language ability is not enough.

As with any linguistic informants, it is important that sign language informants have a certain level of metalinguistic ability.[17] It is essential that informants be able to introspect about language and have enough confidence in their own language use to be assertive about their judgments. Often, the forms elicited and judgments required involve subtle nuances. When elicitation becomes confusing or unclear, or when responses may be compromised, a linguistically sophisticated informant is frequently the first to recognize this. In addition, a linguistically sophisticated informant can often assist in adequately constraining contexts for complicated forms and in eliminating confounding factors introduced by nonoptimal lexical choices and other grammatical aspects of sentences constructed for testing.

The sociolinguistic factors discussed in the previous section can have a direct impact on the elicitation process. Several considerations relevant to conducting elicitation are discussed in the sections that follow.

2.3.2.2   Grammaticality Judgments versus Situational Acceptability
Given the variety of forms of signing that occur, ranging from native ASL to less native forms, it is important that the informant understand what kind of judgment is being sought. For studies of native ASL (of the kind undertaken in this book),[18] the linguist is interested not in forms that the signer might be able to understand, or even forms that the signer might imagine some other deaf person signing, but forms that are part of that native signer's grammar, forms that the signer would use in interactions with other native signers.

A signer might report that a sentence is acceptable because it is *understandable*, not because it is necessarily *grammatical*. As previously mentioned, the heterogeneity of the signing community has engendered a high degree of tolerance for nonnative signing. Signers are exposed to a range of signed forms, anywhere from what a native signer would produce to highly pidginized forms that a native signer would never produce. All these forms are broadly called ASL, and thus may be considered to be ASL by the informant. When asked to judge sentences, native signers tend to be accepting of forms that are interpretable,[19] even forms that they themselves would not sign.

Thus, it is essential that informants actually sign the utterance about which they will be offering a grammaticality judgment, rather than merely evaluating an utterance as signed by someone else. There are several very important reasons for this.

• Sometimes, a signer who has just declared a stimulus sentence to be acceptable discovers, when trying to sign it, that he or she would not sign it that way. This is a crucial distinction.

• Signers may repeat the sentence back in a slightly different form, sometimes correcting a subtle source of ungrammaticality, such as an inappropriate facial expression. They may or may not have consciously noticed the inappropriateness, since they are accustomed to interpreting nonnative signing, but they invariably correct such things when signing back a sentence that they report to be grammatical. (Since linguistically significant facial expressions are central to the grammar of ASL, as will be discussed in subsequent chapters, the ways in which the signer's production may differ from the target can be very significant.)

• If the sentence to be judged is signed by a nonnative signer, informants may not understand what aspect of the utterance they are being asked to judge. Invariably, the nonnative signer's signing is imperfect; there may be imperfections of which the researcher is not aware. It may be hard for an informant to distinguish between sentences that should be considered grammatical and those that should be considered ungrammatical, when they are all defective to some degree.

The researcher should videotape elicitation sessions. For the reasons just mentioned, it is important to analyze the actual sentence that is judged, as signed by the informant, and not assume that this directly corresponds to the stimulus sentence. A signer may make several attempts at the target sentence before making a final judgment on grammaticality.

These attempts may vary, and only the sentence for which a judgment is clearly offered should be included in the data set.

Several other factors, discussed in section 2.2.1, may confound grammaticality judgments. For example, the presence of English in the repertoires of bilingual ASL/English signers has repercussions for acceptability judgments. There are many ways in which this can bias the forms that an informant produces and accepts in an elicitation session.

• If an informant has native command of ASL as well as a high degree of English proficiency, it is possible that grammaticality judgments could become confused. It is vital that the informant be able to distinguish what language he or she is discussing at any one time. An informant might think he or she is giving a grammaticality judgment for an ASL sentence, but actually be offering a judgment that reflects knowledge of English.

• Signers may also display an English bias in reporting their judgments of ASL sentences. In particular, signers who have internalized the notion that ASL is somehow inferior to English may exhibit a preference for ASL structures that are close to English structures over perfectly grammatical ASL structures that differ from English.

• English bias may be intensified in formal situations (such as an elicitation session), where there is a tendency for signers to use more English-like structures.

• Interference from English may take a slightly different form. Some signers may fundamentally mistrust their own judgments about ASL; this is particularly true for signers whose command of English is limited and who have internalized a negative attitude about ASL from educational or other experiences. They may report as most acceptable those sentences that run counter to their intuitions, reflecting the attitude that "good" ASL is ASL that is most English-like (which may, ironically, mean nothing more, in certain instances, than *unnatural* signing).

• Conversely, the signer may feel, consciously or subconsciously, that the *less* English-like a sentence is, the more authentically ASL it is. This may lead signers to err in the other direction, rejecting perfectly acceptable ASL utterances that have word order similar to English, in favor of equally grammatical ASL variants whose structures differ from those found in English.[20] Sometimes, when asked to produce ASL, a signer may systematically avoid typological features or true borrowings from English into ASL that, via historical accretion, have become part of the language.

The elicitation should be designed in such a way as to minimize the potential for interference of these kinds.

2.3.2.3 Elicitation Setting and Procedures It is widely known that informants can change their linguistic production in artificial elicitation situations (Labov 1989). Since researchers work in academic environments and Deaf people have often had negative experiences in educational settings, researchers must be aware that such settings can affect linguistic production.

An important consideration is the relationship of the elicitor to the informant. Most ASL researchers are not native signers. As stated earlier, code-switching is common when native signers converse with nonnative signers. Therefore, it is possible that informants may code-switch (consciously or not) because a nonnative signing researcher is present or because of how they perceive a researcher's language ability.

The manner in which language is elicited can also have an effect. If data are elicited via English, for example, then English influences are more likely to color the results.

In order to elicit sentences that would naturally occur in ASL, among native signers, and eliminate many conditions that trigger code-switching, researchers should pay special attention to the way they set up the elicitation task. There are various techniques that can be used and important considerations to keep in mind.

• Ideally, the elicitor should be a native signer, although in practice, this may not always be possible. A native signing elicitor will maximize the chances for a natural kind of interaction. However, even this alone may not be sufficient. In a formal context such as that of elicitation, the presence of a researcher with a Ph.D. and academic status (even if that researcher is Deaf) could still result in a more English-like form of signing than would naturally occur.

• When it is not possible to have a native signer as elicitor, an elicitor with near-native signing skills is the next best thing, if a Deaf or hearing researcher has this level of language proficiency. If the researcher lacks near-native proficiency, elicitation may be conducted via an interpreter with near-native ASL competency.[21]

This will reduce the alteration of natural communication that might otherwise occur with a nonnative signer (such as the informant slowing down the signing artificially or code-switching). In any event, the researcher must have good receptive skills in order to conduct the elicitation intelligently.

• Ideally, nonnative signing, hearing people should not be present at the elicitation. Even when elicitation is conducted by a native signer, the presence of hearing people in the room may provoke code-switching behaviors and English-like signing.

• Depending on the nature of the data being collected, the presence of more than one Deaf signer at the elicitation session may also assist in creating maximally natural interactions. We have found this useful for eliciting questions, for example.

• The signer should be asked to imagine signing with a person with whom he or she communicates predominantly in ASL. This person can be used as an exemplar of an interlocutor when discussing the grammaticality of various constructions. For example, if this person is the signer's Deaf mother, the signer might be asked, "How would you sign this if you were signing with your mother?"

In our own experience, we have worked with informants who at first reported a sentence as acceptable, but, upon further probing, provided revealing information about the situations in which they might actually sign the given type of sentence. For example, one signer, when asked to sign and judge a sentence, reported it to be acceptable. She was then asked when she would sign that sentence. Her response was that she might use that structure with a teacher, for example, but never with her Deaf mother. This kind of information is extremely important in evaluating an informant's responses. It is therefore important for the elicitor not only to set up the situation optimally, but also to probe deeply, rather than settling for simple grammaticality judgments on given sentences.

2.3.2.4 Involvement of Deaf Researchers A native (or near-native) signing researcher is best able to detect when some aspect of the data elicitation is going awry. It is thus extremely valuable to have a Deaf researcher involved in all aspects of the research, not only in the elicitation process itself, but also in the selection and evaluation of potential informants, and, of course, in the interpretation and analysis of data, as will be discussed below.

2.3.2.5 Practices to Avoid Certain methodologies that have been used by ASL researchers are particularly problematic and should be avoided. For example, elicitation of data via English (or other spoken language) stimuli may skew the results. As previously mentioned, interference from English is a very real possibility in elicitation of ASL data. Care must be taken to minimize such interference. Nonetheless, there are researchers who elicit data by presenting written English sentences and asking that they be signed (see, e.g., Wilbur and Patschke 1998, 279, fn. 3).

Other methodological practices also give cause for concern. Lelièvre (1996), for example, reports an instance where signers were asked to produce signs in LSQ (*la langue des signes québécoise*) in particular orders without regard for the grammaticality of the resulting string and where the judgments offered by signers were systematically ignored. An excerpt of her observations (Lelièvre 1996, 199), both in the original French and in translation, is provided here.

Une expérience que nous avons vécue dernièrement au Centre de recherche illustre bien le problème de l'élicitation. Il s'agissait de travailler sur l'ordre des signes dans des phrases interrogatives simples et complexes. L'élicitation se faisait à partir de phrases composées seulement de gloses (de façon à éviter partiellement l'influence du français). Cependant, il était strictement défendu aux personnes qui signaient de changer l'ordre des gloses.

L'exercice était vraiment très difficile. Il s'agissait de lire les gloses puis d'imaginer des situations qui peuvaient [*sic*] être liées à une structure composée de ces gloses. Il fallait disposer en imagination les personnages et les objets dans l'espace et penser aux mouvements les plus adéquats pour représenter la phrase. Lorsque le tableau était prêt dans notre tête, nous le reproduisions en signes dans l'espace. Mais le corpus recueilli n'était pas fiable car la situation n'était pas naturelle. Le fait d'être obligé de respecter un ordre de signes donné est très perturbant. Lors de l'enregistrement, nous sentions un malaise et c'est en visionnant la vidéo que nous avons réalisé que la langue n'était pas naturelle.

Translation:

A recent experience at the Research Center provides a good illustration of the problem of elicitation. We were working on the order of signs in simple and complex interrogative sentences. The elicitation was done based on sentences made up only of glosses (so as to partially avoid the influence of French). However, the signers were strictly forbidden from changing the order of the glosses.

The exercise was really very difficult. It was a question of reading the glosses and then imagining situations that could be linked to a structure made up of these glosses. It was necessary to situate the characters and objects in space, in our imagination, and to think of the most adequate movements to represent the sentence. When the picture was ready in our mind, we would reproduce it in signs in space. But the corpus that was collected was not reliable because the situation was not natural. The fact of being obliged to respect a given order of signs is very disturbing. At the time of the recording, we felt uneasy and while watching the video we realized that the language was not natural.

The article from which the preceding excerpt was taken appeared in a volume edited by Colette Dubuisson (in whose laboratory Lynda Lelièvre worked) and Denis Bouchard. The article that immediately follows in that volume, by Dubuisson herself, is also revealing with respect to the interactions between researcher and informant in that context. Consider the following excerpt (Dubuisson 1996, 210), again presented first in the original and then in translation:

De façon générale, il faut être particulièrement attentifs à informer les informateurs sourds. Il faut les informer à cause du manque d'accès à l'information mentionné plus tôt et aussi à cause du fait que la peur d'être tenu à l'écart des décisions qui les concerne [sic] est presque devenue héréditaire. Ceci crée certaines difficultés dans une équipe où chaque informateur travaille avec plusieurs chercheurs qui ont chacun leur sujet de recherche. Toujours pressés par le temps, parce qu'il faut produire pour avoir des subventions et avoir des subventions pour produire, les chercheurs se contentent souvent de poser des questions à l'informateur en donnant, si celui-ci insiste, une explication globale du problème, puis ils retournent poursuivre leur réflexion. L'informateur lui aussi poursuit sa réflexion, avec l'information dont il dispose et trouve souvent des explications qui ne sont pas les plus appropriées. Il se fait des idées et c'est ce qu'il faut absolument éviter. Paradoxalement, ce sont les informateurs qui manquent d'information. Ils ont de la difficulté à se contenter du rôle qui consiste à répondre aux questions qu'on leur pose, ils veulent aussi comprendre pourquoi on les leur pose et avoir une part de collaboration plus active dans les recherches.

Translation:

In a general way, one must pay particular attention to informing the deaf informants. It is necessary to inform them because of the lack of access to information mentioned earlier and also because of the fact that the fear of being kept out of the decisions that concern them has practically become hereditary. This creates certain difficulties in a team where each informant works with several researchers who each have their subject of research. Always pressed for time, because it is necessary to produce in order to get grants and to have grants in order to produce, researchers must often be satisfied with asking the informant questions, giving, if the informant insists, a global explanation of the problem, and then they return to pursue their reflection. The informants also pursue their reflection, with the information at their disposal, and often find explanations that are not the most appropriate. They get notions into their head and that is what one must absolutely avoid. Paradoxically, it is the informants who lack information. They find it difficult to content themselves with the role that consists in answering questions asked of them, they also want to understand why the questions are being asked and to have a more active collaborative role in the research.

Data collected under such circumstances, where feedback from the informants is systematically ignored, are suspect.

Thus, it is clear that the way in which the elicitation task is set up is inseparable from the nature and reliability of the results that are obtained. This is something the researcher must always consider carefully.

2.3.2.6 Differences in Data Reported in the Literature   As will be apparent in subsequent chapters, there is a surprising inconsistency in the grammaticality judgments reported in the ASL literature for even simple constructions. Some of this may arise from the factors discussed thus far. For example, results may be skewed by the use of nonnative informants (not all researchers have restricted their study to native signers) or by other methodological problems just described. It is, however, extremely difficult to draw any conclusions about the sources of varying judgments, because data are generally not made available for public inspection and scientific scrutiny. This problem will be addressed in section 2.5.

Some of the reported variation may also be attributable to dialectal or idiolectal differences among signers. In fact, Mougeon and Nadasdi (1998) make the case, basing their argument on a study of Franco-Ontarian adolescents residing in minority Francophone communities, that minority languages are particularly susceptible to high degrees of variation: "We discuss the Labovian view of the speech community against the backdrop of data from research on variation in minority languages. While members of the same speech community normally share a set of norms for social and stylistic constraints on variation and normally share a common grammar, a number of researchers have noted that some speech communities include subgroups of speakers that are unlike the rest of the community in that they observe different rules or constraints on variable usage" (p. 40). Substantial variation does indeed occur within minority languages, and it is likely that there are some "discontinuities" in ASL of the type that Mougeon and Nadasdi describe.

However, it is again difficult to determine the extent to which dialectal and idiolectal differences may account for some of the contradictory reports of grammaticality judgments in the literature. The difficulty here is the general practice of pooling judgments from multiple informants. In our research, we have attempted to study the systematicity of individual signers' judgments across a range of constructions, and we believe that this is an important methodological consideration. Given the range of variation found in ASL (which has yet to be examined carefully), mixing judgments from different signers is likely to obscure the phenomena under study. Ideally, analyses should be based on multiple single-subject studies rather than on randomly pooled judgments from different informants.[22]

2.3.3 Summary

Both naturalistic and elicited data are essential to linguistic research. In both cases, the researcher needs to be acutely aware of potential sources of experimental error. With respect to elicitation, the following considerations are essential:

• careful selection of Deaf native signing informants, with appropriate language background and cultural identification and the ability to make metalinguistic judgments of the kind required for linguistic research,
• elicitation carried out via native or near-native signing elicitors,
• attention to setting up the context of the elicitation and the task itself in such a way as to minimize the likelihood of code-switching and interference from the majority language and to maximize natural signing,
• insistence that signers actually sign for themselves the sentences on which they are to make grammaticality judgments, and
• video recording of data.

The analysis and dissemination of results are discussed in sections 2.4 and 2.5.

2.4 Transcription and Analysis of Data

After data are collected, the next step is transcription and analysis. As already mentioned, it is essential that data be recorded on videotape, so that they can be studied carefully.

Traditionally, researchers have relied on written transcription as part of the process of analyzing signed language data. Given that there is no direct way to represent in written form complex manual and nonmanual behaviors, certain conventions have developed to enable at least partial representation of signed language utterances.[23] The gloss system used in this book, documented more completely in the appendix, is commonly used in the literature, although different researchers' notational conventions vary somewhat. In general, for the representation of manual ASL signs, the nearest English translation of the ASL sign (or some English translation) is written in capital letters. Since there is no one-to-one correspondence between English words and ASL signs, this means that the English glosses often do not permit complete recoverability of the manual signs in the reported utterance. In addition, English glosses do not convey any information about the internal phonological and morphological structure of the ASL sign. Occasionally, however, diacritics may be appended to the beginning or end of the gloss to provide limited phonological or morphological information. For example, there are notations for indicating aspectual and agreement inflections, one-handed versus two-handed variants of signs, stressed or emphatic articulations, and so on.

As will be discussed in chapter 3, signed languages make critical use of nonmanual expressions (gestures of the face or upper body) in parallel with manual signing. Such expressions are indicated in transcriptions by a labeled line drawn over the manual signs with which a marking is coarticulated, where the label identifies the marking. We provide one example to illustrate a typical written representation.

$$\overline{\qquad\qquad\text{neg}\qquad\qquad}$$
(1) JOHN$_i$ NOT $_i$BLAME$_j$ FRANK$_j$
    'John does not blame Frank.'

In this example, the names JOHN and FRANK are actually finger-spelled,[24] although we do not indicate fingerspelling of names explicitly in our glosses in this book.[25] The negative expression consisting in part of a side-to-side headshake (discussed in chapter 3) extends over the indicated signs. The subscripts indicate subject and object verb agreement (also discussed in chapter 3).

The focus and degree of detail of the transcription will, of course, depend on the nature of the research questions being investigated. There are inevitably many behaviors, some of which are or may be linguistically significant, that are omitted from any given transcription.[26] In some cases, because the language has not yet been fully analyzed linguistically, it is unclear which behaviors have linguistic significance. Inevitably, some important information may be omitted—intentionally or unintentionally —by a transcriber. Therefore, any transcription represents, at best, partial information about what was signed, and it is essential, in the course of analysis, to refer directly to the videotape and not rely solely on a written transcription.[27]

Traditionally, the process of accessing data stored on videotapes has been cumbersome and time-consuming, to such an extent that this has seriously hindered linguistic research on signed languages in general. However, such research is now greatly facilitated by current technologies,

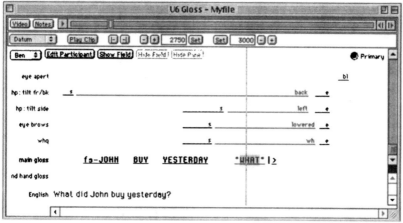

Figure 2.1
SignStream

such as digital video and tools for manipulating that video. Several types
of tools are now available or under development to allow linguistic an-
notation of video-based language data.[28] Such tools generally provide the
ability to search through examples and retrieve relevant utterances for
study, facilitating the testing of linguistic hypotheses (in finite amounts of
time). Access to a library of video data also makes it possible to test new
hypotheses over data sets that were originally collected with different research questions in mind.

One such tool under development by the American Sign Language
Linguistic Research Project (ASLLRP) is SignStream™.[29] SignStream

provides a single computing environment for manipulating video and linking specific frame sequences to simultaneously occurring linguistic events encoded in a fine-grained, multilevel transcription. SignStream allows the user to identify precisely the start and end frames of a particular linguistic behavior, and the program automatically aligns simultaneously occurring linguistic events on screen, as illustrated in figure 2.1. SignStream makes it possible to examine with accuracy the manual and nonmanual components of an ASL utterance as well as their interactions. This type of transcription contrasts with traditional glosses, where co-occurring items are aligned somewhat impressionistically. The availability of SignStream has led to advances in our own understanding of the distributional characteristics of nonmanual markings, which are of central importance to the grammar of ASL (as will become obvious in subsequent chapters).

Just as it is essential to have native signers involved in the process of data collection, so native signers should be involved in the analysis of video data. A native signer (and even a near-native signer who has grown up using the language) will be able to notice things that a nonnative signing researcher may overlook. In addition, a native signer may perceive meaningful facial expressions that the nonnative signing researcher might not identify (particularly since not all linguistically significant nonmanual behaviors have yet been identified). The native signer may also be able to provide subtle information about the meaning of particular constructions, as signed, or detect linguistic detail (such as phonologically assimilated signs) that might otherwise go unnoticed by the nonnative signing researcher.[30]

2.5 Data Dissemination

In this book, we use gloss notation to represent sample sentences. However, since we recognize the inadequacy of the notation, we are making video examples of the key grammatical constructions publicly available.

In general, we have made digital video examples of the constructions we discuss in our publications publicly accessible, although this has not been common practice in the field. Such accessibility is crucial, given the impoverished gloss representation that normally constitutes the only form for presentation of example sentences in the literature.

We also make it a practice to display video exemplars, signed by native signers, of the sentences under discussion when we present our results at conferences. This also is not generally done by ASL researchers. Many presenters, although not native signers, nonetheless sign the examples for the audience themselves. This is extremely problematic. Among other things, the prosody and use of nonmanual expressions, critical for an appropriate analysis of the construction under investigation, are unlikely to be replicated correctly by the researcher. Thus, the signed example can be misleading in crucial respects, often to such an extent that it does not reflect the actual data.[31]

It is essential that video examples of constructions claimed to be grammatical by researchers be inspectable.[32] In the absence of such video material, disputes about the facts of the language cannot be resolved. It is impossible to determine whether different informants genuinely disagree about the status of particular constructions, or whether other differences (including factors discussed in this chapter) may be able to explain the apparent differences in grammaticality judgments.

With current technology, it is easy to disseminate data in a format that is generally accessible.[33] Dissemination of data by ASL researchers is essential to the scientific advancement of ASL linguistics. The sharing of video data on signed languages would have at least as great an impact on our field as the introduction of the CHILDES database (MacWhinney 1995) has had on the study of child language acquisition.

2.6 Chapter Summary

The linguistic study of ASL poses special challenges. The difficulties in isolating the variety of ASL that is used by Deaf native signers in inter-actions with each other may help to explain some of the disputes about ASL data that will be described in subsequent chapters. In the absence of video examples of disputed sentence types, however, it is impossible to determine the extent to which differences in reported judgments may be attributable to methodological problems, misanalysis of data, or genuine dialectal or idiolectal variation.

Chapter 3
Language in the Visual Modality

3.1 Introduction

Since formal study of ASL dates back only to the 1960s, relatively little linguistic research has been conducted on it to date. Much of the early work focused on showing that ASL was indeed a real language, even though it is produced in a different modality from spoken languages. In this chapter, we examine some unique characteristics of language in the visual modality, starting with the basic articulation of signs and then focusing on the linguistic uses of space and facial expressions.

3.2 Articulation of Signs

The basic lexical unit in ASL is the sign. Whereas words in spoken languages are articulated by various movements and interactions along the vocal tract, signs in ASL are articulated by various movements of the hands in visible locations on or near the signer's body.[1] Some signs are produced with both hands; others are produced with only one.[2] Signers generally have a preferred hand for the articulation of one-handed signs; this same hand is used as the primary hand in the articulation of two-handed signs. This preference is usually based on whether the signer is right- or left-handed. The preferred hand is called the signer's "dominant hand." The other hand is referred to as the "nondominant hand."

Signed languages are built upon the same type of basic articulatory units as spoken languages. There are basic discriminatory units that compose and distinguish morphemes, as phonemes do in spoken languages. In fact, the term "phoneme" has been used in the recent literature to describe these units in signed languages. Morphemes are distinguished by differences in handshape, hand orientation, movement, and the

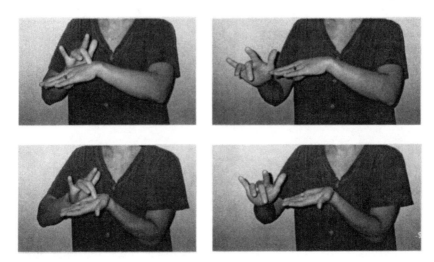

Figure 3.1
Minimal pair: signs for NUDE (top) and RUDE (bottom)

Figure 3.2
Minimal pair: signs for FATHER and FINE

location relative to the signer's body at which the morpheme is articulated. Thus, particular handshapes, orientations, movements, and locations are the equivalent of phonemes.[3] ASL phonemes are coarticulated
in the production of a given morpheme.[4] Each of these parameters of the
sign can be altered to yield (potentially) a new sign with a different
meaning. Thus, ASL has minimal pairs such as the ones illustrated in
figures 3.1 and 3.2.[5] The two signs in figure 3.1 are distinguished by
palm orientation; the two in figure 3.2 are distinguished by place of
articulation.

Figure 3.3
Vehicle classifier

Just as ASL phonology involves coarticulation of phonemes, so ASL morphology frequently involves simultaneous expression of morphemes. Although there are several morphological processes involving concatenation of morphemes in ASL, morphological inflection is often expressed by changes to the root sign. For example, a signer may convey aspectual distinctions (see Kegl 1981; Klima and Bellugi 1979; Newkirk 1979; Padden 1983, 1988) by producing the root sign with different types of repetitive movements.[6]

Another way in which the handshapes and movements interact productively involves the classifier system in ASL.[7] One type of classifier construction involves the interaction of a distinctive handshape and a movement/location root. The handshape consists of a representation of the salient properties of classes of referents (shape {round, twisted, rimmed, ...}, semantic class {small animal, human, vehicle, ...}, physical characteristic {permeable, solid, liquid, ...}, and so on). For example, a car can be represented by a particular handshape associated specifically with certain vehicles (illustrated in figure 3.3).[8] Verbs of motion involve displacement in space of the specific classifier handshape along a path representative of the relevant motion.[9]

Although the discussion thus far has focused on manual articulation, it is important to note that the head and upper body also express crucial information. Such gestures are referred to as "nonmanual markings" and generally occur in parallel with manual signing. Nonmanual markings serve a variety of functions, both linguistic and nonlinguistic. Here we discuss the linguistic use of nonmanual markings for expression of morphological information and abstract syntactic features. Nonmanual markings are discussed further in section 3.4 and in the remainder of the book.

The simultaneous expression of information in two channels, manual and nonmanual, is an important characteristic of languages in the visual modality (Baker 1976b). Study of nonmanual expressions, in relation to manual signs, provides important information about the syntactic structure of the language.

Although ASL is governed by the same organizational principles as spoken languages, there are essential differences based on the fact that ASL is produced in three-dimensional space. In the remainder of this chapter, we introduce issues related to the manifestation of language in the visual modality. In particular, we discuss not only the use of nonmanual markings to convey linguistic information, but also specific uses of space for representation of φ-features (i.e., agreement features) and temporal information.

3.3 Spatial Representation of Linguistic Information

ASL makes use of the three-dimensional signing space in a variety of ways. For an interesting overview of several systematic uses of space, see Emmorey in press. Here, we focus on a few aspects of the use of space that will be relevant in subsequent chapters for examination of syntactic features, such as tense and agreement features.

3.3.1 Representation of φ-Features

ASL and other signed languages make use of locations in space to represent referential entities.[10] Signers assign specific spatial locations to those referents that will be used throughout a stretch of discourse. Interlocutors point to the same locations when referring to those same entities. If the referent is physically present, the referent's real location will be used for this purpose. Otherwise, a location will be established in the signing space. Any other signers who wish to refer to the same referent will point to the previously established spatial location. For example, if Signer A assigns a fixed location in space on his or her left to represent John, Signer B, facing Signer A, accesses the same location (on his or her right) when referring to John,[11] as illustrated in figure 3.4.[12]

Subsequent reference to discourse entities can be accomplished by pointing (in a variety of ways) to the spatial locations that signers associ-

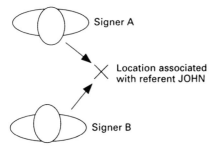

Figure 3.4
Sharing of referents in space

Figure 3.5
Articulation of pronoun

ate with referents. We claim that such use of spatial locations constitutes an overt instantiation of φ-features (specifically, person features)[13] associated with these referential entities, since these locations in space systematically participate in the same linguistic phenomena that involve φ-features crosslinguistically. First person is associated with the signer's body; nonfirst person referents are associated with distinct locations in the signing space.[14] Accessing these first and nonfirst person locations manually can accomplish a variety of linguistic functions, as described below.

3.3.1.1 Pronominals Articulation of a pronoun, glossed as IX, is accomplished by the index finger[15] pointing to the location in space associated with the person features of the intended referent (see figure 3.5).[16]

Figure 3.6
Articulation of possessive

Figure 3.7
Articulation of reflexive/emphatic

3.3.1.2 Possessives Articulation of a possessive marker, glossed as POSS, involves the open palm pointing to (and facing) the location in space associated with the person features of the intended possessor (see figure 3.6). See chapter 6 for more discussion of the ASL possessive construction.

3.3.1.3 Reflexives/Emphatics Articulation of a reflexive or emphatic is accomplished with a closed fist, thumb oriented upward, such that the pad of the thumb faces and points to the location in space associated with the person features of the intended referent (see figure 3.7).

Figure 3.8
ᵢGIVEⱼ: beginning and end of sign

3.3.1.4 Definite Determiners Articulation of a definite determiner involves the index finger pointing to the location in space associated with the person features of the intended referent. This is the same as the articulation of the pronoun form illustrated in figure 3.5 (which is not insignificant, as will be discussed further in chapter 6). It should be noted that the existence of determiners in ASL has been a subject of some controversy. (See BKMN 1995, MacLaughlin 1997, and chapter 6 for more discussion.)

3.3.1.5 Verb Agreement Spatial locations are also involved in the morphological expressions of subject and object agreement. Verbs in ASL differ in their ability to express agreement manually; locative and person-agreeing verbs inflect to show agreement whereas plain verbs do not (Padden 1983, 1988, 1990).[17] Person-agreeing verbs express (subject and/or object) agreement through spatial modification of the sign. For example, the agreeing verb GIVE moves between the spatial locations associated with the subject and the (goal) object (see figure 3.8).[18]

(1) JOHNᵢ ᵢGIVEⱼ MARYⱼ BOOK
    'John gives Mary a book.'

Thus, ASL makes use of a subject agreement prefix and an object agreement suffix,[19] accessing the same spatial locations used for pronominal reference. These affixes constitute the manual expression of the person features of the relevant argument(s).[20]

There are actually two forms that manual subject agreement marking may take. As just described, articulation of the marking may begin at the location associated with the subject. There is also an unmarked form in which the beginning of the sign is articulated close to the signer's body, similar in articulation to first person subject agreement marking (see the first picture of figure 3.9 below).[21] Although this form has been noted before (e.g., Baker and Cokely 1980d; Fischer and Gough 1978; Janis 1995; Kegl 1976a,b; Meier 1981, 1982; Padden 1983, 1988; Supalla 1996), such forms have generally not been analyzed closely (although see Supalla 1996). Some older work has described this form as involving the "citation form" of the sign (Baker and Cokely 1980d), although Bahan (1996) argues that this is incorrect. When verbs with this kind of articulation occur within utterances (i.e., not in isolation), they do display object agreement (as well as subject agreement with respect to number). Bahan proposes that this, in fact, represents an unmarked form of subject agreement, notated as "neutral" ("neu") in the examples.

(2) JOHN $_{neu}$GIVE$_j$ MARY$_j$ BOOK
     'John gives Mary a book.'

Object agreement marking may also take one of two forms, although here the distinction has a different basis. In our recent work, we have discovered a correlation between the spatial characteristics of the location associated with a referent and the definiteness of that referent. Definite referents are associated with points in space; indefinite referents are associated with areas, where the size of the area may vary in relation to the (un)identifiability of the referent (MacLaughlin 1997).[22] Morphological marking of object agreement is sensitive to this distinction.[23] With a definite object, object agreement marking is articulated in such a way that the verb moves to a more precise point in space that is associated with the object. However, with indefinite objects, agreement is associated with an area in space, which may be reflected in the articulation of the morphological object agreement marking. For example, in the manual articulation of the verb GIVE, the fingers and thumb, usually closed throughout the articulation of the verb, may spread as the verb approaches the location associated with the indefinite object (see figure 3.9). This spreading reflects agreement with an area in space.

(3) MARY $_{neu}$GIVE$_{indef}$ SOMEONE BOOK
     'Mary gives someone a book.'

Figure 3.9
$_{neu}GIVE_{indef}$: beginning and end of sign

Crosslinguistically, languages mark the information status of the object argument, in terms of definiteness and specificity, in a number of ways: through case morphology, form of the determiner, word order, or form of agreement marking (the last being characteristic of ASL). For example, in Turkish, objects with overt case morphology are specific; those without are (indefinite) nonspecific (Enç 1991). In Bulgarian, an indefinite object with an overt determiner is interpreted as specific; an indefinite object without a determiner is interpreted as nonspecific (Arnaudova 1996). Specificity of the object has also been claimed to play a role in "object shift," found in the majority of the Germanic languages (see, e.g., Bobaljik 1995; Corver and van Riemsdijk 1991; Holmberg 1986; Vikner 1991), and in other phenomena in Romance (Mahajan 1991).

To summarize, morphological subject and object agreement can be expressed using the same locations in space that are used for other expressions of person features. Subject agreement is manifested in one of two forms: a fully specified (marked) form and a neutral, underspecified (unmarked) form. On the other hand, the manifestation of object agreement is sensitive to information about the definiteness of the object.

3.3.1.6 Summary   In ASL, locations in space are used to express person features in the same types of linguistic constructions where φ-features are involved crosslinguistically.[24] Such locations are accessed in the expression of pronominals, determiners, possessives, reflexives/emphatics, and morphological verb agreement.[25]

The availability of space for this purpose allows for finer person distinctions than are traditionally made in languages that distinguish grammatically only among first, second, and third person. In fact, any number of "persons" can be associated with distinct spatial locations in ASL (although it is rare that more than a few are used within a single stretch of discourse). One consequence of the spatial representation of reference is that overt pronominal reference in ASL is essentially unambiguous.[26]

We have argued that person features are instantiated spatially in ASL. Moreover, characteristics of the spatial location associated with a referent are a function of the referent's (un)identifiability.

The pointing signs described here (determiner/pronominal, reflexive/ emphatic, and possessive marker) are also frequently accompanied by eye gaze to the same location to which the manual sign points. As will be seen in chapters 5 and 6, there is also a more general use of nonmanual markings (head tilt as well as eye gaze) to express syntactic agreement features.

3.3.2   Representation of Temporal Information

Locations in space may also be used to represent temporal information (see an interesting overview of such uses in Emmorey in press). For example, ASL makes use of an abstract "time line." This imaginary line locates the past behind the signer, the present close to the signer's body, and the future in front of the signer (Cogen 1977; Friedman 1975; Frishberg and Gough 1973; Jacobowitz and Stokoe 1988; Klima and Bellugi 1979, chap. 3). Many temporal adverbials are produced along this line.[27] For example, the signs YESTERDAY and TOMORROW are articulated with a backward and forward movement, respectively, as shown in figures 3.10 and 3.11. YESTERDAY is articulated with a closed hand with thumb extended, palm facing forward, the tip of the thumb making initial contact at the cheek and moving back along the jaw line to make contact close to the ear. In contrast, TOMORROW is articulated with a similar handshape but a different orientation, starting at the cheek and moving forward, away from the signer's body, with a pivoting downward motion of the wrist.

Along this time line, relative distance in front of and away from the signer's body may express relative degrees of distance in time from the present. The movement of some adverbs can be modified to express degree of distance from the present. For example, the sign FUTURE$_{adv}$ is articulated with an open hand at the side of the head, palm facing the signer's nondominant side and moving forward. The hand makes an arc-like movement, forward and away from the signer's body, conveying information about the distance in time: the further the hand moves from

Figure 3.10
YESTERDAY: beginning and end of sign

Figure 3.11
TOMORROW: beginning and end of sign

the signer, the further the indicated time is from the present (see figures 3.12 and 3.13).[28]

In addition to adverbials, other kinds of signs may be articulated with respect to the time line. Consider the verbs glossed as POSTPONE and PREPONE, which express a change in the time of an event, moving it either later or earlier than the previously established time. The temporal change is represented spatially (see figures 3.14 and 3.15). The nondominant hand is held in position while the dominant hand moves. If a signer is discussing an event that will be moved further into the future, the dominant hand moves away from the signer. However, if the event is to be moved back in time, the sign is articulated with a backward movement toward the signer. In these cases, the location of the nondominant hand

Figure 3.12
FUTURE_adv 'in the distant future': beginning and end of sign

Figure 3.13
FUTURE_adv 'in the near future': beginning and end of sign

expresses the original time of the event; the movement expresses the relative change in time, either past or present.[29] As with adverbials, relative distance in time may be expressed through variations in articulation. For example, POSTPONE may be articulated with a longer pathlength to indicate that the event will be moved far into the future.

3.4 Uses of Nonmanual Markings

Along with manual signing, ASL makes use of nonmanual markings, that is, movements involving the head and upper body. Such markings are used in a variety of ways in the language, both affectively and grammatically. For example, head and eye movements have linguistic uses not only

Figure 3.14
POSTPONE 'move later': beginning and end of sign

Figure 3.15
PREPONE 'move earlier': beginning and end of sign

at the sentence level, but also with respect to discourse processes. The eyes are crucially involved in turn-taking, and head movements often provide backchannel information (see, e.g., Baker 1976a, 1977; Baker and Padden 1978; Kegl and Poizner 1998). The various functions of the eyes and head can interact in complex ways, as different functions may be overlaid. The essential linguistic functions of facial expressions and movements of the head and upper body may explain why signers tend to focus visually on the area of the face, rather than on the hands, when communicating (see Bahan 1996, 48–49; Baker and Cokely 1980d; Siple 1978). In this section, we describe differences between linguistic and affective uses of facial expressions. With respect to linguistic uses, we focus in particular on several specific sentence-level phenomena.

3.4.1 Affective Markings

Like users of spoken languages, signers convey emotions through facial expressions. However, there is a significant distinction in signed languages between using such expressions for affective purposes and using them for linguistic purposes. Baker-Shenk (1983) noted articulatory differences between affective and linguistic markings with respect to the shape, contour, and timing of the markings, as well as differences in the facial muscles used in the two cases. In addition, neurolinguistic research on signed languages has demonstrated that affective expressions are processed in the right hemisphere, whereas linguistic expressions are processed in the left hemisphere (Bellugi et al. 1989; Corina 1989). Thus, impairment affects linguistic and affective processes differentially (see Kegl and Poizner 1991, 1997; Poizner and Kegl 1992). Further evidence for the distinction between the two types of nonmanual markings comes from both first and second language acquisition studies, which have revealed differences in the acquisition of similar facial gestures used for linguistic and affective purposes (McIntire and Reilly 1988; Reilly and Bellugi 1996; Reilly, McIntire, and Bellugi 1990). In sum, although signers can and do use facial expressions affectively, such uses are distinguishable from linguistic uses.

3.4.2 Lexical Markings

Some lexical signs have specific nonmanual markings associated with them (Baker 1976b; Liddell 1980). Such markings are an integral part of the signs with which they co-occur; these signs would be ill formed without the associated facial expression. The specific nonmanual markings associated with such lexical items occur only over the sign itself; they do not spread to other signs. For example, the sign glossed as NOT-YET has an obligatory nonmanual marking, in the form of a slack protruding tongue.[30] If the same manual sign is articulated without the nonmanual marking, the meaning of the sign changes (in this case, it would mean 'late').[31] The difference is illustrated in figure 3.16. The slack protruding tongue is so strongly associated with the sign NOT-YET that, under certain circumstances, it is possible to articulate the lexical item with only its nonmanual components.

Sometimes, a nonmanual marking characteristically associated with a lexical item can be used with other lexical items more generally. In such cases, the use of the nonmanual marking contributes an additional meaning, as described in the next section. For example, the signs CARELESS and RECENT include the nonmanual markings shown in figures 3.17 and

Figure 3.16
NOT-YET versus LATE

Figure 3.17
CARELESS

Figure 3.18
RECENT

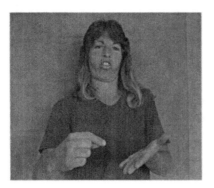

Figure 3.19
Modifying facial expression "th"

3.18. As will be seen in the next section, these same markings may be used productively with other signs as well.

3.4.3   Adverbial Markings

Some facial expressions that co-occur with signs are not an integral part of the sign; instead, they function as modifiers. Although ASL does have manual adverbial signs, nonmanual expressions can also function adverbially. An example is shown in (4) and figure 3.19. This expression, when co-occurring with a verb, contributes the information that the action is performed carelessly.

———th———

(4) JOHN WRITE HOMEWORK
    'John carelessly writes (his) homework.'

Such adverbial expressions are coextensive with the items they modify and do not spread over other signs (e.g., "th" cannot spread over the object of a transitive verb with which it is associated).[32]

Similarly, the notion of proximity in time or space may be expressed nonmanually by a marking that co-occurs with appropriate lexical items. The expression consists of a raising and tensing of one cheek (usually the same side as the signer's dominant hand) and a movement of the cheek toward the shoulder. (The marking is traditionally glossed as "cs" since it crucially involves the cheek and shoulder.) This is the same marking that was shown with the sign RECENT in figure 3.18. The intensity of the marking is related to the degree of proximity; close proximity is expressed

Figure 3.20
'there' with and without "proximity" expression

with a more intense expression. In addition to occurring with temporal signs, this expression may be used with deictic signs expressing physical proximity, such as 'there', as illustrated in figure 3.20. This expression may also appear with certain verbs, such as APPROACH or ARRIVE.

In sum, adverbial expressions, like lexical ones, occur over a single sign.[33] By contrast, as discussed in the next section, syntactic nonmanual expressions may occur over phrasal domains.[34]

3.4.4 Syntactic Markings

ASL also makes systematic use of nonmanual marking for expressing syntactic information. We have found that nonmanual syntactic markings are frequently associated with syntactic features located in the heads of functional projections. These expressions behave in a systematic, predictable fashion that can be described in terms of a few simple generalizations. Here we present those generalizations, using negation for purposes of illustration. In chapters 5, 6, and 7, we discuss the nonmanual correlates of agreement and question features, showing that they are governed by the same generalizations.

3.4.4.1 Generalizations Governing Nonmanual Syntactic Markings   The following generalizations govern nonmanual syntactic markings:

· **Nonmanual syntactic markings are frequently associated with syntactic features residing in the heads of functional projections.**[35]

Figure 3.21
Negative marking. (From Aarons 1994. © Debra Aarons)

Here, we discuss the nonmanual correlate of +neg, which consists most notably of a furrowing of the eyebrows and a side-to-side head shake, as illustrated in figure 3.21.[36] In subsequent chapters, we will also discuss the nonmanual syntactic markings associated with +wh, +y/n, and agreement features. In each case, there is a cluster of nonmanual behaviors that is associated with the particular syntactic feature.[37]

• **The nonmanual marking may spread over the c-command domain of the node with which it is associated (reflecting relations at Spell-Out).**[38]

Negative sentences in ASL can contain both a lexical sign of negation (e.g., NOT) and a corresponding nonmanual marking. In example (5), the nonmanual marking is coextensive with the sign NOT, as shown by the length of the line over the gloss.

<pre>
           neg
(5) JOHN NOT BUY HOUSE
</pre>
    'John is *not* buying a house.'

This nonmanual marking can spread over the c-command domain of Neg, as shown in (6).[39]

<pre>
                           neg
(6) JOHN [NOT [BUY HOUSE]VP]NegP
</pre>
    'John is not buying a house.'

When the negative marking does not spread, as in (5), the sentence receives an emphatic interpretation, as indicated in the English translation.

• **Spread of the nonmanual marking is optional if manual material is available locally. However, in the absence of such manual material, the marking spreads obligatorily so that it may be coarticulated with manual material.**

The optional spread of negative marking in sentences containing a lexical sign of negation is illustrated in (5) and (6). However, negative sentences in ASL do not require an overt lexical sign of negation, but they do require the nonmanual marking; hence the ungrammaticality of (7) in comparison with (9). In cases without an overt manual sign of negation with which the nonmanual marking can be coarticulated, the spread of nonmanual marking is obligatory, as is shown by the contrast in grammaticality between (8) and (9).[40]

(7) *JOHN [NOT]$_{Neg}$ BUY HOUSE

$$\overline{\text{neg}}$$
(8) *JOHN [+neg]$_{Neg}$ BUY HOUSE

$$\overline{\text{neg}}$$
(9)   JOHN [+neg]$_{Neg}$ BUY HOUSE
     'John is not buying a house.'

• **The intensity of the nonmanual marking is greatest at the node of origin and decreases as distance from the source increases.**

With the nonmanual marking of negation, the furrowing of the brows and the angle of head turn are greatest with the articulation of the sign NOT and gradually decrease as the rest of the VP is signed. The head position in relation to manual signing is illustrated in the schematic drawing in figure 3.22 (based on Bahan 1996).

• **As in the manual channel, perseveration (maintenance of a particular articulation that will recur later) is found with nonmanual expressions.**

In ASL, if the same articulatory configuration will be used multiple times, it tends to remain in place between those articulations (if this is possible). This phenomenon occurs systematically in both the manual and non-manual channels. For example, Kegl (1985b, 164–174) describes examples of manual perseveration involving classifier handshapes. Perseveration of manual material is also found in *wh*-question constructions, as discussed

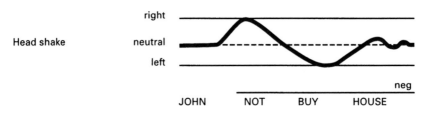

Figure 3.22
Head position during negative head shake

in chapter 7. In what follows, we illustrate nonmanual perseveration of eye gaze within the determiner phrase.[41]

In ASL, a determiner phrase may contain an initial and a final index (pointing) sign, as illustrated in (10). (Determiner phrases will be discussed in chapter 6.)

(10) JOHN KNOW [IX$_i$ MAN IX$_i$]$_{DP}$
'John knows the man there.'

As mentioned earlier, these pointing signs may co-occur with eye gaze ("eg"), "pointing" to the location in space associated with the same referent as the manual index sign, as shown in (11) and (12).

$$\overset{\text{eg}_i}{}$$
(11) JOHN KNOW [$\overline{\text{IX}_i}$ MAN IX$_i$]$_{DP}$
'John knows the man there.'

$$\overset{\text{eg}_i}{}$$
(12) JOHN KNOW [IX$_i$ MAN $\overline{\text{IX}_i}$]$_{DP}$
'John knows the man there.'

These data might lead one to expect that eye gaze could occur over both indexes. However, this is not possible, as shown by the unacceptability of (13). Instead, the eye gaze perseverates obligatorily over the manual material that intervenes between the two sources of the nonmanual marking, as in (14). Thus, (13) is unacceptable because the obligatory perseveration of eye gaze has not occurred.

$$\overset{\text{eg}_i}{}\quad\overset{\text{eg}_i}{}$$
(13) *JOHN KNOW [$\overline{\text{IX}_i}$ MAN $\overline{\text{IX}_i}$]$_{DP}$

$$\overset{\text{eg}_i}{}$$
(14) JOHN KNOW [$\overline{\text{IX}_i \text{ MAN IX}_i}$]$_{DP}$
'John knows the man there.'

Perseveration of eye gaze and head position within DP is discussed in more detail in Bahan 1996 and especially MacLaughlin 1997. In chapter 7, we address perseveration of the nonmanual marking associated with *wh*-question constructions.[42]

Finally, note that the distribution of nonmanual syntactic markings reflects hierarchical relations that hold at Spell-Out.[43] For example, the nonmanual marking of negation does not occur over the subject in a sentence like (6) or (9), even though the subject is generally assumed to originate in a VP-internal position.[44] Further examples supporting this claim are contained in subsequent chapters.

3.4.4.2 Significance of Nonmanual Syntactic Markings   Nonmanual syntactic markings in ASL, associated with abstract syntactic features such as +neg, are governed by generalizations that account for their distribution and intensity. The study of such markings can yield important information about syntactic structure. In particular, spread of such markings over phrasal domains provides evidence of particular hierarchical constituents. Moreover, the distribution, spread, intensity, and perseveration of such markings provide evidence about the location of abstract syntactic features.

3.4.5   Summary
ASL uses nonmanual markings to encode a variety of types of information. Affective facial expressions can be distinguished from linguistic facial expressions both on the basis of muscles used and on the basis of timing; moreover, these two types of expressions can co-occur and remain separable (Baker-Shenk 1983). Affective facial expressions are also involuntary and universal (Ekman 1992; Ekman and Friesen 1978; Izard 1971). Further support for such a distinction comes from the differential acquisition and impairment of affective and linguistic expressions.

There are two types of nonmanual markings that occur solely over individual signs. Lexically associated markings are those that are an integral part of the sign with which they co-occur; such signs are well formed only when accompanied by the appropriate nonmanual marking. Adverbial markings are modifiers that can co-occur with signs. Like lexically associated markings, they are coextensive with the sign they modify; however, they are not intrinsically a part of the sign.

Nonmanual syntactic markings differ from the other types in their distribution. When such markings appear, they necessarily co-occur with any manual material that occupies the node containing the features with which they are associated and optionally spread over the c-command domain of that node. The otherwise optional spread becomes, in essence, obligatory if spread is required in order for there to be manual material with which the nonmanual marking can be articulated.[45]

3.5   Conclusions

We have considered two interesting ways in which syntactic features are expressed in ASL. Agreement features are associated with locations in space, which may be accessed manually. Syntactic features in general may also have nonmanual correlates, which spread over precise and predictable syntactic domains, as was illustrated with respect to +neg. Careful examination of the characteristics of these markings provides critical information about hierarchical syntactic structure in ASL. As we will show in chapters 5 and 6, agreement features also have nonmanual correlates that are governed by the same generalizations discussed here. The distribution and intensity of these nonmanual markings of agreement provide evidence that may help to resolve recent controversies about the existence of agreement projections crosslinguistically. In addition, the properties of *wh*-marking, discussed in chapter 7, provide important evidence for rightward *wh*-movement in ASL, which has ramifications for a proper understanding of universal constraints on phrase structure and movement processes.

Chapter 4

Delimiting CP

4.1 Introduction

Before we investigate the internal structure of CP, it is important to distinguish CP-internal and CP-external constituents, to avoid potential misanalysis of data. Therefore, in section 4.2, we briefly describe several constructions involving constituents that may adjoin to the left or right of CP:

- topics,
- tags, and
- pronominal right dislocations.

We will not focus on a detailed analysis of these constructions;[1] however, identification and isolation of these phenomena are critical to any investigation of the internal structure of CP. For clarity of exposition, we will use commas in the ASL glosses to set off elements (i.e., topics, tags, and pronominal right dislocations) that are external to CP. The commas are not intended to indicate a pause, although there are prosodic characteristics associated with these constructions, as will be discussed.

In section 4.3, we lay out the basic underlying word order of the ASL sentence. Although early work on ASL structure included observations of many possible word orders, with careful attention to prosody and non-manual markings, it is possible to distinguish unmarked word orders from those that involve movement or contain topics, tags, or right-dislocated pronominals.[2] Once CP-external material is properly identified and null arguments are recognized, it becomes apparent that the underlying word order is SVO. Although there is generally consensus about this in the current literature, we do discuss briefly (and argue against) a suggestion by Bouchard and Dubuisson (1995) that ASL has essentially free word order rather than an underlying hierarchical structure.

4.2   Common Clause-External Constructions

We begin with topics, which occur to the left of CP, bear particular non-manual markings, and are often set off from CP prosodically by a pause (i.e., the end of the topic sign and the nonmanual marking are held briefly).

4.2.1   Topics

ASL makes productive use of several types of topics, as demonstrated convincingly in Aarons 1994, although most other ASL linguists have generally not differentiated them (even subsequent to Aarons 1994). In this section, we discuss the distinctions among these types of topics, their distribution, and the importance of recognizing the distinctions among topics for a proper syntactic analysis of ASL.

4.2.1.1   Moved versus Base-Generated Topics   Aarons (1994) argues for a distinction among three types of topics. She demonstrates that there is a fundamental difference between moved and (two distinct kinds of) base-generated topics, which is relevant to a proper account of their syntactic distribution. Moved and base-generated topics are associated with different nonmanual markings. Consider first moved topics, which bear what Aarons calls "topic marking 1" or "tm1," which we identify here as "t1-mv," found in sentences like (1), which has contrastive focus.[3]

    <u>t1-mv</u>
(1) JOHN$_i$, MARY LOVE t_i
    '*John* Mary loves.'

According to Aarons, the nonmanual realization includes raised eyebrows, widened eyes, head tilted slightly back and to the side, with the head moving down and forward, as illustrated in figure 4.1.

   In contrast, a base-generated topic of the kind found in (2) and (3) has a different nonmanual marking, "t2-bg," labeled "tm2" by Aarons. The nonmanual marking t2-bg is expressed with a large movement of the head back, eyes very wide, with the head moving down and forward, as shown in figure 4.2.

    <u>t2-bg</u>
(2) JOHN$_i$, IX$_i$ LIKE MARY
    'As for John, he likes Mary.'

Figure 4.1
Marking found on moved topics: t1-mv. (From Aarons 1994. © Debra Aarons)

Figure 4.2
Marking found on base-generated topics conveying 'as for': t2-bg. (From Aarons 1994. © Debra Aarons)

<u>   t2-bg   </u>
(3) VEGETABLE, JOHN PREFER CORN
    'As for vegetables, John prefers corn.'

The use of the base-generated topic changes the discourse topic, as suggested by the English translation. It is necessarily associated with an
argument in the following clause. In (2), there is a pronominal referring back to the topic. That pronominal need not be overt. As will be
shown later, ASL allows null pronominals in appropriate configurations.
(The licensing of null pronominals is discussed in chapter 5.) Alternatively, there may be a class:member relation, as in (3), between the base-
generated topic marked with t2-bg and the associated argument in the
following clause.

    Finally, a third kind of topic identified by Aarons (1994, 163–164) is
marked with what she calls "tm3," and what we will label "t3-bg."

The head is down at a slightly forward angle, and jerked up and down, the mouth
is open with the upper lip somewhat raised, the eyebrows are raised, as in other
topic marking, but the eyes are opened very wide and maintain a fixed gaze and
there is a series of very slight rapid headnods, followed by a pause in which the
expression is held, before the signing of the rest of the sentence.

This is illustrated in figure 4.3. This kind of base-generated topic is used
only with known referents, and it introduces a major change in discourse
topic, as shown in (4).

Figure 4.3
Marking found on base-generated 'you know' type topics: t3-bg. (From Aarons
1994. © Debra Aarons)

$$\overline{\text{t3-bg}}$$
(4) JOHN$_i$, MARY LOVE IX$_i$
'(You know) John – Mary loves him.'

Thus, moved and base-generated topics in ASL can be distinguished by the nonmanual markings with which they occur, and by their discourse functions. They also differ in their distributional characteristics, as we will now discuss.

4.2.1.2 Positions in Which Topics Appear An ASL clause allows a maximum of two topics (Aarons 1994; ABKN 1992; Kegl 1985b). As Aarons demonstrates, a moved topic must occupy the topic position closest to the CP, as in (5). This is shown by the ungrammaticality of (6).[4]

$$\overline{\text{t3-bg}}\quad\overline{\text{t1-mv}}$$
(5) JOHN$_j$, MARY$_i$, IX$_j$ LOVE t_i
'You know John, *Mary* he loves.'
(Aarons 1994, 179, ex. (80))

$$\overline{\text{t1-mv}}\quad\overline{\text{t3-bg}}$$
(6) *MARY$_i$, JOHN$_j$, IX$_j$ LOVE t_i
(Aarons 1994, 179, ex. (80))

It is possible to find two base-generated topics in either order,[5] as illustrated by the following examples from Aarons 1994:

$$\overline{\text{t2-bg}}\quad\quad\overline{\text{t2-bg}}$$
(7) CHINA IX$_i$, VEGETABLE, PEOPLE PREFER fs-BROCCOLI
'In China, as far as vegetables are concerned, people prefer broccoli.'
(Aarons 1994, 175, ex. (67))

$$\overline{\text{t2-bg}}\quad\quad\overline{\text{t2-bg}}$$
(8) VEGETABLE, CHINA IX$_i$, PEOPLE PREFER fs-BROCCOLI
'As for vegetables, in China, people prefer broccoli.'
(Aarons 1994, 176, ex. (68))

We have claimed that topics in ASL are adjoined to CP. As we will argue in chapter 7, [Spec, CP] in ASL occurs to the right of TP, whereas topics occur CP-initially.[6] Therefore, it is clear that topics do not occupy [Spec, CP] in ASL. Evidence from the distribution of nonmanual *wh*-marking shows that topics are external to the c-command domain of C. In addition, on the basis of the distribution of nonmanual topic marking, we suggest that topics in ASL do not occur within a functional projection headed by a +topic feature. Under such an analysis, one might expect topic marking (like other nonmanual markings associated with syntactic features) to be able to spread over the c-command domain of the head of the topic projection, and therefore over the following clause, which it never does.

4.2.1.3 Importance of Distinguishing between Moved and Base-Generated Topics
Discussions about topics in the literature have often disregarded the distinction between moved and base-generated topics. This distinction is critical for a proper syntactic analysis. For example, the status of a null element associated with a topic, whether a *pro* coreferential with the topic noun phrase or a trace that is part of a chain, is not insignificant, as binding and movement are subject to different constraints.

Various claims have been made about the syntax of ASL that crucially rely on the analysis of topic constructions, especially in Lillo-Martin 1986, 1990, 1991, 1992, and subsequent publications by others based upon these works. Lillo-Martin does not distinguish between moved and base-generated topics. She treats all topics as involving the same syntactic process, which she terms "topicalization," but her analysis of topic constructions seems to involve properties of both moved and base-generated topics simultaneously. The following quotation about topic structures is representative of her approach:

Thus, the name 'left dislocation' would be more appropriate for these structures. I will, however, continue to refer to them as topicalization structures, and discuss them using the terminology of extraction, without implying a movement analysis. To indicate the non-movement nature of this relationship, I will use the term 'extraction' in single quotes. (Lillo-Martin 1991, 55)

Despite the "non-movement nature" of topic constructions explicitly assumed in Lillo-Martin 1991, Lillo-Martin (1990, 1992) uses evidence from topic constructions to support her proposed constraints on movement rules in ASL.

The distinction between moved and base-generated topics is also crucial for proper analysis of the licensing of null arguments in ASL. As will be discussed again in chapter 5, Lillo-Martin proposes that topics license null arguments of certain types of verbs in ASL. Under such an analysis, the distinction between a *pro* (requiring licensing) and a trace (subject to different constraints) is of critical importance. Lillo-Martin's conflation of different types of topics is particularly problematic,[7] as her conclusions have served as the basis for other research in the field.

The main point here is that ASL does have both moved and base-generated topics. These are distinguishable in terms of their syntactic properties and their nonmanual markings.

4.2.2 Right Dislocation

Pronominal right dislocation of both subjects and objects occurs quite frequently in ASL.[8] This involves a (base-generated)[9] sentence-final un-stressed pronoun coreferential with a prior noun phrase. The pronoun is part of the same prosodic unit as the preceding material; it is normally not preceded by a pause. Examples are given in (9) and (10).

(9) JOHN$_i$ LEAVE, IX$_i$
    'John left, him.'

(10) IX$_{1p}$ SEE$_j$ JOHN$_j$ YESTERDAY, IX$_j$
    'I saw John yesterday, him.'

This construction is comparable to pronominal right dislocation in other languages.

(11) *French*
    Jean$_i$ est parti, lui$_i$.
    'John left, him.'

(12) *Norwegian*
    Anton$_i$ har vært i Egypt, han$_i$.
    'Anton has been to Egypt, he.'
    (from Fretheim 1996)

Although further research on the discourse conditions associated with pronominal right dislocation in ASL is needed, preliminary investigation suggests that essentially the same discourse factors are relevant to the use of pronominal right dislocation in languages such as French, Norwegian, and ASL.[10]

However, unlike French and Norwegian, ASL allows only pronominal elements (but not full noun phrases) in a right-dislocated position. In French and Norwegian, it is possible to find right dislocation of a full noun phrase.

(13) *French*
    Il est parti, Jean.
    'He left, John.'

(14) *Norwegian*

Han$_i$ var gift med søskenbarnet mitt en gang i tida, Axel Aarvoll$_i$.
'He$_i$ was once married to my cousin, Axel Aarvoll$_i$.'
(from Fretheim 1995)

Such constructions would not be well formed in ASL, however, as illustrated by the ungrammaticality of (15).

(15) *IX$_i$ LEAVE, JOHN$_i$

This difference may be attributable to the unambiguous spatial representation of pronominal reference in ASL, as mentioned in chapter 3.

Given the prevalence of pronominal right dislocation in the language, it is surprising to find claims that right dislocation does not exist in ASL. Wilbur (1994b) states that ASL "appears to make little or no use of Right Dislocation" (p. 677), claiming that "[w]hat is needed to confirm that ASL does indeed have Right Dislocation is examples where the pronoun is in the main clause and the full NP follows (after an intonation break)" (p. 666). In essence, then, Wilbur concludes that since right dislocation of full noun phrases does not occur in ASL, pronominal right dislocation cannot occur.

The occurrence of sentence-final pronominals in ASL has been widely recognized, but different constructions involving such pronominals have not been carefully distinguished. As just discussed, a right-dislocated pronominal may occur in sentence-final position. In the next section, we introduce the tag construction in ASL, which may also contain a pronominal (among other elements) in final position.

4.2.3 Tags

In ASL, as in many other languages, sentence-final tags (consisting of a repeated but reduced version of basic material from the main clause) occur productively. As we argue in chapter 5, a modal or tense marker may occur in the head of TP; not coincidentally, this modal or tense marker frequently recurs in the tag.[11] A pronoun coreferential with the main-clause subject is also commonly found in the tag. One significant characteristic of such reduced elliptical clauses is the presence of a distinctive head nod first described by Liddell (1980), which is associated with null verbal material. Liddell observes that the affirmative head nod is found with null copular constructions, gapping, verb phrase deletion, and similar constructions, all of which involve null verbal material.[12] In addition, when base-generated topics occur in conjunction with a clause lacking overt verbal material, this same head nod ("hn") is found, as in (16).

$$\overline{\text{t2-bg}} \quad \overline{\text{hn}}$$
(16) LOVE MARY, JOHN
    'As for loving Mary, John (does).'

An affirmative declarative tag is also accompanied by this repeated head nod.[13] The examples in (17) through (19) illustrate the ASL tag construction.

$$\overline{\text{hn}}$$
(17) JOHN FUTURE$_{tns}$ GO, FUTURE$_{tns}$
    'John will go, (he) will.'

$$\overline{\text{hn}}$$
(18) JOHN CAN GO, CAN
    'John can go, (he) can.'

$$\overline{\text{hn}}$$
(19) JOHN$_i$ FUTURE$_{tns}$ GO, IX$_i$
    'John will go, he (will).'

Sentence-final tags in ASL necessarily agree with the main clause in tense, polarity, and question status. Thus, in (17) and (19), the tag is understood as an affirmative declarative in the future tense.[14] Although (17) contains an overt repetition of the tense marker FUTURE$_{tns}$, it is not necessary to repeat this material, as is demonstrated in (19).

An affirmative head nod is optional within clauses that do not contain null verbal material. When an affirmative head nod is present in the main clause as well as in the tag (see (20)), it is generally possible to distinguish two peaks in the intensity of the head movement. The head nod in the main clause exhibits its maximal movement at the beginning of its articulation and damps as the remainder of the clause is articulated; a second maximal articulation occurs over the tag (see figure 4.4).[15]

$$\overline{\text{hn}} \qquad \overline{\text{hn}}$$
(20) JOHN FUTURE$_{tns}$ GO PARTY, FUTURE$_{tns}$
    'John will go to the party, he will.'

The presence of the head nod allows us to distinguish between tags containing only a pronoun and instances of right dislocation. Compare (19) with the right dislocation example in (21).

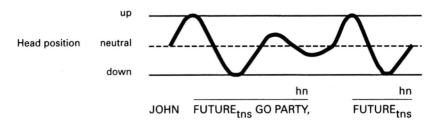

Figure 4.4
Head position in the tag construction

(21) JOHN$_i$ FUTURE$_{tns}$ GO, IX$_i$
    'John will go, him.'

In fact, it is possible to find right dislocation at the end of a tag, as in (22).[16]

$$\overline{\hspace{4cm}\text{hn}\hspace{0.5cm}}$$
(22) JOHN$_i$ FUTURE$_{tns}$ GO, FUTURE$_{tns}$, IX$_i$
    'John will go, (he) will, him.'

4.2.4 Summary

Before investigating the internal structure of CP, it is essential to differentiate constituents that precede or follow CP from CP-internal elements. As we have shown, ASL makes productive use of up to two topics left-adjoined to CP as well as right-dislocated pronominal elements and tag constructions that occur sentence-finally.

4.3 Word Order and Hierarchical Structure

Failure to distinguish between CP-internal and CP-external material could give a false impression of free word order within the clause. For example, there are cases where it might appear that the subject may occur after the verb rather than in TP-initial position. This word order is not surprising, given the prevalence of both null pronominal subjects and right-dislocated pronominals in ASL, as illustrated in (23).

(23) pro$_i$ $_i$BLAME$_j$ FRED$_j$, IX$_i$
    '(He/She) blames Fred, him/her.'

Since the only overt pronominal is TP-external, this kind of example provides no evidence of the TP-internal position of subjects.

Similarly, the occurrence of a modal or pronominal in a clause-final tag position provides no evidence of CP-internal structure. Petronio and Lillo-Martin (1997), who do not recognize the existence of a tag consisting of a reduced clausal constituent, propose that the modal in an example like (20), for instance, occupies a sentence-final C position. Such assumptions form the basis for their claims regarding the internal structure of CP. As demonstrated in chapter 7, their proposal cannot account for the ASL facts.

4.3.1 Basic SVO Order
When CP-internal constituents alone are considered, it is readily apparent that the underlying "unmarked" word order is SVO. In a sentence like (24), the subject necessarily precedes the VP, and the object follows the verb; no other word order yields the interpretation indicated.[17]

(24) MARY LOVE JOHN
     'Mary loves John.'

Other word orders require use of sentence-peripheral positions. For example, the object may be topicalized, as in (1), repeated here.

```
      tl-mv
```
(1) JOHN$_i$, MARY LOVE t_i
     '*John* Mary loves.'

Likewise, a null pronominal can occur in subject position, with or without a tag and/or a right-dislocated pronominal in sentence-final position, as shown in (23), repeated here.

(23) *pro*$_i$ $_i$BLAME$_j$ FRED$_j$, IX$_i$
     '(He/She) blames Fred, him/her.'

In fact, there is essentially consensus in the recent literature that ASL clauses have an underlying hierarchical SVO word order. Deviations from this word order—which we would analyze as involving topics, tags, or right-dislocated elements (or other movement processes)—are, we argue, distinguishable by nonmanual cues and prosody (see note 2).

4.3.2 Alternative Claims of Free Word Order in ASL
The early ASL literature, where less attention was paid to nonmanual markings and prosodic evidence, includes claims that word order in ASL is essentially free (see, e.g., Tervoort 1968, which proposed free word

order, or Friedman 1976a, which claimed that word order is relatively free, with the exception that the verb tends to be last). This claim has been clearly refuted (see Chinchor et al. 1976; Fischer 1974, 1975; Kegl 1977, 1985b; Liddell 1977, 1980; Padden 1983, 1988).

The claim of free word order has recently resurfaced, however, in Bouchard and Dubuisson 1995 (see also Bouchard 1997), although Bouchard and Dubuisson go one step further. They suggest not only that signed languages generally exhibit free word order, but also that signed languages, as well as some spoken languages, are not characterized by an underlying hierarchical phrasal structure and instead make use of entirely different organizing principles. The alternative account that they offer is not complete or precise, and hence not testable. They resort to such principles as "fluidity of articulation," suggesting (Bouchard and Dubuisson 1995, 107) that "articulatory economy ... often determines the preference for the order of signs, over and above other factors."[18] They explain (Bouchard and Dubuisson 1995, 131–132) what they describe as word order "tendencies" in terms of ground-figure relations. The "ground-figure pattern ... is favored in a language with a four-dimensional mode." What we interpret to be the underlying word order, they instead characterize as a kind of "elsewhere condition." In the absence of any other determinative factors governing word order, "ASL reverts to order as a means to express information such as the grammatical functions involved; the order in such cases appears to be SVO. Our impression is that this is the status of order in sign languages in general" (Bouchard and Dubuisson 1995, 109).[19] Thus, they conclude (Bouchard and Dubuisson 1995, 132), "Since there are other means that a language can use to indicate what elements combine, a language does not have to have a specific order that reflects these combinations. We therefore conclude that not all languages have a basic order: only languages in which word order has a high functional role will exhibit a basic order."

Problems with their proposed analysis of ASL are addressed in detail in KNMHB 1996 and will not be discussed further here.[20] However, it is interesting to note that Bouchard and Dubuisson's claims are based primarily on their own research on LSQ (*la langue des signes québécoise*), and their LSQ data and interpretation appear to be problematic. Their finding of free word order may not be unrelated to their methodology. As is evident from the excerpts from Lelièvre 1996 and Dubuisson 1996 presented in chapter 2, the informants' actual judgments of the acceptability of differing word orders was, in essence, disregarded.

Thus, Bouchard and Dubuisson's claims about LSQ are dubious. In any event, they then extend their claims of free word order in LSQ to ASL (on the basis of a small sample of glossed examples from the literature). It is clear that noncanonical word orders do occur in ASL. Nonetheless, we have argued and we maintain that the variety of surface word orders (and the distribution of nonmanual syntactic markings and prosodic characteristics of those sentences) are best accounted for in terms of an underlying hierarchical clausal structure.

Evidence that the language is hierarchically organized comes from many sources, including not only basic word order facts, but also nonmanual markings and prosodic cues that reflect the underlying hierarchical syntactic structures. These structures are best understood once CP-internal and CP-external constituents are carefully differentiated, as we have argued in this chapter. As we will show in subsequent chapters, the spread of nonmanual correlates of syntactic features over c-command domains provides additional strong evidence in favor of hierarchical phrase structure of the same kind that has been shown to account for the syntax of spoken languages.

4.4 Chapter Summary

There is strong language-internal evidence to support the claim that ASL has the same kind of hierarchical syntactic structure as has been proposed for other languages. Some apparent deviations from canonical SVO word order can be attributed to the presence of CP-peripheral elements, such as topics (of which there are several types), tags, and pronominal right dislocations, constructions that have been described in this chapter.

In the next chapter, we begin our investigation of the internal structure of the ASL clause. We argue that the clause is fundamentally a projection of tense. We also present evidence supporting the postulation of distinct subject and object agreement projections.

Chapter 5

Tense and Agreement in the Clause

5.1 Introduction

In this chapter, we focus on the analysis of tense and agreement in the ASL clause. We provide evidence for the following conclusions:

• Agreement in the ASL clause may be realized both manually and non-manually. Morphological agreement inflections are expressed manually, whereas abstract agreement features located in the heads of agreement phrases may be expressed by nonmanual markings. The distribution of nonmanual expressions of agreement provides important evidence relevant to a number of issues concerning the nature of agreement and the licensing of null arguments.

• Tense and agreement constitute distinct functional projections, and TP dominates the Agr projections, as argued by Pollock (1989, 1997). Evidence for these conclusions comes primarily from the distribution of nonmanual markings of agreement: the spread of these markings shows that T is outside the c-command domain of the Agr heads with which the markings are associated.

The representation of agreement and tense are considered in sections 5.2 and 5.3, respectively.

5.2 Agreement

Agreement in ASL may be expressed not only by morphological inflections on the verb (described in chapter 3), but also nonmanually, through the use of head tilt and eye gaze. Head and eye movements during signing have long been noticed; however, the use of such behaviors to mark syntactic agreement had not been recognized prior to Bahan 1996.[1]

Although the head and eyes serve many important functions within ASL, their use in expressing agreement is systematic. Nonmanual agreement markings are not generally required for grammaticality, but they occur quite frequently. We interpret these nonmanual markings as manifestations of abstract agreement features located in the heads of functional projections. They exhibit the same distributional characteristics as other nonmanual syntactic markings, spreading over the c-command domain of the head of the functional projection with which they are associated. The distribution of nonmanual syntactic markings of agreement provides evidence relevant to several important theoretical issues, such as the existence and proper representation of abstract agreement features.

5.2.1 Head Tilt and Eye Gaze as Nonmanual Expressions of Agreement

Like other syntactic features, agreement features may be expressed nonmanually. The examples in (1) and (2) illustrate basic transitive ASL sentences containing nonmanual markings of syntactic agreement. As the examples show, these markings are found both with clauses containing an agreeing verb, like BLAME,[2] and with clauses containing a nonagreeing verb, like LOVE.

$$\overline{ \text{head tilt}_i}$$
$$\overline{ \text{eye gaze}_j}$$
(1) ANN$_i$ [+agr$_i$]$_{Agr_s}$ [+agr$_j$]$_{Agr_o}$ $_i$BLAME$_j$ MARY$_j$
    'Ann blames Mary.'

$$\overline{ \text{head tilt}_i}$$
$$\overline{ \text{eye gaze}_j}$$
(2) JOHN$_i$ [+agr$_i$]$_{Agr_s}$ [+agr$_j$]$_{Agr_o}$ LOVE MARY$_j$
    'John loves Mary.'

In these sentences, the head tilts toward the spatial location associated with the subject, and the eyes gaze to the location associated with the object. These nonmanual expressions of subject and object agreement are illustrated in figure 5.1 (with the verb GIVE).

Support for interpreting these markings as expressions of subject and object agreement comes from the following facts:

· Head tilt and eye gaze reference the same spatial locations that are used to express manual agreement marking.
· The nonmanual markings of agreement exhibit the same duality of forms as manual agreement marking (section 5.2.2).

Figure 5.1
Nonmanual realizations of agreement marking. (From Bahan 1996. © Benjamin Bahan)

- Head tilt and eye gaze can license null arguments (section 5.2.4.1).
- The same markings express agreement within DP (chapter 6).

In the remainder of this section, we analyze the nonmanual syntactic markings of agreement within the clause in detail.

5.2.2   Nonmanual Agreement in Transitive Clauses

In transitive constructions, head tilt may be used to express subject agreement, and eye gaze may be used to express object agreement (see (1) and (2)).[3] Careful study of the timing and intensity characteristics of these markings reveals important clues about the underlying structure of the ASL transitive clause. The head begins tilting just prior to the articulation of the VP. After the head begins tilting, the eye gaze changes. However, because the head moves more slowly than the eyes, the eyes generally reach their destination before the head does. The head and eyes remain in position during the articulation of the VP, although the intensity of the markings diminishes as the VP is articulated. In other words, the head and eyes may begin returning to neutral position during the articulation of the VP.[4]

These facts about the timing and intensity characteristics of the nonmanual agreement markings follow from the same generalizations that govern the distribution of other syntactic markings, if we assume that the nonmanual markings of subject and object agreement are associated with agreement features in the heads of two distinct functional projections, as depicted in (3).

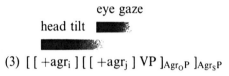

eye gaze

head tilt

(3) $[\,[\,+agr_i\,]\,[\,[\,+agr_j\,]\,VP\,]_{Agr_OP}\,]_{Agr_SP}$

The finding that head tilt begins immediately prior to eye gaze follows from the proposed analysis, since Agr$_S$ c-commands Agr$_O$ (as we will show in section 5.2.3, the timing of these markings in transitive clauses contrasts in an important way with what is found in intransitive clauses, where there is only one Agr head). On the assumption that these functional heads contain no manual material,[5] the nonmanual markings are predicted to spread obligatorily over the c-command domains of their nodes of origin, and this is indeed what occurs. The markings are most intense at the source, diminishing as distance from the source increases.

5.2.2.1 Two Forms of Subject Agreement   The examples thus far have illustrated one possible form that the nonmanual marking of subject agreement may take. In addition to this fully agreeing form, there is a neutral form (labeled "neu" in the glosses). This is analogous to what is found with manual subject agreement marking on verbs, as described in chapter 3. Just as with manual agreement on the verb, the neutral form of head tilt is a first-person-like form, as illustrated (co-occurring with the verb GIVE) in figure 5.2. Note that this head position contrasts with the overt expression of subject agreement illustrated in figure 5.1.[6] The neutral form of subject agreement marking may co-occur with nonmanual object agreement marking and with either agreeing or nonagreeing verbs, as shown in (4) and (5).

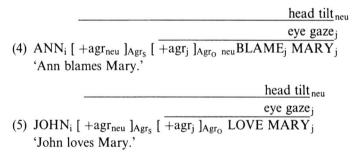

$$\text{head tilt}_{neu}$$
$$\text{eye gaze}_j$$
(4) ANN$_i$ [$+agr_{neu}$]$_{Agr_S}$ [$+agr_j$]$_{Agr_O \; neu}$BLAME$_j$ MARY$_j$
    'Ann blames Mary.'

$$\text{head tilt}_{neu}$$
$$\text{eye gaze}_j$$
(5) JOHN$_i$ [$+agr_{neu}$]$_{Agr_S}$ [$+agr_j$]$_{Agr_O}$ LOVE MARY$_j$
    'John loves Mary.'

Figure 5.2
"Neutral" nonmanual subject agreement marking. (From Bahan 1996. © Benjamin Bahan)

Thus, manual and nonmanual subject agreement markings exhibit a similar duality of form. It is revealing to examine the co-occurrence restrictions among the possible forms. The previous examples have shown that it is possible to combine fully agreeing forms (see, e.g., (1)) and neutral forms (see (4)). Interestingly, the sentence in (6), with fully specified nonmanual agreement marking and neutral manual agreement inflection, is also possible.

$$\overline{\textbf{head tilt}_i}$$
$$\overline{\text{eye gaze}_j}$$

(6) ANN$_i$ [+agr$_i$]$_{Agr_s}$ [+agr$_j$]$_{Agr_o}$ $_{neu}$BLAME$_j$ MARY$_j$
      'Ann blames Mary.'

The existence of sentences like (6) shows that nonmanual and manual expressions of agreement are not merely reflections of the same underlying agreement features. This supports the postulation of dual representations of features, on lexical items and in functional projections. Sentences like (6) show that the two sets of features can be instantiated separately, although the relevant features must be compatible for well-formedness. If one assumes a feature-checking approach to agreement, then the acceptability of (6) demonstrates that underspecified lexical features on the verb are compatible with fully specified features in Agr.

Significantly, the opposite case, where nonmanual syntactic agreement is in the neutral form and morphological agreement takes the fully agreeing form, is unacceptable, as shown in (7).

$$\overline{\text{head tilt}_{neu}}$$
$$\overline{\text{eye gaze}_j}$$
(7) *ANN$_i$ [+agr$_{neu}$]$_{Agr_s}$ [+agr$_j$]$_{Agr_o}$ $_i$BLAME$_j$ MARY$_j$

If one assumes that feature checking is asymmetric (contra suggestions in Chomsky 1995a), one can account for the contrast between (6) and (7). In this kind of feature-checking relationship, the agreement features on the verb must be checked by the abstract features in Agr; the features in Agr do not themselves need to be checked.[7] Thus, one might view feature checking in this instance as a process that licenses or validates morphological features on a lexical item. Assuming that neutral (underspecified) features on V may be checked by compatible features (either neutral or fully specified) in Agr, we can account for the acceptability of both (6) and (4). However, fully specified features on V can only be checked by (compatible) fully specified features in Agr; thus, (7) is unacceptable.

We have shown that, like other syntactic features, subject agreement features have nonmanual correlates that spread over precisely defined syntactic domains. Like manual agreement marking, nonmanual subject agreement marking, in the form of head tilt, exhibits both a fully agreeing and a neutral form. Table 5.1 delimits the possible combinations of fully agreeing and neutral forms of morphological and syntactic expressions of subject agreement. The subject agreement facts provide evidence that agreement features are represented in two places, on lexical items (presumably added before the lexical item is inserted into the syntax) and in the heads of functional projections. Given the allowable combinations of agreement forms, the checking relation involved in the licensing of agreement features is proposed to be asymmetric.

Table 5.1
Combinations of forms of subject agreement

Agreement on V	Agreement in Agr (expressed nonmanually)	
	Neutral	Fully agreeing
Neutral	√	√
Fully agreeing	*	√

5.2.2.2 Definite and Indefinite Forms of Object Agreement   In chapter 3, we discussed two forms of morphological object agreement marking: definite and indefinite. Nonmanual object agreement marking, expressed by eye gaze, also exhibits two forms, depending on the definiteness of the object. When the object is definite, the eyes gaze to the precise location associated with the object. However, indefinite objects are associated with an area in space, rather than a point. When nonmanual agreement with an indefinite object is marked, the eyes gaze over this area; they may wander slightly within the area or they may take on an unfocused stare.[8] An example with the indefinite form of nonmanual object agreement is given in (8).

$$\text{t1-mv}$$
(8) $\overline{\text{BOOK}_i,}$

$$\text{indefinite gaze}$$

JOHN [$+\text{agr}_{\text{neu}}$]$_{\text{Agr}_S}$[$+\text{agr}_{\text{indef}}$]$_{\text{Agr}_O}$ $_{\text{neu}}$GIVE$_{\text{indef}}$ SOMEONE t_i

'*The book*, John gave (to) someone.'

Thus, eye gaze to the location in space associated with the object's agreement features constitutes a nonmanual expression of object agreement.[9]

5.2.2.3 Summary   In transitive clauses, subject and object agreement may optionally be expressed nonmanually through head tilt and eye gaze, respectively.[10] These nonmanual markings are taken to be the expressions of abstract agreement features located in the heads of two functional projections: Agr$_S$P and Agr$_O$P. Examination of the distribution and intensity characteristics of these markings provides evidence for the proposed analysis. The markings spread obligatorily over their c-command domains (i.e., over VP), as the functional heads with which they are associated contain no manual material with which the marking may co-occur.

5.2.3 Nonmanual Agreement in Intransitive Clauses

In intransitive clauses, where there is only a single argument with which agreement may be expressed, either nonmanual device may be used. That is, head tilt, eye gaze, or both may express agreement with the single syntactic argument, as shown in (9) and (10).[11]

$$\text{head tilt}_i$$
(9) a. JOHN$_i$ [$+\text{agr}_i$]$_{\text{Agr}}$ BATHE

$$\text{b. JOHN}_i\ [\ +\text{agr}_i\ ]_{\text{Agr}}\ \overline{\overset{\text{eye gaze}_i}{\text{BATHE}}}$$

$$\text{c. JOHN}_i\ [\ +\text{agr}_i\ ]_{\text{Agr}}\ \overline{\overset{\text{head tilt}_i}{\overset{\text{eye gaze}_i}{\text{BATHE}}}}$$

'John is bathing.'

$$(10)\ \text{a. JOHN}_i\ [\ +\text{agr}_i\ ]_{\text{Agr}}\ \overline{\overset{\text{head tilt}_i}{\text{ARRIVE}}}$$

$$\text{b. JOHN}_i\ [\ +\text{agr}_i\ ]_{\text{Agr}}\ \overline{\overset{\text{eye gaze}_i}{\text{ARRIVE}}}$$

$$\text{c. JOHN}_i\ [\ +\text{agr}_i\ ]_{\text{Agr}}\ \overline{\overset{\text{head tilt}_i}{\overset{\text{eye gaze}_i}{\text{ARRIVE}}}}$$

'John is arriving.'

When both head tilt and eye gaze are employed, they begin and end together, supporting the claim that there is only one syntactic agreement projection in intransitive clauses, as depicted in (11). This contrasts with what is found with transitive clauses, where head tilt begins before eye gaze. Thus, compare (11) with the transitive (3), repeated here.

eye gaze
head tilt

(11) $[\ [\ +\text{agr}\ ]\ \text{VP}\ ]_{\text{Agr}_s\text{P}}$

eye gaze
head tilt

(3) $[\ [\ +\text{agr}_i\ ]\ [\ [\ +\text{agr}_j\ ]\ \text{VP}\ ]_{\text{Agr}_o\text{P}}\ ]_{\text{Agr}_s\text{P}}$

5.2.4 Implications

In addition to being expressed morphologically, agreement may be expressed nonmanually through head tilt and eye gaze toward the location associated with the relevant ϕ-features.[12] The distribution of these nonmanual markings reveals important information about the underlying structure of the ASL clause. These results have significant implications for both ASL linguistics and syntactic theory in general. In section 5.2.4.1, we show that a proper analysis of syntactic agreement reveals that null arguments in ASL are uniformly licensed by realizations of agreement (and that other licensing strategies that have been proposed in the literature are incorrect). In sections 5.2.4.2 and 5.2.4.3, we discuss more general theoretical implications of these data for the representation of agreement, arguing for agreement projections and feature checking.

5.2.4.1 Agreement and Null Arguments in ASL Null arguments are permitted with verbs of all morphological classes, regardless of whether the verb itself overtly expresses morphological agreement. There has been some controversy concerning how to account for the distribution of null arguments in ASL (see, e.g., Lillo-Martin 1986, 1991; BKLMN in press NBMLK 1998). However, once the nonmanual realizations of syntactic agreement are recognized, a simple account of the distribution of *pro* emerges: *pro* in ASL is licensed by an appropriate (manual or nonmanual) expression of agreement.[13] Two types of licensing strategies have been proposed: licensing by agreement (Borer 1984; Chomsky 1981, 1982; Rizzi 1982a, 1986; Taraldsen 1980), found in languages with rich agreement systems, and licensing by topic (Huang 1982, 1984), claimed to be associated with languages that lack agreement. We argue that ASL, which expresses agreement both manually and nonmanually, licenses null arguments in the same way as other languages with rich agreement systems.

Examples throughout this chapter have shown that nonmanual markings of agreement occur with verbs of all morphological classes (i.e., agreeing and nonagreeing). These nonmanual markings of agreement can license null arguments in ASL. Compare the grammatical and ungrammatical null subject and object examples in (12)–(15), which involve the nonagreeing verb LOVE. The examples demonstrate that a null subject or object is permitted only if there is an expression of agreement, which, in these cases (since LOVE is a plain verb), can only be nonmanual.[14]

$$\overline{\hspace{4cm}\text{head tilt}_i}$$

(12) pro_i [$+agr_i$]$_{Agr_s}$ [$+agr_j$]$_{Agr_o}$ LOVE MARY$_j$
     '(He/She) loves Mary.'

(13) *pro LOVE MARY
     '(He/She) loves Mary.'

$$\overline{\hspace{5cm}\text{eye gaze}_j}$$

(14) JOHN$_i$ [$+agr_i$]$_{Agr_s}$ [$+agr_j$]$_{Agr_o}$ LOVE pro_j
     'John loves (him/her).'

(15) *JOHN LOVE *pro*
     'John loves (him/her).'

It is interesting to note that in other languages as well, there are distinctions between constructions in which agreement is overtly expressed and those in which it is not, precisely in terms of the ability to license null arguments. Such languages include Arabic (Jelinek 1983), Hebrew (Borer 1984; Chomsky 1981), and Irish (McCloskey and Hale 1983).

In sum, the data presented here provide evidence that null arguments in ASL are uniformly licensed by an expression of agreement (either manual or nonmanual). These facts contradict the following claims put forward by Lillo-Martin (1986, 1991):

• There is a direct relation between manifestation of morphological agreement on the verb and presence of abstract syntactic agreement features in the clause; that is, syntactic agreement is present in clauses containing overtly agreeing verbs (like GIVE) but not in clauses containing nonagreeing verbs (like LOVE).

• Null subjects in ASL may be licensed either by syntactic agreement (if present) or by a topic. More specifically, null subjects of agreeing verbs are *pro*, licensed by Agr;[15] null subjects of nonagreeing verbs are variables licensed by a (lexically filled or null) topic, as in Chinese.[16] According to Lillo-Martin (1986, 432), null pronouns occur "with nonagreeing verbs in just the same places in which null pronouns occur in Chinese."

The occurrence of nonmanual markings of agreement with both agreeing and nonagreeing verbs clearly shows that Lillo-Martin's first claim is incorrect. The absence of morphological agreement inflection on the verb does not imply the absence of syntactic agreement features.

With respect to Lillo-Martin's second claim, a licensing-by-topic account of the distribution of null subjects with nonagreeing verbs was first considered by Kegl (1985b, 484–485, 488). However, Kegl noted cases involving null subjects of plain verbs that such a mechanism could not account for (sentences for which no topic was available to license the null element).[17] Additional evidence against the topic-licensing account, based on straightforward facts about the distribution of topics and null arguments in ASL, is offered by ABKN (1992, 1994), who found that several predictions of the topic-licensing hypothesis fail to hold for ASL. ABKN present cases like (16) (ABKN 1992, ex. (72)), where a null subject disjoint in reference from both topics is acceptable.[18]

Context: John is arranging the catering for a dinner for members of his family, Bill, Sue, and Mary. John knows everyone's tastes and preferences. He is discussing the vegetable course. He knows that as far as his brother, Bill, is concerned, he likes artichokes. He also knows that as for his sister Sue, she likes asparagus.

$$\frac{\text{t2-bg}}{} \qquad \frac{\text{t2-bg}}{} \qquad \frac{\text{head tilt}_k}{}$$

(16) $\overline{\text{MARY}_i, \overline{\text{VEGETABLE}_j, e_k \text{ KNOW IX}_i \text{ LIKE CORN}}}$
    'As for Mary, as for vegetables, (he = John) knows she likes corn.'

Since an ASL sentence allows a maximum of two topics (Aarons 1994; Kegl 1985b; see also chapter 4), one cannot resort to postulating a (third) null topic to explain how the null subject may be licensed. Lillo-Martin would predict sentences like (16) to be ungrammatical; however, they are acceptable in an appropriate discourse context. Thus, ABKN (1992) show that null subjects of nonagreeing verbs do not, in fact, exhibit the same patterns of distribution as null subjects in Chinese, counter to Lillo-Martin's claim.

Lillo-Martin offers no explicit argument to support her claim that ASL sentences involving nonagreeing verbs should be analyzed in the same way as Chinese sentences with respect to the distribution of null arguments. Although she states (1986, 428), "I will argue here that there is an analysis of null arguments with nonagreeing verbs," she does not actually argue for any analysis as it applies to ASL. She presents Huang's (1984) account for Chinese. She then shows that ASL qualifies as a discourse-oriented language according to Huang's criteria. Finally, she says (1986, 431) that Huang's account "will work equally well for ASL."

Lillo-Martin's proposal is especially puzzling, since she states, as justification for exploiting Huang's analysis of the licensing of null arguments in Chinese, that null subjects of nonagreeing verbs in ASL occur in the same places as null arguments in Chinese. Significantly, in Chinese, the relation between the topic and the null element with which it is coindexed does *not* obey Subjacency. This is precisely what leads Huang to argue that the null elements are base-generated and bound by topics and that movement is not involved in the Chinese structures that Lillo-Martin equates with ASL sentences containing nonagreeing verbs. (Thus, Lillo-Martin is incorrect when she says (1991, 83) that Huang (1984) "argues that these empty categories are not pronominals, but variables left by the movement of an empty topic which is then coindexed with an appropriate preceding topic.") Nonetheless, Lillo-Martin uses evidence from

Subjacency effects in ASL to support her claim that null arguments of
nonagreeing verbs should be analyzed in the same way as null arguments
in Chinese.

This is not the only respect in which the ASL data involving sentences
with nonagreeing verbs do not parallel Chinese. One further piece of evidence that Huang offers for analyzing null arguments as variables is the
fact that such elements cannot be A-bound (and thus obey Principle C).

(17) *Chinese*
     Zhangsan shuo [Lisi bu renshi *e*].
     Zhangsan say   Lisi not know
     'Zhangsan said that Lisi did not know [him].'
     (from Huang 1984, 537, ex. (19d))

Huang (1984, 538) says of (17) that "the embedded object EC [empty
category] may refer only to someone whose reference is fixed outside of
the entire sentence, but not to the matrix subject *Zhangsan*."

Although Lillo-Martin (1991, 92–101) discusses issues surrounding the
Chinese data in (17) at some length, as well as similar data in Japanese
(from Hasegawa 1984–85), she does not examine the comparable case in
ASL. In fact, in ASL, the null object of a nonagreeing verb (accompanied
by nonmanual agreement marking) can refer to the matrix subject.

$$
\begin{array}{ll}
 & \underline{\hspace{2.5cm}\text{head tilt}_j} \\
 & \underline{\hspace{2.5cm}\text{eye gaze}_i} \\
(18)\ \text{JOHN}_i\ \text{IX}_i\ \text{THINK MARY}_j & \text{LOVE}\ e_i
\end{array}
$$

     'John$_i$ thinks Mary loves (him$_i$).'

The ability of the null element in (18) to be A-bound supports analyzing it
as *pro*, not as a variable. The fact that nonmanual agreement marking is
required in such a sentence shows that it is the expression of agreement
that is licensing the null pronominal.

Lillo-Martin does, however, observe differences in the distribution of
null elements co-occurring with agreeing and nonagreeing verbs, which
she suggests can be explained by postulating different licensing mechanisms in the two cases. The basis for Lillo-Martin's pursuit of the idea
that null arguments of plain and agreeing verbs are licensed by different
mechanisms seems to be the (correct) observation that—when one re-
stricts attention to sentences that do not contain nonmanual expressions
of syntactic agreement, as Lillo-Martin does (albeit unknowingly)—the
distribution of null arguments of plain verbs is more limited than the dis-

tribution of null arguments of agreeing verbs. However, the grammatical sentences that she presents involving a nonovert argument of a plain verb ostensibly licensed by an overt topic actually involve moved rather than base-generated topics.[19] Although Lillo-Martin does not distinguish between moved and base-generated topics (see section 4.2.1.3), she does claim that the null argument of a plain verb is not allowed in constructions that she appears to analyze as involving long-distance extraction of a topic out of an island (Lillo-Martin 1986, 1991, 1992).

Thus, although the presence of the topic is not incidental to the grammaticality of the sentences Lillo-Martin presents containing null arguments of plain verbs, the grammaticality of such sentences does not bear on the licensing mechanism(s) for null arguments. It would seem that, although Lillo-Martin has uncovered evidence for two kinds of null elements (as suggested in the title of her 1986 paper), she has not discovered a *pro* licensed by agreement as opposed to a *variable* licensed by topic (as proposed by Huang for Chinese). Instead, she has found evidence for distinguishing *pro* from traces.

To summarize, the ASL data show that agreement can be expressed nonmanually in clauses containing verbs without overt morphological agreement inflection, and that these nonmanual expressions of agreement are capable of licensing null arguments. A topic-licensing account of the distribution of null arguments with nonagreeing verbs, as proposed by Lillo-Martin, makes predictions that are not supported by the ASL facts. This is, of course, not to say that there are no discourse-level considerations that enter into determining when pronouns (null or otherwise) are used in language.

We conclude, then, that null arguments in ASL are uniformly licensed by overt expressions of agreement. Thus, the strategy for licensing null elements in ASL is the same as has been proposed for other languages with rich agreement systems.

5.2.4.2 The Nature of Agreement Features The existence and distribution of nonmanual markings of agreement in ASL support the postulation of functional projections (independent of tense and aspect projections, as will be demonstrated in section 5.4) containing abstract agreement features (counter to proposals in Baker 1996 and Chomsky 1995a).[20] Further, syntactic agreement features appear to have the same status as other abstract syntactic features (like +neg, discussed in chapter 3, and +wh, to be discussed in chapter 7): they have nonmanual expressions whose distribution follows the same generalizations that have been shown to hold for other nonmanual syntactic markings in the language. Thus, the evidence from ASL argues against eliminating abstract agreement features and agreement projections from syntactic theory.

5.2.4.3 Duality of Features and Feature Checking The analysis of clausal agreement put forth in this chapter relies crucially on a feature-checking mechanism, whereby features are located both on lexical items (added to the lexical item prior to its insertion into the syntax) and in the heads of functional projections. It has been shown that, with respect to agreement, both sets of features receive expression in ASL: agreement features on the verb are expressed through morphological inflection, and agreement features in functional heads may be expressed nonmanually, through head tilt and/or eye gaze. The ASL agreement phenomena support the postulation of a feature-checking mechanism over an alternative conception in which lexical items acquire features in the course of the syntactic derivation (e.g., through head raising), as in Pollock 1989. This kind of direct evidence for the dual representation of syntactic features and a feature-checking mechanism has been hard to come by. This is just one example where data from ASL (and signed languages generally) yield important evidence relevant to issues in syntactic theory.

5.3 Tense

Evidence from ASL supports the position that TP constitutes a functional projection distinct from AgrP, and that TP dominates AgrP. Before examining that evidence, however, we address prior claims that ASL lacks grammatical tense (see, e.g., Fischer and Gough 1978; Fischer and Janis 1989, 289; Friedman 1975; Padden 1983, 1988; Perlmutter 1991; Wilbur 1979, 45). We argue that ASL has a set of lexical tense markers that occur in the head position of TP, and that these markers are distinct from morphologically related temporal adverbials; they have different articulatory and distributional properties.

Many of the lexical tense markers that we have identified, listed in table 5.2, are similar in articulation to related time adverbials, which frequently occur in sentence-initial or sentence-final positions. The similarity between tense markers and time adverbials may be partly to blame for claims that ASL lacks grammatical tense. However, tense markers and time adver-

Table 5.2
Lexical tense markers. (Note that the tense markers used by a signer may vary somewhat from one individual to the next.)

Marker	Meaning	Articulation
PAST$_{tns}$	Past tense	Bent B handshape taps (or moves toward) the shoulder
RECENT-PAST$_{tns}$	Past tense, restricted to the recent past	Articulated either like PAST$_{tns}$ but with more restrained movement, or like RECENT, in either case co-occurring with the "cs" (cheek-to-shoulder) facial expression
FORMERLY$_{tns}$	Formerly	A 5 handshape moving in a small circular motion with thumb side brushing near collar bone
#EX	Habitual past	Identical to the fingerspelled loansign used as a nominal prefix
UP-TO-NOW (often glossed SINCE)	From some time in the past to the present	Articulated with two index fingers, bent at the first knuckle, palm downward, fingertip points contacting upper shoulder and moving in an arcing motion to a palm-up orientation at about chest height in front of the body
IMMED-PRESENT$_{tns}$	Immediate present	Similar to the manual sign NOW but articulated closer to the body, co-occurring with a nonmanual marking in which teeth are clenched, lips are stretched, and mouth corners are pulled downward
FUTURE$_{tns}$	Future tense	B handshape oriented palm sideward starting near the dominant side of the face and moving forward along a fixed pathlength

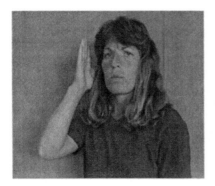 

Figure 5.3
FUTURE$_{tns}$

bials can be distinguished on the basis of differences in articulation and distribution.

5.3.1 Articulatory Properties of Tense Markers and Time Adverbials

Although the articulation of many time signs may vary to express greater or lesser distance in time, as discussed in chapter 3, such modulations are prohibited with time signs that occur in the preverbal "modal" position. The generalization that emerges is that although adverbials permit this articulatory variation, tense markers are more restricted, in terms of both articulatory properties and syntactic distribution.

For example, the future tense marker (glossed as FUTURE$_{tns}$) does not vary in its articulation. A fixed pathlength is required for the future tense marker, as well as for other lexical tense markers related to time adverbials that display variability. The (only possible) articulation of FUTURE$_{tns}$ is illustrated in figure 5.3. This contrasts with the possibilities demonstrated for FUTURE$_{adv}$ illustrated in chapter 3.[21]

Thus, it would appear that many lexical tense markers constitute frozen forms of time adverbials. However, not all tense markers have related time adverbials. Consider the tense marker #EX, which is used by some (but not all) signers. This marker actually represents a fusion of past tense and habitual aspect, yielding the habitual past, analogous (in many cases) to the English analytic habitual past *used to* construction (see, e.g., Comrie 1976).[22] The sign #EX is related to the prefix found in expressions such as these:

(19) #EX+PRESIDENT
'ex-president'

(20) #EX+WIFE
'ex-wife'

For many signers, this morpheme can also be used as a lexical marker of the habitual past.

$$\overline{\qquad\qquad\qquad\text{neg}\qquad}$$
(21) JOHN #EX NOT LIKE CHOCOLATE
'John didn't used to like chocolate.'

However, #EX does not have an adverbial function. #EX cannot appear sentence-initially or sentence-finally (in positions where adverbials may appear), as shown in (22) and (23).

(22) *JOHN LIKE CHOCOLATE #EX

(23) *#EX JOHN LIKE CHOCOLATE

Thus, the case of #EX provides additional support for the existence of distinct classes of lexical tense markers and time adverbials.

5.3.2 Distribution of Lexical Tense Markers

In contrast to adverbials, lexical tense markers have a highly restricted syntactic distribution. Lexical tense markers and modals occur in a single syntactic position,[23] one in which adverbials do not appear.[24] In fact, tense markers exhibit the same distribution as do modals.

· A modal or tense marker comes between the subject and the verb.

(24) JOHN CAN BUY HOUSE
'John can buy a house.'

(25) JOHN MUST BUY HOUSE
'John must buy a house.'

(26) JOHN FUTURE$_{tns}$ BUY HOUSE
'John will buy a house.'

(27) JOHN PAST$_{tns}$ LIVE CHICAGO
'John lived in Chicago.'

· In negative sentences, a modal or tense marker precedes the negative sign (with which it may contract).

$$\overline{\text{neg}}$$
(28) JOHN SHOULD $\overline{\text{NOT BUY}}$ HOUSE
'John should not buy a house.'

$$\overline{\text{neg}}$$
(29) JOHN $\overline{\text{SHOULD}^\wedge\text{NOT BUY HOUSE}}$
'John shouldn't buy a house.'

$$\overline{\text{neg}}$$
(30) JOHN FUTURE$_{tns}$ $\overline{\text{NOT BUY}}$ HOUSE
'John will not buy a house.'

$$\overline{\text{neg}}$$
(31) JOHN $\overline{\text{FUTURE}_{tns}^\wedge\text{NOT BUY HOUSE}}$
'John won't buy a house.'

• A modal or tense marker precedes a lexical marker of aspect.[25]

(32) JOHN SHOULD FINISH READ BOOK
'John should have read the book.'

(33) JOHN FUTURE$_{tns}$ FINISH READ BOOK
'John will have read the book.'

• Neither a modal nor a lexical tense marker can occur in an infinitival clause.[26] Temporal adverbials are permitted in such environments.[27]

(34) JOHN PREFER GO MOVIE
'John prefers to go to a movie.'

(35) *JOHN PREFER FUTURE$_{tns}$ GO MOVIE

(36) *JOHN PREFER CAN GO MOVIE

(37) JOHN PREFER GO MOVIE TOMORROW
'John prefers to go to a movie tomorrow.'

(38) JOHN WANT SELL CAR
'John wants to sell (his/a/the) car.'

(39) *JOHN WANT FUTURE$_{tns}$ SELL CAR

(40) *JOHN WANT SHOULD SELL CAR

(41) JOHN WANT SELL CAR FUTURE$_{adv}$
'John wants to sell his car in the future.'

These distributional facts provide strong evidence for analyzing signs like FUTURE$_{tns}$ as tense markers that, like modals, occur in the head of

TP.[28] Additional support comes from the distribution of tense markers and modals in sentence-final tags (see discussion of tags in chapter 4). A modal or tense marker frequently occurs as part of a tag. Significantly, temporal adverbials related to tense markers are not acceptable in the tag.

$$\overline{\qquad\qquad\text{hn}}$$
(42) JOHN FUTURE$_{\text{tns}}$ GO, FUTURE$_{\text{tns}}$

$$\overline{\qquad\qquad\text{hn}}$$
(43) *JOHN FUTURE$_{\text{tns}}$ GO, FUTURE$_{\text{adv}}$

$$\overline{\qquad\qquad\text{hn}}$$
(44) FUTURE$_{\text{adv}}$ JOHN GO, FUTURE$_{\text{tns}}$

$$\overline{\qquad\qquad\text{hn}}$$
(45) *FUTURE$_{\text{adv}}$ JOHN GO, FUTURE$_{\text{adv}}$

Given the analysis of T as the head of the clause, it is not surprising that the tag, which consists of a repetition of essential grammatical material from the main clause, frequently contains a modal or lexical tense marker, but prohibits an adverbial.

To summarize, in this section, we have examined the distribution of tense markers and related time adverbials. Tense markers exhibit a restricted distribution, different from that of time adverbials. The position in which a tense marker (or modal) may appear is T. Tense elements may also be found as part of a sentence-final tag.

5.3.3 Use of Lexical Tense Markers

The preceding discussion has established that ASL has several lexical tense markers that occur in the head of TP. However, overt tense markers do not appear in every ASL sentence. For example, there is no overt tense marker for simple present tense.

(46) JOHN LIKE CHOCOLATE
     'John likes chocolate.'

(47) JOHN BUY HOUSE
     'John is buying a house.'

Clauses without overt tense marking can sometimes be interpreted as referring to events that will occur in the future.

(48) NEXT-WEEK JOHN GO NEW-YORK
     'Next week, John is going to New York.'

This is not unlike what is found in English and other languages, in sentences such as the following:

(49) Tomorrow, I'm going to Switzerland.

(50) *French*
      Demain, je pars pour la Suisse.
      'Tomorrow, I leave for Switzerland.'

In fact, we would suggest that sentences like (48) are syntactically in the present tense; present tense just happens to not be overtly marked in ASL.

It is also possible to find cases where a clause with no overt tense marking receives a past tense interpretation.

(51) LAST-WEEK JOHN GO NEW-YORK
      'Last week, John went to New York.'

Various factors, such as the presence of temporal adverbials, semantic properties of the verb, and aspectual markings, may affect which interpretation is most salient in the absence of a lexical tense marker. However, further study is required to determine more precisely what conditions govern the use of lexical tense markers in ASL.

The absence of a lexical tense marker in sentences such as (48) and (51) may have contributed to claims that the presence of time adverbials, rather than grammatical tense, determines time information in ASL. As we have shown, however, the language does make use of a set of lexical items occurring in T.

5.3.4 Summary

In this section, we have demonstrated the existence of lexical tense markers, different from related time adverbials in their articulation and distribution. Whereas time adverbials exhibit variations in articulation, reflecting differing degrees of distance in time, lexical tense markers are restricted in their articulation. It is interesting to note that similar articulatory constraints are found in the nominal system as well. In chapter 6, we describe differences in articulation between related morphological forms occurring as determiners or locative adverbials. Determiners, like tense markers, require a restricted articulation. Thus, the articulatory restrictions described here may be characteristic of functional categories in ASL generally.

Modals and lexical tense markers occur in the canonical syntactic position in which tense elements have been shown to appear crosslinguistically. Like main verbs in other languages, main verbs in ASL may subcategorize for tensed or tenseless clauses; as predicted, lexical tense markers and modals are prohibited in tenseless clauses. Thus, the selectability of tense features supports the claim that T constitutes the head of the clause. The prevalence of modals and lexical tense markers in tags, which contain a repetition of essential grammatical material from the main clause, is also consistent with the claim that T heads the clause. Further evidence that T (as opposed to Agr) is the head of the clause, based on the distribution of tense in relation to nonmanual expressions of agreement, is presented in the next section.

5.4   The Hierarchical Structure of the ASL Clause

There has been some debate over whether TP dominates AgrP or AgrP dominates TP. Pollock (1989, 1997) argues for the former position; the latter position is represented by Belletti (1990) and Chomsky (1991) and has been adopted by numerous other researchers.[29] The data from ASL provide evidence that TP dominates both Agr_SP and Agr_OP in ASL. As shown in (52), nonmanual agreement markings begin after a lexical tense marker.[30]

$$\overline{ \text{head tilt}_i}$$
$$\overline{ \text{eye gaze}_j}$$

(52) $JOHN_i$ $FUTURE_{tns}$ [$+agr_i$]$_{Agr_S}$ [$+agr_j$]$_{Agr_O}$ $VISIT_j$ $MARY_j$
    'John will visit Mary.'

Examples like (52) demonstrate that tense markers are located in a structural position that lies outside the c-command domain of the Agr heads, that is, that TP dominates the Agr projections. The nonmanual markings of agreement essentially provide overt evidence about which elements lie within the scope of the Agr heads. Since the lexical tense marker is not contained within the scope of the agreement markings, it is not in a position that is c-commanded by the Agr heads. Thus, we conclude that TP dominates AgrP in ASL.

Examples (53) through (55) further delineate the hierarchical structure of the ASL clause. They show, respectively, that NegP dominates AgrP, Asp(ect)P dominates AgrP, and NegP dominates AspP, leading to the structural analysis in (56).[31]

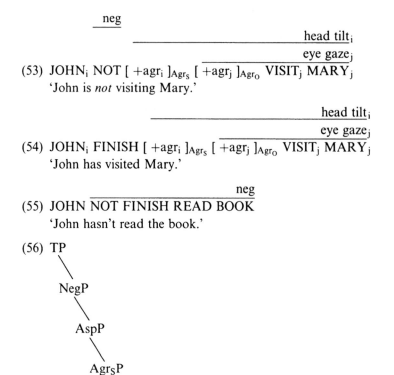

(53) JOHN$_i$ NOT [+agr$_i$]$_{Agr_s}$ [+agr$_j$]$_{Agr_o}$ VISIT$_j$ MARY$_j$
'John is *not* visiting Mary.'

(54) JOHN$_i$ FINISH [+agr$_i$]$_{Agr_s}$ [+agr$_j$]$_{Agr_o}$ VISIT$_j$ MARY$_j$
'John has visited Mary.'

(55) JOHN NOT FINISH READ BOOK
'John hasn't read the book.'

(56) TP

In sum, the distribution of nonmanual markings of agreement in ASL provides evidence that TP dominates AgrP, as has been argued by Pollock (1989, 1997).[32]

5.5   Chapter Summary

The examination of the agreement and tense systems of ASL has resulted in several significant conclusions relevant both to our understanding of the structure of ASL and to syntactic theory more generally. As we have shown, abstract agreement features are like other syntactic features in that they may be expressed nonmanually in ASL. The distribution of non-manual agreement markings can be captured by the same generalizations that describe the distribution of other nonmanual syntactic markings in the language. Thus, agreement features are on a par with other abstract syntactic features.

The dual expression of agreement in ASL (manual and nonmanual) lends support to a feature-checking approach in which agreement features are represented both on a lexical item and in a functional head. Features in Agr may be expressed nonmanually, through head tilt and eye gaze; agreement features present on the verb may be expressed through morphological inflection. In fact, the features on the verb and the features in Agr may take on different (but compatible) forms. Restrictions on the combinations of forms are explained in terms of asymmetric feature checking.

The co-occurrence of nonmanual expressions of agreement with all types of ASL verbs and their ability to license null arguments provide evidence against several long-standing claims made by Lillo-Martin (1986, 1991). The absence of morphological agreement inflection on a verb does not correlate with the absence of syntactic Agr, as "plain" verbs can co-occur with nonmanual expressions of agreement. Additionally, the finding that such nonmanual markings license null arguments in clauses containing plain verbs obviates the need for a "mixed" system for the licensing of null arguments, as proposed by Lillo-Martin (a proposal that in any event cannot account for the facts of ASL, as we have shown). This is a welcome result, as ASL therefore does not represent an oddity with respect to the typology of null argument languages. Like other languages, ASL makes use of a single strategy for licensing *pro*. Specifically, in ASL, *pro* is uniformly licensed by an expression of agreement, whether that expression be manual or nonmanual.

Finally, we have shown that, in ASL, TP and AgrP constitute distinct functional projections, and TP dominates AgrP. This conclusion is based on the distribution of lexical tense markers and nonmanual expressions of agreement. Specifically, tense markers (in T) occur outside the scope of nonmanual agreement markings. Thus, the ASL facts support the analysis of clause structure originally proposed by Pollock (1989) in which TP dominates AgrP.

Chapter 6

Determiners and Agreement
in DP

6.1 Introduction

Recent work on noun phrase structure in a variety of languages has led to proposals that the structure of noun phrases parallels what has been proposed for clauses.[1] Just as clauses are analyzed as containing a VP shell, so noun phrases are analyzed as being composed of an NP shell, above which there may be a number of functional projections associated with a variety of abstract syntactic features, such as number, person, and definiteness. From this perspective, the noun is viewed as the "ultimate head" of the noun phrase (Radford 1993) (the verb being the ultimate head of the clause), and the highest functional projection in the noun phrase is generally taken to be headed by a determiner. For this reason, noun phrases are generally viewed as determiner phrases, or DPs.[2]

In this chapter, we address the structure of DP in ASL, focusing in particular on the manifestation of D elements and agreement[3] in nonpossessive and possessive constructions.[4] For further detail about the analysis of DP constructions in ASL, see MacLaughlin 1997. Here we present the following facts:

• ASL has both a definite and an indefinite determiner, which occur in an initial D position. These same elements also function as pronouns, supporting proposals that pronouns are determiners.

• Like agreement in clauses, agreement in DP may be expressed both manually and nonmanually, through head tilt and eye gaze. Nonmanual expressions of agreement within DP exhibit essentially the same patterns of distribution as in the clause: possessive DPs pattern like transitive clauses and nonpossessive DPs pattern like intransitive clauses.

The distribution of nonmanual agreement marking in DP further supports the conclusions of chapter 5 with respect to agreement. Agreement features are similar to other syntactic features in heading their own functional projections and receiving nonmanual expression in ASL. The similarities in the patterns of agreement marking found in the clause and in the noun phrase show that noun phrases and clauses are parallel in structure, and that agreement plays an important role in both domains.

6.2 Determiners

The ASL literature contains conflicting statements about whether ASL possesses determiners, ranging from claims that signed languages in general lack determiners (De Vriendt and Rasquinet 1989) to suggestions that in ASL, index (pointing) signs, which are found both prenominally and postnominally within noun phrases, may function as determiners in either position (Hoffmeister 1977, 1978; Kegl 1977; Wilbur 1979; Zimmer and Patschke 1990). We have argued (BKMN 1995; MacLaughlin 1997) that ASL has both definite and indefinite determiners, occurring in an initial D position, and that DP-internal postnominal indexes are locative adverbials.

6.2.1   Definite Determiners

We claim that there is a characteristic index sign found prenominally within DP that functions as a definite determiner. This determiner index sign, illustrated in figure 6.1, is distinguishable from other index signs that serve different functions, on the basis of semantic properties. When a DP contains such an index in prenominal position, the DP is interpreted as definite, as shown in (1).[5]

Figure 6.1
The definite determiner

(1) [IX_{det_i} BOY]$_{DP}$ LIKE CHOCOLATE
    'The boy likes chocolate.'

Index signs may also occur postnominally within the noun phrase, although with a different function that had not previously been distinguished from that of the prenominal index.[6] We claim that these postnominal indexes are, in fact, locative adverbials, of the same kind that are found elsewhere in the language, as in (2).

(2) JOHN LIVE IX_{adv_i}
    'John lives there.'

When such indexes occur in postnominal position within DP, they provide information about the location of the referent, but they do not contribute information about definiteness. In fact, such indexes are found in both definite and indefinite noun phrases, as the following examples demonstrate. In (3), the adverbial index co-occurs with the definite determiner;[7] in (4), it co-occurs with (what we analyze to be) the indefinite determiner, SOMETHING/ONE$_{det}$ (as we will discuss in section 6.2.2).

(3) JOHN KNOW [IX_{det_i} MAN IX_{adv_i}]$_{DP}$
    'John knows the man over there.'

(4) JOHN KNOW [SOMETHING/ONE$_{det}$ MAN IX_{adv_i}]$_{DP}$
    'John knows a man over there.'

The controversy surrounding the existence of a definite determiner in ASL may stem, in part, from the fact that not all noun phrases that receive a definite interpretation necessarily contain an overt manual sign functioning as a definite determiner. A DP without a prenominal index may be interpreted as either definite or indefinite, as in (5).[8]

(5) JOHN READ BOOK
    'John read a/the book.'

This is true whether or not the DP contains a postnominal index.

(6) [BOY IX_{adv_i}]$_{DP}$ LIKE CHOCOLATE
    '(A/the) boy over there likes chocolate.'

However, note that (7), which differs from (6) only in that it contains an additional prenominal index, requires a definite reading (as does example (1)).

(7) [IX_{det_i} BOY IX_{adv_i}]$_{DP}$ LIKE CHOCOLATE
    'The boy over there likes chocolate.'

Thus, within the noun phrase, the prenominal index that we have identified here is a definite determiner, whereas the postnominal index is a locative adverbial. We analyze this prenominal index, associated with a definite interpretation, as a determiner occurring in D. Postnominal indexes, in contrast, receive an adverbial interpretation and may occur in both definite and indefinite DPs. We suggest that the adverbial is an adjunct right-adjoined to an intermediate position within DP (evidence for the adjunction site of postnominal DP-internal modifiers, based on the distribution of nonmanual agreement marking within DP, is discussed in section 6.4.2.3).

6.2.2 Indefinite Determiners
In addition to the definite determiner, ASL has a singular indefinite determiner, which we gloss as SOMETHING/ONE$_{det}$ (since this sign can, when used without a following overt NP, be translated by the English *something* or *someone*).

Context: A videotape is missing. John asks where it it is. Bill answers:

(8) [SOMETHING/ONE$_{det}$ STUDENT]$_{DP}$ HAVE VIDEOTAPE
    'A student has the videotape.'

Like the definite determiner, the indefinite determiner occurs only in pre-nominal position.[9] Notice that there are fewer confounding effects in analyzing indefinite DPs, since, unlike the index used for the definite determiner, there is no distinct adverbial sign that has the same form as the indefinite determiner.

  Like the definite determiner, the indefinite determiner need not appear in every indefinite noun phrase. This is illustrated in the following example, which could also be used in the situation described in (8):

(9) STUDENT HAVE VIDEOTAPE
    'A student has the videotape.'

  The articulation of the indefinite determiner displays interesting characteristics that are directly related to the way in which ASL makes use of space for indefinite reference. The indefinite determiner is articulated with the same handshape used for the definite determiner (a G handshape), but with the palm oriented inward and index finger pointing upward (see figure 6.2), with a slight tremoring motion in the upper forearm. This sign is generally accompanied by a nonmanual expression of uncertainty, which includes a wrinkled nose, furrowed brows, and a slight rapid head shake.[10] Both the degree of tremoring motion in the forearm and the intensity of the nonmanual expression may vary in relation to the degree of

Figure 6.2
The indefinite determiner SOMETHING/ONE_det

(un)identifiability that is associated with a referent. For a highly identifiable referent, the tremoring motion essentially disappears to the point that the indefinite determiner is articulated similarly to the numeral ONE.[11] At the other extreme, for a largely unknown referent, SOMETHING/ONE may exhibit more tremoring and a lengthier articulation, and the nonmanual expression is more intense.

Notice that the manual articulation of the indefinite determiner contrasts with that of the definite determiner, in that the indefinite determiner is articulated in an area of space, whereas the definite determiner is associated with a point. This distinction reflects the more general difference in the spatial representation of definites versus indefinites in ASL, discussed in chapter 3.

The indefinite determiner occurs only in prenominal position within DP. We analyze the indefinite determiner as occurring in D, the same position that houses the definite determiner.[12]

6.2.3 Pronouns
Both definite and indefinite determiners can function as pronouns, occurring with no following nominal material. This supports suggestions by Postal (1969) and Abney (1987), among others, that pronouns are essentially determiners.

(10) IX_det_i ARRIVE
'He/She/It arrived.'

(11) SOMETHING/ONE_det ARRIVE
'Someone/Something arrived.'

In the rest of this chapter, we will use the notation IX_{pro} (or SOMETHING/
ONE_{pro}) when IX_{det} (or SOMETHING/ONE_{det}) functions as a pronominal, for purposes of clarity.

The fact that determiners and (strong) pronouns are identical in form
in ASL would seem to present a counterexample to Cardinaletti's (1994)
claim about strong and weak (clitic) pronouns and determiners. She proposes that weak pronouns are intransitive determiners, occurring in D,
whereas strong pronouns are N heads that raise to D. Evidence for this
analysis comes, in part, from the observation that weak pronouns and
determiners frequently exhibit the same form. Within Cardinaletti's account, both are D elements. However, strong pronouns are not expected
to have the same form as determiners, since strong pronouns are Ns. In
ASL, though, strong pronouns, both definite and indefinite, exhibit the
same form as the definite and indefinite determiners.

6.2.4   Articulatory Differences: Determiners, Pronominals, and Adverbials
Although, as we have mentioned, a variety of different indexes, occurring
in different syntactic positions and having different functions, may be
found within DP, they nonetheless exhibit articulatory differences. Specifically, the articulation of an adverbial may vary in order to express
precise information about the relevant location. For example, to identify
a distant location, an adverbial index can be articulated with a tremoring
hand movement and a large, slow arc, as shown in figure 6.3 (along with a
characteristic nonmanual expression). The index sign may also trace a
path to the location, simulating moving around corners, for example.
Such variations in articulation are found within DP on indexes in final
position; definite determiner indexes do not allow this variation.

far

(12) $JOHN_{j\ j}GIVE_i$ [IX_{det_i} MAN IX_{adv_i} "far"]$_{DP}$ NEW COAT
       'John gave the man way over there a new coat.'

It should be noted, however, that it is not impossible to find variably
articulated indexes occurring before the noun. In such cases, this index
also precedes the determiner (if there is one).

far

(13)   JOHN $_{neu}GIVE_{indef}$ IX_{adv_i} "far" [SOMETHING/ONE_{det}
       WOMAN] BOOK
       'John gave a woman over there a book.'

Figure 6.3
Articulation of IX_{adv} "far": beginning and end of sign

Thus, it is clear in such cases that the variably articulated index is not functioning as a determiner.[13]

In sum, adverbial indexes exhibit variations in articulation, whereas definite determiners exhibit a restricted articulation. This is reminiscent of what was described in chapter 5 with respect to tense markers and related temporal adverbials. In both cases, functional elements (T and D) are restricted in their articulatory properties, whereas related adverbials permit variations in articulation.

6.2.5 Summary

ASL has two determiners, IX_{det} and $SOMETHING/ONE_{det}$, which are associated with definite and indefinite interpretations, respectively. These signs occur in an initial D position within DP. The same signs may function pronominally when they are not followed by any other overt material within DP. A DP, whether definite or indefinite, may also contain a postnominal index, functioning as a locative adverbial. Indexes that function as determiners differ from those that function as adverbials in terms of their semantic, distributional, and articulatory properties.

6.3 Possessive Constructions

The ASL possessive construction is characterized by the word order [(PossessorDP) Possessive-Marker NP]$_{DP}$.[14] Examples are shown in (14) and (15).

(14) FRANK$_i$ POSS$_i$ NEW CAR
   'Frank's new car'

(15) POSS$_i$ NEW CAR
   'his/her new car'

The possessive marker POSS is an indexical sign formed with an open handshape such that the palm is oriented toward the location associated with the possessor, as illustrated in figure 6.4.[15] There is also a neutral form of POSS (see figure 6.5), which may be used with indefinite possessors and in *wh*-possessive constructions (*wh*-possessives are discussed further in chapter 7). In such cases, the sign is articulated in a kind of

Figure 6.4
Articulation of POSS$_i$

Figure 6.5
Articulation of POSS$_{neu}$

neutral position, close to the signer's body, and this spatial location does not carry referential information.

(16) SOMETHING/ONE$_{pro}$ POSS$_{neu}$ BOOK
    'someone's book'

(17) WHO POSS$_{neu}$ BOOK
    'whose book'

In certain cases, the notion of possession may be expressed without an overt POSS marker. This occurs frequently with kinship relations, and often with inalienable possession as well, as in (18) and (19).[16]

(18) JOHN (POSS) BROTHER
    'John's brother'

(19) JOHN (POSS) LEG
    'John's leg'

In most cases, POSS is required. For example, 'whose' questions cannot normally be expressed without POSS, as shown in (20).[17]

(20) WHO *(POSS) BOOK
    'whose book'

Finally, POSS may never be omitted if there is no overt possessor phrase (i.e., if POSS is functioning pronominally).

(21) *(POSS) BOOK
    'his/her/your book'

The basic structure that we adopt for ASL possessive DPs is shown in (22).

(22)

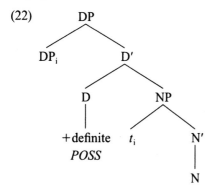

We assume that the possessor phrase is generated as the subject of the NP.

In ASL, it surfaces in [Spec, DP], as evidenced by the word order facts. We analyze POSS as occurring in D. More specifically, we suggest that POSS occurs in a +definite D, given that prenominal possessive constructions pattern like definite DPs in a number of respects. First, although a possessive construction can be used to introduce a new referent into the discourse (a property normally associated with indefinite phrases), possessives carry a uniqueness presupposition, which is characteristic of definites (Barker 1995). Additionally, possessive constructions exhibit the "definite" pattern of nonmanual agreement marking (see section 6.4). Finally, analyzing POSS as occurring in D immediately explains the incompatibility of determiners in ASL possessive constructions: since the determiner position is occupied by the possessive marker, there is no position available for a determiner.

6.4   Agreement

Within DP, agreement is expressed both manually and nonmanually, via the same nonmanual markings found in the clause: head tilt and eye gaze. There is a strong interdependence between expressions of definiteness and agreement. Both manual and nonmanual expressions of agreement may vary in form, depending on the definiteness of the element with which agreement is being expressed. We propose that the D position contains both definiteness features and agreement features, at least by Spell-Out. We show that nonmanual agreement marking within DP is parallel to what is found in the clause; in particular, nonpossessive DPs pattern like intransitive clauses, and possessive DPs pattern like transitive clauses.

6.4.1   Manual Expressions of Agreement

Lexical elements in D may manually express agreement features.[18] In fact, the definite determiner IX_{det} obligatorily expresses agreement; it is not possible to articulate the definite determiner without referencing the point in space associated with the DP. In contrast, the indefinite determiner, $SOMETHING/ONE_{det}$, optionally expresses agreement by being articulated at or oriented toward the spatial location associated with the DP. At the same time, the indefinite determiner may also express information about the degree of (un)identifiability of the referent, by moving through a smaller or larger region of space. Thus, like the definite determiner, the indefinite determiner may simultaneously convey information about (in)definiteness and agreement features.

In possessive constructions, the possessive marker POSS expresses the agreement features of the possessor. The articulation of POSS does not vary in relation to the definiteness of the possessor. With both definite and indefinite possessors, POSS points to the location in space associated with the referent. This is consistent with the claim that POSS occurs in a +definite D; we assume, therefore, that POSS is also +definite. The neutral form of the possessive marker, which is generally used with indefinite possessors that are not associated with any location in space (e.g., in 'whose' constructions), does not express any agreement features.

In sum, elements that occur in D (IX_{det}, SOMETHING/ONE$_{det}$, and POSS) are capable of expressing agreement manually by accessing (pointing to or orienting toward) the appropriate spatial location. At the same time, these elements express the definiteness features in D; expressions of definiteness and agreement features are essentially inseparable (as in many other languages). We assume that these manual expressions of person agreement are a reflection of inflectional features present on the lexical items in D. These agreement features (as well as definiteness features) are then associated with the D head into which those lexical items are inserted. Further support for the existence of person agreement features within D comes from the nonmanual realization of agreement features within DP, discussed in the next section.

6.4.2 Nonmanual Expressions of Agreement
Agreement features in DP may be expressed nonmanually through head tilt and eye gaze, the same nonmanual devices that express agreement in the clause. As in the clause, these markings are essentially optional, although they occur quite frequently. In the next two subsections, we describe the manifestation of nonmanual agreement markings in nonpossessive and possessive DPs, respectively. We then show how careful study of the distribution of nonmanual agreement markings in DP can provide evidence relevant to determining the structural analysis of certain DP-internal postnominal modifiers.

6.4.2.1 Nonpossessive DPs In definite DPs, agreement may be expressed nonmanually by either head tilt or eye gaze (or both) toward the location in space associated with the DP's agreement features. We claim that these nonmanual markings reflect agreement features located in D. The nonmanual agreement markings achieve their maximal intensity simultaneously with the articulation of the definite determiner. Thus, the maximal degree of head tilt co-occurs with the maximal extension of the pointing sign.[19] The timing of these markings in relation to the articulation of the determiner supports the claim that they express agreement features contained in D.

The distribution of the nonmanual markings associated with agreement features follows from the generalizations about nonmanual syntactic markings presented in chapter 3, under the assumption that the agreement features are contained in D. When a definite determiner is present (providing manual material with which the nonmanual correlates of the agreement features may be coarticulated), spread of the nonmanual markings over the c-command domain of D is optional. In such cases, then, there are six possible realizations of nonmanual agreement marking, taking into account different combinations of head tilt and eye gaze, as shown in the examples in (23), all of which have the same English gloss.[20]

(23) a. $\text{IX}_{\text{pro}_{1p}}$ KNOW [$\overline{\text{IX}_{\text{det}_i}}^{\text{eg}_i}$ OLD MAN]$_{\text{DP}}$
     'I know the old man.'

   b. $\text{IX}_{\text{pro}_{1p}}$ KNOW [$\overline{\text{IX}_{\text{det}_i}}^{\text{ht}_i}$ OLD MAN]$_{\text{DP}}$

   c. $\text{IX}_{\text{pro}_{1p}}$ KNOW [$\overline{\text{IX}_{\text{det}_i}}^{\substack{\text{ht}_i \\ \text{eg}_i}}$ OLD MAN]$_{\text{DP}}$

   d. $\text{IX}_{\text{pro}_{1p}}$ KNOW [$\overline{\text{IX}_{\text{det}_i} \text{ OLD MAN}}^{\text{eg}_i}$]$_{\text{DP}}$

   e. $\text{IX}_{\text{pro}_{1p}}$ KNOW [$\overline{\text{IX}_{\text{det}_i} \text{ OLD MAN}}^{\text{ht}_i}$]$_{\text{DP}}$

   f. $\text{IX}_{\text{pro}_{1p}}$ KNOW [$\overline{\text{IX}_{\text{det}_i} \text{ OLD MAN}}^{\substack{\text{ht}_i \\ \text{eg}_i}}$]$_{\text{DP}}$

When there is no determiner, the nonmanual markings (if present) must spread, as shown by the contrast in (24).[21]

(24) a. *$\text{IX}_{\text{pro}_{1p}}$ KNOW [$\overline{\text{OLD MAN}}^{\substack{\text{ht}_i \\ \text{eg}_i}}$]$_{\text{DP}_i}$

   b. $\text{IX}_{\text{pro}_{1p}}$ KNOW [$\overline{\text{OLD MAN}}^{\substack{\text{ht}_i \\ \text{eg}_i}}$]$_{\text{DP}_i}$
     'I know the old man.'

This obligatory spread is predicted, since there is no manual material in D with which the nonmanual marking may be coarticulated.

Finally, note that when the nonmanual agreement markings spread beyond D, they must spread over the entire c-command domain of D. The markings cannot end early, as shown by the unacceptability of (25).

$$\overline{\qquad\qquad\text{ht}_i}$$
$$\overline{\qquad\qquad\text{eg}_i}$$
(25) *$\text{IX}_{\text{pro}_{1p}}$ KNOW [$\overline{\text{IX}_{\text{det}_i}}$ OLD MAN]$_{\text{DP}}$

Although agreement features in indefinite DPs may also be expressed nonmanually via eye gaze, the eye gaze takes the indefinite form, described in chapter 5 in relation to indefinite object agreement, where the eyes gaze or wander over an area in space. Thus, just as the manual articulation of SOMETHING/ONE involves articulation in an area rather than a point, so the eye gaze associated with indefiniteness (when it marks agreement within the clause or the noun phrase) targets a more diffuse area than the eye gaze associated with a definite referent.

This nonmanual marking shows the same distribution as nonmanual markings in definite DPs. When an indefinite determiner is present, the nonmanual marking may occur over the determiner alone, or it may spread over the c-command domain of D. In the absence of a determiner, the nonmanual marking, if present, spreads obligatorily.

$$\overline{\qquad\text{indefinite gaze}_i}$$
(26) a. [SOMETHING/ONE$_{\text{det}}$ WOMAN]$_{\text{DP}_i}$ ARRIVE
        'A woman arrives.'

$$\overline{\qquad\qquad\qquad\text{indefinite gaze}_i}$$
    b. [SOMETHING/ONE$_{\text{det}}$ WOMAN]$_{\text{DP}_i}$ ARRIVE
        'A woman arrives.'

$$\overline{\text{indefinite gaze}_i}$$
(27) a. *[WOMAN]$_{\text{DP}_i}$ ARRIVE
$$\overline{\qquad\qquad\text{indefinite gaze}_i}$$
    b. [WOMAN]$_{\text{DP}_i}$ ARRIVE
        'A woman arrives.'

There is one difference, however, between definite and indefinite DPs with regard to the nonmanual realization of agreement features. Within indefinite DPs, nonmanual expression of agreement via head tilt is not possible (except in special contrastive contexts, where the head tilt has a different function). Thus, it would appear that head tilt as an expression of agreement within DP is restricted to definite DPs (as we will show, head tilt also occurs within possessive DPs, which are postulated to be +definite).[22]

To summarize, nonmanual agreement markings in nonpossessive DPs exhibit the expected behavior, if these markings are analyzed as expressions of agreement features located in D. The markings occur simultaneously with a manual determiner sign, if one is present. Possibilities for the spread of these markings are determined by the presence or absence of a manual sign in D. The simultaneous expression of definiteness and agreement in ASL (both manually and nonmanually) supports an analysis of DP in which D houses both definiteness and agreement features, as shown in (28).[23]

(28)

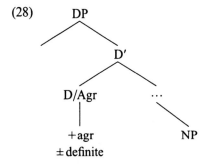

6.4.2.2 Possessive DPs In possessive constructions, both the agreement features associated with the possessor and those associated with the noun phrase (the possessee) may be expressed nonmanually, through head tilt and eye gaze, respectively. The possibilities for nonmanual markings within possessive DPs are summarized in the examples in (29). In (29a), the head tilt associated with possessor agreement spreads over the remainder of the phrase; in (29b), it occurs only over the possessive marker.[24]

$$\underline{\hspace{3.5cm}}\text{ht}_i$$
$$\underline{\hspace{2.5cm}}\text{eg}_j$$
(29) a. [JOHN$_i$ POSS$_i$ $\overline{\text{FRIEND}}_j$]$_{DP}$ HAVE CANDY
    'John's friend has candy.'

$$\underline{\hspace{1.2cm}}\text{ht}_i$$
$$\underline{\hspace{2.5cm}}\text{eg}_j$$
b. [JOHN$_i$ POSS$_i$ $\overline{\text{FRIEND}}_j$]$_{DP}$ HAVE CANDY
    'John's friend has candy.'

The nonmanual markings in these constructions are analyzed as expressions of two distinct sets of agreement features contained in two functional Agr heads, D/Agr$_S$ and Agr$_O$, as shown in the structure in (30).

(30)

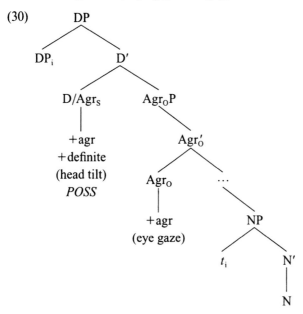

Head tilt co-occurs with POSS; the head begins tilting after the articulation of the possessor DP, if any,[25] and it reaches its maximum at the same time that POSS reaches its maximal extension. Spread of head tilt over the c-command domain of D is optional because POSS supplies manual material with which the head tilt may be coarticulated.

It is significant that head tilt is not possible in conjunction with the neutral form of the possessor, as shown in (31).

$$\overline{}\,ht_i$$

(31) *[SOMETHING/ONE$_{pro}$ POSS$_{neu}$ CAR]$_{DP}$ STOLEN

This contrasts with what was noted for agreement in the clause, where an overt head tilt can co-occur with neutral subject agreement marking on the verb. However, the construction in (31) differs from the situation in the clause in an important way, one that provides an immediate explanation for the facts. In (31), the nonmanual head tilt and the manual agreement marking on POSS are expressions of a single set of agreement features: those contained in D. Any expressions of this set of features must reflect the same feature values; thus, the combination of neutral and fully specified expressions is not possible. In contrast, in the clause, the combination of an overt head tilt and neutral manual agreement marking on the verb is allowed because the two manifestations of agreement are expressing different sets of (compatible) agreement features located in different positions: features in Agr and features associated with the agreement inflection on the verb. Although those features are required to be compatible, in the sense described in chapter 5, they are distinct and may be expressed independently.

Recall from the discussion of nonmanual agreement markings in non-possessive DPs that head tilt appears to be restricted to definite DPs. This claim is consistent with the distribution of head tilt in possessive DPs (which are postulated to be +definite). Interestingly, head tilt is possible in possessive constructions, whether the possessor phrase is definite or indefinite.

$$\overline{\qquad\qquad\text{ht}_i\qquad}$$
(32) [SOMETHING/ONE$_{pro}$ POSS$_i$ CAR]$_{DP}$ STOLEN
     'Someone's car was stolen.'

The fact that head tilt can occur with an indefinite possessor, as in (32), shows that head tilt is not restricted to expressing agreement with a definite argument. We conclude that head tilt in DP must be associated with a position containing a +definite feature; the agreement features in that same position need not be associated with a +definite possessor.

Whereas head tilt expresses the agreement features of the possessor, eye gaze expresses the agreement features of the possessee (i.e., those of the overall DP). Eye gaze exhibits different distributional characteristics from head tilt, supporting the analysis in (30) whereby head tilt and eye gaze are associated with agreement features located in distinct functional heads. First, eye gaze to the spatial location associated with the possessee begins after the possessive marker is signed (and hence after head tilt has reached its maximum) but immediately before any other lexical material in the DP. Second, eye gaze spreads obligatorily over the remainder of the DP (see (33) through (35)); unlike the distribution of head tilt, the distribution of eye gaze is not affected by the presence or absence of a possessive marker. These distributional facts are expected under the proposed analysis, as there is never any manual material in the Agr$_O$ position with which eye gaze may be coarticulated.[26]

$$\text{eg}_j$$
(33) [JOHN POSS$_i$ $\overline{\text{OLD HOUSE}_j}$]$_{DP}$ SOLD YESTERDAY
      'John's old house was sold yesterday.'

$$\text{eg}_j$$
(34) *[JOHN POSS$_i$ $\overline{\text{OLD}}$ HOUSE$_j$]$_{DP}$ SOLD YESTERDAY

$$\text{eg}_j$$
(35) *[JOHN POSS$_i$ OLD $\overline{\text{HOUSE}_j}$]$_{DP}$ SOLD YESTERDAY

The indefinite ("wandering") form of eye gaze, which is found in indefinite nonpossessive DPs and is associated with indefinite object agreement in the clause, is not possible in possessive DPs. This fact further supports analyzing possessive DPs as +definite.

In sum, in possessive constructions, two distinct sets of agreement features, associated with the possessor and the head noun, respectively, may be expressed nonmanually via head tilt and eye gaze. The distribution of these nonmanual markings provides evidence for postulating two distinct functional heads within DP that contain agreement features. Possessive constructions pattern with definite nonpossessive DPs in permitting head tilt and the definite form of eye gaze.[27]

6.4.2.3 Nonmanual Agreement and the Position of Postnominal Modifiers
The distribution of nonmanual agreement markings can provide important evidence about the internal structure of DP. For example, as we have just shown, the study of these markings supports the postulation of two sets of agreement features in distinct functional heads within possessive constructions. Here, we show that the data also provide evidence for the structural position of postnominal DP modifiers in ASL.

In ASL, a DP may contain one or more of a variety of postnominal modifiers, including predicative adjectives, predicative possessives, and locative adverbials. For present purposes, we focus on adjectives. DP-internal adjectives in ASL may occur either in prenominal position (as illustrated in earlier examples) or in postnominal position. Postnominal adjectives are restricted to a predicative interpretation; prenominal adjectives are not.[28] Following Cinque (1994), MacLaughlin (1997) analyzes prenominal adjectives as specifiers of functional projections above NP. Postnominal adjectives are viewed as modifiers right-adjoined within DP.[29] Evidence from the distribution of nonmanual agreement marking in DP shows that the adjunction site of postnominal adjectives lies within the c-command domain of the agreement features.

$$\overline{eg_i}$$

(36) a. SUE BUY [$\overline{\text{IX}_{\text{det}_i}}$ CAR BLUE]$_{\text{DP}}$
        'Sue is buying the blue car.'

$$\overline{eg_i}$$

  b. SUE BUY [$\overline{\text{IX}_{\text{det}_i} \text{ CAR BLUE}}$]$_{\text{DP}}$
        'Sue is buying the blue car.'

$$\overline{eg_i}$$

  c. SUE BUY [$\overline{\text{CAR BLUE}}$]$_{\text{DP}}$
        'Sue is buying the blue car.'

$$\overline{eg_i}$$

(37) *SUE BUY [$\overline{\text{IX}_{\text{det}_i} \text{ CAR BLUE}}$]$_{\text{DP}}$

As these data demonstrate, the c-command domain of D, where the agreement features are located, includes the position of postnominal adjectives. When the nonmanual agreement markings spread over this c-command domain, they occur over any postnominal adjectives as well. It is ungrammatical for the nonmanual markings to terminate prior to the articulation of a postnominal adjective, as shown by the unacceptability of (37).[30] Thus, the distribution of nonmanual agreement markings in DP provides evidence about the positioning of postnominal DP-internal adjectives.

6.4.3 Parallels with Agreement in the Clause

As we have shown, agreement features within the ASL DP are expressed nonmanually through head tilt and eye gaze. In possessive DPs, where there are two distinct sets of agreement features, head tilt is associated with possessor agreement, and eye gaze expresses the agreement features of the possessee. In nonpossessive DPs, there is only one set of agreement features, which may be expressed by either (or both) of the two available nonmanual devices.

The nonmanual expression of agreement features in DP is strikingly parallel to the nonmanual marking of agreement in the clause, described in chapter 5. In transitive clauses, subject and object agreement may be expressed through head tilt and eye gaze, respectively. In intransitive constructions, either nonmanual device (or both) may be used. More generally, then, we could say that, when a structural domain (a nominal phrase or a clause) contains a single set of agreement features, those features may be expressed nonmanually by either or both of the available

Table 6.1
Nonmanual expression of agreement in the noun phrase and in the clause

	Transitive	Intransitive
Clause	head tilt$_i$ eye gaze$_j$ DP$_i$ [+agr]$_{Agr_i}$ [+agr]$_{Agr_j}$ V DP$_j$	head tilt$_i$ eye gaze$_i$ DP$_i$ [+agr]$_{Agr_i}$ V
Noun phrase	head tilt$_i$ eye gaze$_j$ DP$_i$ [POSS]$_{Agr_i}$ [+agr]$_{Agr_j}$ NP$_j$	head tilt$_i$ eye gaze$_i$ [IX$_{det}$]$_{Agr_i}$ NP$_i$

nonmanual agreement devices. However, when a structural domain contains two distinct sets of agreement features, one set is expressed via head tilt and the other via eye gaze. In both the clause and the noun phrase, it is the higher set of agreement features, those associated with the subject (if the possessor is viewed as a subject), that is normally expressed through head tilt; eye gaze is associated with the lower set of agreement features. The parallels between nonmanual agreement marking in the clause and in the noun phrase are summarized in table 6.1.

Similar correspondences, with respect to case and agreement marking in transitive clauses and possessive DPs, on the one hand, and intransitive clauses and possessor-less DPs, on the other, have been observed cross-linguistically. For example, Abney (1987, chap. 2) notes that in Yup'ik, possessive noun phrases pattern like transitive clauses and nonpossessives like intransitives, with respect to agreement morphology. In Aleut, for nouns with possessors, the number agreement marking is identical to the object agreement marking on verbs; for nouns without possessors, it is like the subject agreement marking on verbs (Bergsland and Dirks 1981). Bittner and Hale (1996, 60) also report, "Many languages that employ the ergative Case use it both for the subject of a transitive VP and for the subject of a possessed NP, that is, the possessor. This holds not only for classical ergative languages, like Inuit, but also for languages with three-way or split Case systems." Thus, the parallelism in the manifestation of agreement relations in the clause and noun phrase in ASL is in keeping with the parallelism between clauses and noun phrases in other languages (see also Ouhalla 1991b; Szabolcsi 1987).

There are, however, some interesting (yet predictable) differences in the distribution of nonmanual agreement markings in the clause and the noun phrase. These differences stem from the possibility, in the noun phrase, of finding manual material in D with which a nonmanual expression of agreement may be coarticulated. When manual material is present, the spread of any associated nonmanual agreement marking is optional. In the clause, however, there is never any manual material in the Agr heads; thus, spread of nonmanual agreement markings in the clause is always obligatory. Obligatory spread is found in noun phrases as well, however, when there is no manual material in the relevant Agr head. In possessive constructions, for example, eye gaze marking agreement with the possessee must spread, as there is never any manual material in the position that houses the associated agreement features. In addition, nonmanual markings associated with D spread obligatorily when D contains no manual sign. In any case, the distribution of nonmanual agreement markings, both in the noun phrase and in the clause, follows the same generalizations that account for the distribution of other nonmanual syntactic markings in the language.

The similarities between nonmanual expressions of agreement in the noun phrase and the clause support the interpretation of these markings as reflections of syntactic agreement. Moreover, such findings provide further evidence that, crosslinguistically, noun phrases have an underlying structure analogous to that of the clause and that agreement features play an important role in both domains.

6.5 Chapter Summary

In this chapter, we have analyzed the structure of the ASL DP, focusing on determiners and agreement. On the basis of the evidence presented here, the following conclusions can be drawn:

• ASL has both a definite and an indefinite determiner, which occur in the head of a functional determiner phrase.
• In addition to definiteness features, the determiner position houses agreement features, which may be expressed nonmanually.
• In nonpossessive DPs, the single set of agreement features in D may be expressed nonmanually by head tilt and/or eye gaze. Head tilt is restricted to +definite DPs. The form of eye gaze varies depending on the definiteness of the DP.
• In possessive DPs, head tilt expresses "subject" agreement, and eye gaze expresses "object" agreement. These nonmanual markings occur

over different syntactic domains, supporting the postulation of two distinct functional heads housing two different sets of agreement features.

• Nonmanual realization of agreement in DP parallels what is found in the clause, thereby supporting the claim that agreement features play an important role in both domains, and that the structure of noun phrases is similar to that of clauses.

Chapter 7

Wh-Questions

7.1 Introduction

In this chapter, we focus on our analysis of *wh*-questions in ASL. We argue that *wh*-movement in ASL results in *wh*-phrases moving rightward to a [Spec, CP] position. The evidence for this analysis comes both from word order facts and from the pattern of distribution of nonmanual markings associated with the +wh feature. Since it has been claimed (Kayne 1994) that syntactic movement universally occurs only leftward, the data from question constructions in ASL have important theoretical consequences.

We should note that, although there is consensus in the literature that in ASL questions the *wh*-phrase need not move, but may remain in situ, there has been some controversy about whether *wh*-movement, when it occurs, involves movement to the left or right periphery of the sentence.[1] This controversy is due, in part, to disagreements about the allowable positions for a *wh*-phrase corresponding to the subject or object in simple ASL sentences. In section 7.2, we present the judgments of our informants and our own analysis of the data. In section 7.3, we discuss differing claims about these data and possible explanations for discrepancies in reported data. In section 7.4, we evaluate alternative accounts of *wh*-question constructions in ASL that rely on leftward *wh*-movement. We argue that those proposals cannot account for the ASL facts. We therefore maintain that Universal Grammar must allow for rightward movement.

7.2 The Case for Rightward *Wh*-Movement in ASL

We begin by considering sentences that have a single *wh*-phrase corresponding to the subject or object. Although there is also a common construction in ASL in which more than one occurrence of a *wh*-phrase corresponds to a single questioned argument (to be discussed in section 7.2.2), the directionality of movement is established most easily through consideration of the simple cases.

7.2.1 Sentences with a Single *Wh*-Phrase

In *wh*-questions, a *wh*-phrase occurs either in situ or in a clause-final position. These facts may be explained straightforwardly in terms of rightward *wh*-movement. The word order facts are decisive on this point (although there have been some disagreements about the data, which will be addressed later). Further evidence for this analysis is provided by the distribution and intensity of nonmanual *wh*-marking.

7.2.1.1 Word Order   A *wh*-phrase corresponding to a subject may occur either in the canonical, preverbal, subject position, as in (1), or at the right periphery of the sentence, as in (2).

$$\overline{\hspace{3cm}\text{wh}\hspace{1.5cm}}$$
(1) WHO LOVE JOHN
    'Who loves John?'

$$\overline{\hspace{3cm}\text{wh}\hspace{1.5cm}}$$
(2) t_i LOVE JOHN WHO$_i$
    'Who loves John?'

This is consistent with an analysis according to which the *wh*-phrase in (2) has moved rightward to a clause-final position.

In contrast, a *wh*-phrase corresponding to an object may not appear in sentence-initial position. Example (4), signed exactly as glossed,[2] is not acceptable to our informants.[3]

$$\overline{\hspace{3.5cm}\text{wh}\hspace{1cm}}$$
(3)   JOHN LOVE WHO
    'Who does John love?'

$$\overline{\hspace{3.5cm}\text{wh}\hspace{1cm}}$$
(4) *WHO JOHN LOVE

Although it seems clear from examples like (4) that the *wh*-object does not move leftward, it might, at first glance, appear difficult to test whether a *wh*-object in a sentence like (3) remains in VP or moves rightward. Nonetheless, by examining constructions containing TP-final adverbials,

Perlmutter (1991) demonstrates that the *wh*-object may move rightward out of VP. Consistent with an account in terms of rightward *wh*-movement to [Spec, CP], the *wh*-object may occur either VP-internally, as in (5), or in a right-peripheral position, as in (6).

$$\overline{\hspace{6cm}\text{wh}\hspace{0.5cm}}$$

(5) TEACHER LIPREAD WHO YESTERDAY
    'Who did the teacher lipread yesterday?'

$$\overline{\hspace{6cm}\text{wh}\hspace{0.5cm}}$$

(6) TEACHER LIPREAD t_i YESTERDAY WHO$_i$
    'Who did the teacher lipread yesterday?'

This sentence-final position is not a position in which a non-*wh* noun phrase occurs, as the ungrammaticality of (8) demonstrates.

(7) TEACHER LIPREAD JOHN YESTERDAY
     'The teacher lipread John yesterday.'

(8) *TEACHER LIPREAD YESTERDAY JOHN

In sum, when *wh*-movement occurs, it results in the *wh*-phrase appearing at the right periphery of the sentence.[4] We assume that the landing site in such cases is the canonical position into which *wh*-phrases move crosslinguistically; thus, we conclude that the *wh*-phrase moves rightward to a sentence-final specifier position that we identify as [Spec, CP].

Note that nothing hinges on the *label* of this projection. If evidence bears out the need for a more articulated C structure, as proposed, for example, in Rizzi 1997, it may turn out that crosslinguistically, *wh*-phrases move to the specifier position of some other functional projection: perhaps a focus projection, as Rizzi suggests. Crucially, we observe that *wh*-phrases move rightward to a specifier position of a functional projection higher than TP. For present purposes, we identify that projection as CP.

7.2.1.2 Distribution of Nonmanual *Wh*-Marking   *Wh*-questions in ASL obligatorily occur with a specific nonmanual expression. This nonmanual *wh*-marking consists, most notably, of furrowed brows, squinted eyes, and a slight side-to-side head shake (Baker and Cokely 1980d; Baker and Padden 1978; Baker-Shenk 1983, 1985), as illustrated in figure 7.1. Nonmanual *wh*-marking is associated with the +wh feature.[5] Thus, this marking is not only characteristic of +wh clauses in ASL; it is also found

Figure 7.1
Wh-marking with sign "WHAT". (From Aarons 1994. © Debra Aarons)

with +wh signs produced in isolation. It is precisely the inherent +wh feature contained within the lexical signs (e.g., WHO) heading *wh*-phrases[6] that enables such phrases to check the +wh feature posited in C when they move to [Spec, CP]. In this section, we examine the distribution of nonmanual *wh*-marking. As we will show, the distribution of *wh*-marking provides indirect support for the feature-checking approach to *wh*-movement taken in recent literature (e.g., Chomsky 1993).

In each of the sentences presented thus far, (1) through (6), *wh*-marking extends over the entire question. However, in certain constructions, *wh*-marking need not spread over the entire clause. The generalizations about the distribution of nonmanual markings in ASL established in chapter 3 correctly predict the cases of optional and obligatory spread of nonmanual *wh*-marking, but only on the assumption of rightward *wh*-movement.

The distinction between constructions in which the *wh*-marking may appear solely over the *wh*-phrase and those in which this marking obligatorily spreads over the entire question is explained as a function of the availability of manual material in [Spec, CP]. In cases where *wh*-movement has resulted in the occurrence of manual material to the right of TP, in [Spec, CP] position, the *wh*-marking associated with the +wh feature in C is able to be coarticulated with manual material, and, therefore, the spread over TP is optional.[7] As predicted, then, in the cases analyzed as involving rightward movement of the *wh*-phrase to [Spec, CP], the *wh*-marking may occur solely over the *wh*-phrase or may spread over the rest of CP. Corresponding to examples like (2) and (6), for example, with spread of *wh*-marking over the entire question, we find examples like (9) and (10).

$$\overline{\text{wh}}$$
(9) [t_i LOVE JOHN]$_{TP}$ WHO$_i$
'Who loves John?'

$$\overline{\text{wh}}$$
(10) [TEACHER LIPREAD t_i YESTERDAY]$_{TP}$ WHO$_i$
'Who did the teacher lipread yesterday?'

In contrast, in examples where the *wh*-phrase remains in situ, *wh*-marking spreads obligatorily over the entire CP. This is because there is no manual material available locally to be coarticulated with the *wh*-marking associated with the +wh feature in C unless the marking spreads over its c-command domain. Thus, there is no counterpart to sentences like (1) and (5) in which *wh*-marking occurs solely over the *wh*-phrase in situ, or solely over the +wh feature in C (assumed for the time being, to be to the right of TP),[8] as shown by the ungrammaticality of examples like (11) through (14).

$$\overline{\text{wh}}$$
(11) *WHO LOVE JOHN [+wh]$_C$

$$\overline{\text{wh}}$$
(12) *WHO LOVE JOHN [+wh]$_C$

$$\overline{\text{wh}}$$
(13) *TEACHER LIPREAD WHO YESTERDAY [+wh]$_C$

$$\overline{\text{wh}}$$
(14) *TEACHER LIPREAD WHO YESTERDAY [+wh]$_C$

Thus, the optional versus obligatory spread of *wh*-marking follows from independent generalizations about the distribution of nonmanual syntactic markings, but only under the assumption of rightward *wh*-movement.

7.2.1.3 Intensity Characteristics of *Wh*-Marking The rightward-movement analysis proposed here also correctly accounts for the intensity characteristics of *wh*-marking in those constructions where the marking spreads over the entire clause. Specifically, as predicted, the intensity is greatest nearest the source of the +wh feature with which the marking is associated, and it diminishes as distance from that node increases. Because the +wh feature is postulated to occur in a C node located at the right edge of the clause, the observed effect in examples such as (2), (3), and (6) is that the marking increases in intensity as the question is signed (Bahan 1996).[9]

7.2.1.4 Summary In all respects, then, the rightward-movement analysis allows an account of the distribution and intensity characteristics of nonmanual *wh*-marking in terms of independently established generalizations.

7.2.2 *Wh*-Questions with More Than One *Wh*-Phrase

Questions containing more than one *wh*-phrase corresponding to a single questioned argument are quite common in ASL.[10] This occurs frequently in two rather different constructions, described in sections 7.2.2.1 and 7.2.2.2, involving a *wh*-phrase within CP (either in situ or in [Spec, CP]) and a coreferential phrase occurring in the tag or in topic position (constructions discussed in chapter 4).

7.2.2.1 Final Tags Including a *Wh*-Phrase As shown in chapter 4, the tag consists of a reduced repetition of the matrix clause. A tag that follows a *wh*-question also necessarily contains a *wh*-phrase. Just as affirmative and negative tags have a characteristic head movement associated with them (an affirmative head nod or a negative head shake), so there is a characteristic head movement associated with *wh*-phrases occurring in a tag position.[11] This is illustrated in (15).[12]

$$\frac{\overline{\qquad\qquad\qquad\qquad\quad \text{hs}}}{\overline{\qquad\qquad\qquad\qquad\qquad\quad \text{wh}}}$$

(15) WHO LIKE JOHN, WHO
    'Who likes John, who (does)?'

This head movement was described by Aarons (1994, 129), who attributes this observation to Karen Petronio (personal communication). As with other tags, there may be a slight prosodic break before the tag in a sentence like (15).[13]

7.2.2.2 Initial *Wh*-Topics A *wh*-phrase may also occur in a clause-initial position preceding a *wh*-question, as illustrated in (16).[14]

$$\overline{\qquad\qquad\qquad\qquad\text{wh}\qquad\qquad\qquad}$$

(16) "WHAT", JOHN BUY "WHAT"
    'What, what did John buy?'

The main-clause question may contain the *wh*-phrase either in situ or in [Spec, CP], although there is a preference for the latter. We suggest that the initial *wh*-phrase is yet another type of base-generated topic. As shown in chapter 4, different types of topics differ with respect to their discourse function, their distribution relative to other types of topics, their nonmanual marking, and so on. We suggest that *wh*-topics are a type of base-generated topic, different from the two types of base-generated topics labeled as t2-bg and t3-bg.

As discussed in Aarons 1994, ABKN 1992, and NKBAM 1997, evidence that these initial *wh*-phrases are, in fact, base-generated topics comes from (1) the nonmanual marking found on these phrases, (2) the position of such *wh*-phrases in relation to other topics, and (3) their relation to the following *wh*-question and subsequent coreferential *wh*-phrase. We will consider these pieces of evidence in turn.

Nonmanual Marking of Wh-*Topics* Given that topics in ASL bear distinctive nonmanual markings involving (among other characteristics) raised eyebrows, one might expect that *wh*-topics would also bear such marking. However, there are conflicting articulatory demands placed on *wh*-topics, since *wh*-marking (associated with the +wh feature that is part of the *wh*-topic phrase) itself includes lowered brows. This articulatory conflict may be resolved in a number of ways, resulting in a nonmanual marking that, according to Aarons (1994, 124), "appears to be a combination of *wh*-marking and topic marking." As described by Aarons (1994, 150), *wh*-topics may involve raised brows (combined with "a narrowing of the eyes and the backward tilt of the head that is normally associated with wh-marking"). Often, however, they retain the lowered brows associated with *wh*-marking and are additionally topic-marked "by raised chin and a slight tensing of the muscles of the upper cheekbones" (an observation that Aarons attributes to Karen Petronio, personal communication). The nonmanual marking associated with *wh*-topics, illustrated in figure 7.2, thus exhibits some variability and does not always distinguish *wh*-topics from nontopic *wh*-phrases.

Figure 7.2
Wh-phrase in topic position. (From Aarons 1994. © Debra Aarons)

One difference between *wh*-topics and the other types of topics mentioned in chapter 4 should be noted. Other types of topics are typically followed by a slight pause; *wh*-topics generally are not.

Distributional Properties of Wh-*Topics*   *Wh*-topics display the same distributional properties as other base-generated topics. First, when a sentence contains a *wh*-topic, only one additional topic is allowed. This would be expected if the *wh*-phrase were indeed a topic, since a maximum of two topic phrases may occur left-adjoined to CP, as discussed in chapter 4. Second, if a *wh*-phrase co-occurs with a moved topic, it must precede the moved topic, just as any other base-generated topic would.[15] Finally, if a *wh*-topic co-occurs with another base-generated topic, it may either precede or follow that topic, as illustrated by examples (17) and (18).[16]

      wh   t2-bg   wh

(17) WHO, VEGETABLE, PREFER POTATO WHO
     'Who, as for vegetables, who prefers potatoes?'

          t2-bg   wh

(18) VEGETABLE, WHO, PREFER POTATO WHO
     'As for vegetables, who, who prefers potatoes?'

These co-occurrence patterns are characteristic of base-generated topics, as shown by Aarons (1994).

Relation between the Wh-*Topic and the Following* Wh-*Question* Like other base-generated topics, a *wh*-topic must be related to some element in the clause to which it is adjoined. In ASL, a *wh*-topic necessarily occurs in conjunction with a subsequent *wh*-phrase, contained within the following *wh*-question. The *wh*-phrase within the *wh*-question refers back to the initial *wh*-topic. ASL is somewhat unusual in having a generic *wh*-sign, glossed as "WHAT" (sometimes glossed elsewhere as "*wh*-generic"), that can be used to ask where, who, how, what, why, and so on, and that may refer back to a more specific question phrase. This generic *wh*-sign is frequently used to refer back to a *wh*-topic, just as a pronoun frequently refers back to a noun phrase topic.

$$\overline{\quad \text{t2-bg} \quad}$$
(19) JOHN$_i$, IX$_i$ LIKE MARY
'As for John, he likes Mary.'

$$\overline{\qquad\qquad\qquad\qquad\qquad\qquad \text{wh}}$$
(20) WHO, LOVE JOHN "WHAT"
'Who, who [generic *wh*-phrase] loves John?'

In neither case is the reverse relation (a more specific phrase referring back to a less specific phrase) well formed.[17]

$$\overline{\quad \text{t2-bg} \quad}$$
(21) * IX$_i$, JOHN$_i$ LIKE MARY
'As for him, John likes Mary.'

$$\overline{\qquad\qquad\qquad\qquad\qquad\qquad \text{wh}}$$
(22) *"WHAT", LOVE JOHN WHO
'Who [generic *wh*-phrase], who loves John?'

Thus, although many languages do not allow *wh*-phrases in topic position, ASL—perhaps because of the existence of generic *wh*-phrases in the language—does allow base-generated *wh*-topics.[18]

7.2.2.3 Distribution and Intensity of Nonmanual *Wh*-Marking Constructions involving *wh*-topics necessarily exhibit *wh*-marking over the entire utterance, whether or not the *wh*-phrase has moved rightward within CP. This contrasts with *wh*-questions containing a single *wh*-phrase that has moved rightward, where the *wh*-marking may occur solely over the *wh*-phrase. In this section, we consider the distribution of nonmanual *wh*-marking in constructions that involve +wh features in more than one position, sentences that therefore have more than one source of non-manual *wh*-marking. We show that the distribution of *wh*-marking in these *wh*-topic constructions is predictable, given the general phenomenon of perseveration.

As mentioned in chapter 3, if the same articulatory configuration will be used multiple times in close proximity, it tends to remain in place between those articulations (if this is possible). This phenomenon, referred to as "perseveration," occurs in both the manual and nonmanual channels. One interesting example of manual perseveration relevant to the present discussion involves the perseveration of the nondominant hand used for the sign "WHAT" in a sentence that contains two occurrences of that sign, as illustrated in (23).[19]

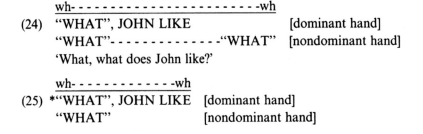

In this sentence, the nondominant hand retains the handshape of "WHAT" while the rest of the sentence is articulated with the dominant hand, finishing with the full two-handed articulation of "WHAT".[20]

In fact, the final "WHAT" sign may be articulated solely by the perseverating nondominant hand (and need not have a distinct onset). The presence of this final sign has generally gone unnoticed, with the notable exception of descriptions in Baker and Cokely 1980a,b,c. NKB (1994) offered the first account of this phenomenon in terms of nondominant handshape perseveration. This phenomenon may explain some of the discrepancies in the reported judgments on *wh*-questions that contain an initial *wh*-sign (not corresponding to an in-situ subject). Our informants normally accept such sentences only if there is another *wh*-phrase in the sentence, either in situ or clause-finally.

In particular, although some researchers have reported sentences like (25) to be grammatical, it is possible that the actual signed utterances corresponded to sentences like (24). It is impossible to determine whether this is the case, however, since the relevant videotaped data have not been made accessible.[21]

NKB (1994) also report perseveration in the nonmanual channel; further detail is provided in Bahan 1996 and NKBAM 1997. Specifically, the nonmanual *wh*-marking perseverates (i.e., is maintained) between the multiple occurrences of the +wh feature in the sentence. This was illustrated, for example, in (24), where the nonmanual *wh*-marking is maintained throughout the sentence.[22] Similar phenomena in the nonmanual channel, involving head tilt and eye gaze in determiner phrases (as discussed in chapter 3), confirm that perseveration is general and systematic in the nonmanual as well as the manual channel.

As shown in Bahan 1996, the maximal intensity of *wh*-marking correlates with the syntactic locations where the +wh features occur. When two such features are present, the maximal articulation is maintained between those two nodes. There are two types of *wh*-constructions where this happens. First, in the construction with an initial *wh*-topic, the analysis proposed here entails the existence of a +wh feature both initially, as an inherent feature of the *wh*-item occurring in topic position, and to the right of TP, in C. (There is also a third +wh feature associated with the *wh*-item that occurs either in situ or in [Spec, CP].) As discussed in Bahan 1996, the articulation of *wh*-marking is maximally intense at these positions, and this intensity is maintained over the intervening material, as indicated by the extent of the thick black line in sentences like (26).[23]

```
wh- - - - - - - - - - - - - - - - - - - - - - - - - - - - - - - - - - - - - - - - -wh
```

(26) "WHAT" [[JOHN BUY t_i YESTERDAY]$_{TP}$ [+wh]$_C$ "WHAT"$_i$]$_{CP}$ [dh]
     "WHAT" - "WHAT"$_i$ [ndh]
     'What, what did John buy yesterday?'

Thus, our account explains not only the distribution of nonmanual *wh*-marking, but also the intensity of its realization.

Second, we find a similar effect involving simple *wh*-questions with a *wh*-phrase in situ, as shown in (27) and (28).

wh- - - - - - - - - - - - - - - - -wh

(27) [[WHO LOVE JOHN]_{TP} [+wh]_C]_{CP}
'Who loves John?'

        wh- - - - - - - - - - - - - - - - -wh

(28) [[JOHN SEE WHO YESTERDAY]_{TP} [+wh]_C]_{CP}
'Who did John see yesterday?'

The spread of the nonmanual *wh*-marking over the entire question is obligatory, since there is otherwise no manual material with which the +wh feature in C can be articulated. The maximally intense articulation begins with the first occurrence of the +wh feature (i.e., the in-situ *wh*-phrase) and perseverates through the rest of the sentence, until the position associated with the second +wh feature (C) is reached. Thus, the perseveration of the maximally intense *wh*-marking provides support for postulating that +wh features occur in two locations in these constructions.

Note that the evidence from intensity in such constructions supports the claim that C is to the right of TP in ASL. Different intensity effects would be predicted if the clause-level +wh feature were located to the left of TP. For example, a sentence like (27) would be predicted to have maximal intensity at the beginning, with intensity decreasing toward the end, and a sentence like (28) would be expected to have maximal intensity from the beginning until the in-situ *wh*-phrase, after which intensity would decline.

In conclusion, as discussed in section 7.2.1, a sentence containing a single *wh*-phrase that has moved rightward to [Spec, CP] is analyzed as containing a +wh feature in C and a *wh*-phrase in [Spec, CP]. Spread of *wh*-marking is optional, since there is manual material locally (the *wh*-phrase in [Spec, CP]) with which it may be coarticulated. When spread over the c-command domain (the rest of the clause) occurs, the intensity is greatest at the end of the question, since all the +wh features in the sentence are at the right edge of the clause.

The constructions considered in this section involve multiple occurrences of +wh features, in *different* locations at Spell-Out, within a single sentence. In such cases, the nonmanual expression of these features remains in place, at maximal intensity, between their first and last occurrences. As distance from this domain increases, intensity diminishes (as shown in (28)). Thus, the characteristics of nonmanual *wh*-marking are predictable from the previously stated generalizations about the distribution, intensity, and perseveration of nonmanual syntactic markings.

It is also worth noting that the distribution and intensity of nonmanual *wh*-marking support the syntactic analysis proposed here. That is, the pattern of *wh*-marking follows from the generalizations that have been discussed only if the sentence is understood to contain a +wh feature in a post-TP position. The facts about distribution and intensity of *wh*-marking indirectly support the assumption—essential to a feature-checking account of the motivation for *wh*-movement—of a +wh feature in C that must be checked by a *wh*-phrase, also containing a +wh feature, generated elsewhere in the sentence.

7.2.2.4 Summary   A sentence-initial *wh*-phrase (that is not an in-situ subject) is analyzed as a base-generated *wh*-topic, left-adjoined to a CP that contains another *wh*-phrase, either in situ or in a clause-final [Spec, CP] position. The latter *wh*-phrase, which refers back to the *wh*-topic, frequently takes the form of the generic *wh*-sign, glossed as "WHAT", a sign that may, furthermore, be expressed solely through a perseverating nondominant hand. Failure to recognize this final sign may account for published reports of the grammaticality of sentences that appear to involve leftward movement. Such sentences may, in fact, involve a second occurrence of a *wh*-phrase articulated solely by the nondominant hand.

7.2.3 Extraction from Embedded Clauses
The rightward *wh*-movement account correctly predicts that *wh*-phrases extracted out of embedded clauses occur at the right edge of the main clause, as illustrated in (29) and (30). This is contrary to some other claims in the literature (e.g., Lillo-Martin (1990) states that extraction out of embedded clauses is impossible, whereas in subsequent work, Petronio and Lillo-Martin (1997) say that it is grammatical but unattested; see discussion in section 7.3.3).

$$\overline{\qquad\qquad\qquad\qquad\qquad\qquad\qquad\qquad\text{wh}\quad}$$
(29) [[TEACHER EXPECT [[t_i PASS TEST]$_{TP_2}$ t_i]$_{CP_2}$]$_{TP_1}$ $\overline{\text{WHO}_i}$]$_{CP_1}$
     'Who does the teacher expect to pass the test?'

$$\overline{\qquad\qquad\qquad\qquad\qquad\qquad\qquad\qquad\qquad\qquad\quad\text{wh}\quad}$$
(30) [[TEACHER EXPECT [[t_i PASS TEST]$_{TP_2}$ t_i]$_{CP_2}$]$_{TP_1}$ $\overline{\text{WHO}_i}$]$_{CP_1}$
     'Who does the teacher expect to pass the test?'

In such constructions, the distribution of nonmanual *wh*-marking is as predicted. It may occur solely over the *wh*-phrase in [Spec, CP] of the matrix clause, as in (29); otherwise, it spreads over the c-command domain of that node (i.e., the rest of the matrix question), as in (30). It cannot occur, for example, solely over the embedded clause, as illustrated by the ungrammaticality of (31).

$$\overline{\hspace{5cm}\text{wh}}$$

(31) *[[TEACHER EXPECT [[t_i PASS TEST]$_{\text{TP}_2}$ t_i]$_{\text{CP}_2}$]$_{\text{TP}_1}$ WHO$_i$]$_{\text{CP}_1}$
    'Who does the teacher expect to pass the test?'

Thus, rightward *wh*-movement accounts correctly for extraction from embedded clauses.[24]

7.2.4   Other Types of Questions

The essential analysis presented in this chapter also accounts for other question constructions in ASL, such as yes-no questions and rhetorical questions. Both involve nonmanual markings whose distribution and intensity are comparable to those found in *wh*-questions.

7.2.4.1   Yes-No Questions   Yes-no questions are analogous to *wh*-questions in several respects. Although the nonmanual yes-no marking is different in form from *wh*-marking, as illustrated in figure 7.3,[25] the distribution of the two markings obeys the same generalizations. Yes-no questions may contain a manual sign, glossed "QMwg" (a sign made with

Figure 7.3
Yes-no marking. (From Aarons 1994. © Debra Aarons)

a wiggling index finger), although this sign is not required. Nonmanual marking often suffices to convey that the utterance is a yes-no question. The distribution of yes-no question marking is as predicted. In the absence of the manual sign, the marking spreads obligatorily over the clause. Otherwise, the marking may occur solely over QMwg, which we assume occurs in C,[26] or it may spread optionally over the remainder of CP. This is illustrated by examples (32) through (34).

              y-n

              ▬▬

(32) JOHN LOVE MARY QMwg
     'Does John love Mary?'

              y-n

(33) JOHN LOVE MARY QMwg
     'Does John love Mary?'

              y-n

(34) JOHN LOVE MARY [+y/n]$_C$
     'Does John love Mary?'

Even in cases where no manual QMwg sign is present, as in (34), the intensity of y-n marking increases, with maximal intensity at the right edge of the clause. This supports postulating that C, containing the relevant question features, occurs to the right of TP. (If QMwg does, in fact, occur in C, then its position in (32) and (33) reveals the position of C relative to TP.)[27]

Like *wh*-phrases in *wh*-questions, the QMwg sign may also occur in initial position in yes-no questions. In such cases, the same perseveration effects found with *wh*-questions are found with yes-no questions.

      y-n   y-n
(35) *QMwg, JOHN LOVE MARY QMwg

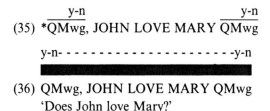

y-n- -y-n

(36) QMwg, JOHN LOVE MARY QMwg
     'Does John love Mary?'

As predicted in such cases, yes-no marking is at its maximal intensity throughout the clause, as shown in (36), rather than increasing in

Figure 7.4
Rhetorical *wh*-question marking. (From Aarons 1994. © Debra Aarons)

intensity, as in (33) and (34). Thus, yes-no questions pattern with *wh*-questions with respect to the distribution and intensity of nonmanual question marking.

7.2.4.2 Rhetorical Questions The same distribution and intensity characteristics of nonmanual marking are also found in rhetorical question-answer sequences, used in discourse to introduce new information. In such constructions, the signer asks a question and then provides the answer.

The question portion of the rhetorical question-answer sequence, be it a *wh*-question or a yes-no question, has the same syntactic characteristics as the corresponding information-seeking question, even though rhetorical questions involve distinct, characteristic nonmanual markings.[28] The marking found in rhetorical *wh*-questions is illustrated in figure 7.4. For example, a *wh*-phrase may occur either in situ (as in (37) or (38)) or at the right periphery of the rhetorical question (as in (39) through (42)).[29] Nonmanual rhetorical question marking spreads obligatorily over the rhetorical question ((37), (38)) unless there is manual material to the right of TP,[30] in which case the nonmanual rhetorical question marking accompanies the manual material and optionally spreads over the rest of the rhetorical question ((39)/(40), (41)/(42)).

$$\overline{}^{\text{rh/wh}}$$
(37) [[WHO TELL$_j$ BILL$_j$]$_{TP}$ [+wh]$_C$]$_{CP}$ MARY
'Who told Bill? Mary.'

$$\overline{}^{\text{rh/wh}}$$
(38) [[JOHN BUY "WHAT" YESTERDAY]$_{TP}$ [+wh]$_C$]$_{CP}$ BOOK
'What did John buy yesterday? A book.'

$$\overline{}^{\text{rh/wh}}$$
(39) [[t_i TELL$_j$ BILL$_j$ YESTERDAY]$_{TP}$ WHO$_i$]$_{CP}$ MARY
'Who told Bill yesterday? Mary.'

$$\overline{}^{\text{rh/wh}}$$
(40) [[t_i TELL$_j$ BILL$_j$ YESTERDAY]$_{TP}$ WHO$_i$]$_{CP}$ MARY
'Who told Bill yesterday? Mary.'

$$\overline{}^{\text{rh/wh}}$$
(41) [[JOHN BUY t_j YESTERDAY]$_{TP}$ "WHAT"$_j$]$_{CP}$ BOOK
'What did John buy yesterday? A book.'

$$\overline{}^{\text{rh/wh}}$$
(42) [[JOHN BUY t_j YESTERDAY]$_{TP}$ "WHAT"$_j$]$_{CP}$ BOOK
'What did John buy yesterday? A book.'

As in information-seeking *wh*-questions, there may be a *wh*-phrase in topic position as well as a *wh*-phrase either in situ or in [Spec, CP] of the rhetorical question, as in (43) and (44). In such cases, the nonmanual marking perseverates.

$$\overline{}^{\text{rh/wh}}$$
(43) [WHO [[t_i TELL$_j$ BILL$_j$]$_{TP}$ "WHAT"$_i$]$_{CP}$]$_{CP}$ MARY
'Who, who told Bill? Mary.'

$$\overline{}^{\text{rh/wh}}$$
(44) [WHO [JOHN SEE "WHAT"]$_{CP}$]$_{CP}$ MARY
'Who, who did John see? Mary.'

Likewise, the *wh*-phrase in a rhetorical question may be extracted from an embedded clause.

$$\overline{}^{\text{rh/wh}}$$
(45) [[JOHN SEE [[t_i THROW APPLE]$_{TP_2}$ t_i]$_{CP_2}$]$_{TP_1}$ WHO$_i$]$_{CP_1}$
MARY
'Who did John see throw the apple? Mary.'

$$\text{rh/wh}$$

(46) [[JOHN SEE [[t_i THROW APPLE]$_{TP_2}$ t_i]$_{CP_2}$]$_{TP_1}$ WHO$_i$]$_{CP_1}$
MARY
'Who did John see throw the apple? Mary.'

Thus, the account just provided for the structure of *wh*-questions and yes-no questions applies as well to the question portion of rhetorical question-answer sequences.

The traditional view (see, e.g., Baker and Cokely 1980d) that this construction is really what it appears to be, essentially a question-answer sequence, has recently been challenged, and the status of rhetorical questions has been the subject of some controversy. Several ASL linguists have claimed that the question clause and the answer in this construction are actually contained within a single matrix clause (Fischer 1990; Petronio 1991; Wilbur 1994a,b, 1996);[31] others maintain that these constructions are, as suggested here, composed of a question followed by an answer (Aarons 1994; NKBAM 1997). See especially HNMKB 1997 for arguments that the latter view is correct.[32] The relevance of rhetorical questions to the issue at hand is simply that the word order and distribution of nonmanual markings of rhetorical questions is comparable to that found in information-seeking *wh*- and yes-no questions, further supporting the analysis of question constructions proposed here.

7.2.5 Summary
We have argued in this section that the data from several types of questions in ASL are consistent with the claim that *wh*-movement, when it occurs, results in movement of a *wh*-phrase to a sentence-final position. The simple cases, involving a single *wh*-phrase corresponding to a questioned argument, show that the predictions of this analysis are correct: the *wh*-phrase may move to a clause-final position, but may not move to a clause-initial position. Spread of nonmanual *wh*-marking is optional if there is manual material in [Spec, CP] with which the marking may otherwise be coarticulated. When optional spread of *wh*-marking over CP occurs, the marking occurs with greatest intensity at the right edge of the sentence. If no manual material is present in [Spec, CP] (as is the case if the *wh*-phrase remains in situ), then spread over the c-command domain of the C node housing the +wh feature is obligatory. Thus, the evidence from the distribution and intensity of nonmanual markings supports the proposal that both C and [Spec, CP] are to the right of TP in ASL.

The account of the distribution and spread of *wh*-marking was extended to cases involving multiple sources of +wh features. We have suggested that cases containing an initial *wh*-phrase preceding a *wh*-question involve a *wh*-topic. In such cases, the *wh*-marking perseverates between the *wh*-topic position and the other occurrences of +wh features in the question (including the +wh feature at the right edge of the sentence), so that *wh*-marking occurs across the entire question. We have shown that this analysis accounts for the intensity of *wh*-marking in other constructions in which there is more than one source of +wh features, as well. For example, sentences in which the *wh*-phrase remains in situ involve a +wh feature within the *wh*-phrase internal to TP as well as a +wh feature in C. Thus, the *wh*-marking is most intense between those two positions. Such evidence supports the existence of +wh features in more than one location, as is posited under a feature-checking account of *wh*-constructions. Therefore, we maintain that, in ASL, *wh*-phrases move to a [Spec, CP] position that is to the right of TP.

7.3   Agreements and Disagreements about the Data

The interpretation of data is critical to claims that have been made about the appropriate analysis of particular *wh*-constructions. Surprisingly, the literature contains contradictory claims about the grammaticality of even very basic sentence types (in some cases, with differing judgments reported by the same researchers in different years). For this reason, we consider in this section some of the most important constructions relevant to deciding between leftward and rightward accounts of *wh*-movement in ASL about which contradictory claims have been made. As will become evident, the differences in reported judgments may be somewhat less dramatic than they might at first appear.

7.3.1   Left-Peripheral *Wh*-Objects in Simple Sentences
As mentioned earlier, simple sentences such as (4) and (47) involving sentence-initial *wh*-objects, predicted to be grammatical under a leftward-movement account, are rejected by our informants when signed exactly as glossed (see note 21).

wh

(47) *WHO JOHN HATE
     'Who does John hate?'

Comparable sentences have been reported to be grammatical in the literature (Lillo-Martin 1990; Lillo-Martin and Fischer 1992).

The judgments reported by Petronio (1991) for *native signers* concur with those of our (native) informants: they reject the sentence. However, Petronio also consulted nonnative signers, whose judgments on such sentences did not always agree with those of her native signers.[33] Petronio (1993, 99) summarizes these findings as follows: "In previous work (Petronio 1991), I reported that some ASL signers accept whOSV in direct questions while others reject it." She does not mention her previous finding that *native* signers generally rejected such sentences. Although Petronio and Lillo-Martin (1997, 50–51) discuss this construction, they report "varying judgments" and make no explicit claim about the grammaticality of the critical sentences. They summarize their own previous reports on such sentences as follows: "Lillo-Martin 1990 and Lillo-Martin & Fischer 1992 report them as grammatical, and Petronio 1993 reports that they receive mixed judgments." Petronio's (1993) characterization of the findings reported in Petronio 1991 is thus perpetuated in Petronio and Lillo-Martin 1997; again, no mention is made of the fact that the native signers tested by Petronio generally reject such sentences.

Moreover, it is also possible that, to the extent that native signers have reported sentences with initial *wh*-objects to be grammatical, the sentences they are actually judging may differ in significant ways, as discussed in section 7.2.2.3. Without access to the relevant video data, this is impossible to ascertain. As discussed in chapter 2, there are many possible explanations for conflicting reports of grammaticality judgments. For example, given that the construction under consideration exhibits English word order, influence from English may contribute to the reported acceptance of such sentences. In any case, despite conflicting grammaticality judgments reported in the literature, sentences with initial *wh*-objects (such as (25)), signed exactly as glossed, are generally rejected by native signers (according to Petronio 1991 and according to our own findings).

7.3.2 Right-Peripheral *Wh*-Subjects in Simple Sentences
In contrast, examples such as (2), (9), (48), and (49) have not received much attention in the literature.

$$\overline{\hspace{3.5cm}\text{wh}\hspace{0.5cm}}$$
(48) t_i HATE JOHN WHO$_i$
'Who hates John?'

(49) t_i HATE JOHN $\overline{\text{WHO}_i}^{\text{wh}}$
      'Who hates John?'

Petronio (1991, 212, 214) offers (50) and (51) as grammatical examples.

(50) TAKE-UP EXPLAIN $\overline{\text{WHO}}^{\text{rhq}}$, ANN
      'It is Ann who will do the explaining.'
      (Petronio 1991, ex. (4a))

(51) $\overline{\text{TAKE-UP EXPLAIN WHO}}^{\text{rhq}}$, ANN
      'It is Ann who will do the explaining.'
      (Petronio 1991, ex. (4b))

Because she reports that *wh*-questions and rhetorical questions exhibit the same patterns with respect to both the spread of the nonmanual marking and the positioning of the *wh*-element (see note 33), she would thus appear to be claiming that sentences such as (48) and (49) are also acceptable.

In contrast, Petronio (1993, 168, fn. 11) reports that sentences such as (52) and (53) are "odd or ungrammatical" (as indicated by her "%" notation) for most signers. Example (53) is offered as a *grammatical* sentence in Lillo-Martin et al. 1996 (as shown in (54)).

(52) %LIKE JOHN $\overline{\text{WHO}}^{\text{whq}}$
      (Petronio 1993, 153, ex. (68))

(53) %BUY CAR $\overline{\text{WHO}}^{\text{whq}}$
      (Petronio 1993, 153, ex. (69))

(54) BUY CAR $\overline{\text{WHO}}^{\text{whq}}$
      (Lillo-Martin et al. 1996, 13, ex. (2b))

Petronio and Lillo-Martin (1997, 36) say of such sentences, "[W]e find that when [they] are presented in isolation, judgments vary—some signers accept them, but others do not."[34]

It would seem that even Petronio and Lillo-Martin essentially agree with us that this is a grammatical construction when used in appropriate contexts.[35] According to our findings, at any rate, this construction, predicted to be grammatical by a rightward-movement analysis, is indeed grammatical for native signers.

7.3.3 Questions Involving Extraction from Embedded Clauses

Varying claims have been made about extraction from embedded clauses in ASL. Lillo-Martin (1990) claimed that extraction out of embedded clauses is impossible in ASL (a claim based in part on her observation that "Wh-words are generally not fronted out of embedded clauses" (p. 214)).[36] Petronio and Lillo-Martin (1997) now claim, however, that long-distance extraction is *not* ungrammatical, and that it operates leftward, even though the predicted examples, such as (55), are not attested.[37]

$$\overline{\text{wh}}$$

(55) *WHO JOHN THINK MARY LIKE
      'Who does John think Mary likes?'
      (Petronio and Lillo-Martin 1997, 52, ex. (112a))

Petronio and Lillo-Martin (1997, 52) state that the cases of leftward extraction of *wh*-phrases from embedded clauses to a sentence-initial position that their analysis predicts to be grammatical "are rarely observed in natural conversation and judgments by consultants vary. Such sentences were reported to be ungrammatical in Lillo-Martin 1990 and ABKN; similar examples were found grammatical by Boster 1996 and received mixed judgments in Petronio 1993."[38] Petronio and Lillo-Martin (1997, 52) point out that there are signers who accept such constructions only if there is a *wh*-sign on the *right* edge of the clause.

In contrast, grammatical examples of extraction of *wh*-phrases from embedded clauses to the right periphery of the matrix clause, as in (29) and (30), repeated here, have been presented in ABKN 1992, Aarons 1994, NKB 1994, NKBA 1994, and NKBAM 1997. Notably, no examples of this kind are addressed in Petronio and Lillo-Martin's discussion of long-distance *wh*-movement in ASL.

$$\overline{\text{wh}}$$

(29) [[TEACHER EXPECT [[t_i PASS TEST]$_{TP_2}$ t_i]$_{CP_2}$]$_{TP_1}$ WHO$_i$]$_{CP_1}$
      'Who does the teacher expect to pass the test?'

$$\overline{\text{wh}}$$

(30) [[TEACHER EXPECT [[t_i PASS TEST]$_{TP_2}$ t_i]$_{CP_2}$]$_{TP_1}$ WHO$_i$]$_{CP_1}$
      'Who does the teacher expect to pass the test?'

In sum, the facts concerning the occurrence of *wh*-phrases extracted from embedded clauses do not (any longer) seem to be contested. Extraction does occur, and extracted *wh*-phrases occur only in the right periphery of the matrix clause, consistent with rightward *wh*-movement.

7.3.4 Distribution of Nonmanual Marking

Constructions involving optional versus obligatory spread of *wh*-marking described in section 7.2.1.2 have been discussed in the literature. In fact, one of the aims of Lillo-Martin and Fischer 1992 was to account for a subset of the cases we have discussed here, under the assumption that *wh*-movement in ASL results in *wh*-phrases occurring in a [Spec, CP] position at the left edge of the clause. Lillo-Martin and Fischer (1992) describe the spread of *wh*-marking as optional in sentences like (3), which they analyze as containing an in-situ object, but obligatory in constructions in which they claim that leftward *wh*-movement has taken place (such as (4)) or in sentences containing an in-situ subject (such as (1)).[39] Those examples are repeated here.

```
                          wh
```
(1) WHO LOVE JOHN
     'Who loves John?'
     (Lillo-Martin and Fischer: subject leftward-moved or in situ—
     obligatory spread)

```
     (          )   wh
```
(3) JOHN LOVE WHO
     'Who does John love?'
     (Lillo-Martin and Fischer: object necessarily in situ—optional spread)

```
                      wh
```
(4) *WHO JOHN LOVE
     (Lillo-Martin and Fischer: leftward-moved object, grammatical for
     Lillo-Martin and Fischer with obligatory spread)

Lillo-Martin and Fischer's description does not correctly extend to sentences like (2) and (9), repeated here, involving right-peripheral subjects with and without spread of *wh*-marking (although they do not consider such examples).

```
                          wh
```
(2) t_i LOVE JOHN WHO$_i$
     'Who loves John?'

$$\overline{\text{wh}}$$
(9) [t_i LOVE JOHN]$_{TP}$ WHO$_i$
'Who loves John?'

Moreover, their descriptive generalization does not account for the contrast in grammaticality between (10) and (13), repeated here, containing *wh*-objects that we analyze as in situ versus moved (a distinction not available to Lillo-Martin and Fischer (1992), who admit only leftward movement and claim that spread is optional in sentences like (3) because the object is in situ).

$$\overline{\text{wh}}$$
(10)   TEACHER LIPREAD t_i YESTERDAY WHO$_i$
'Who did the teacher lipread yesterday?'

$$\overline{\text{wh}}$$
(13) *TEACHER LIPREAD WHO YESTERDAY

Again, Lillo-Martin and Fischer do not consider such examples. In any event, Lillo-Martin and Fischer apparently agree that cases of optional rather than obligatory spread exist, although their generalization about the distinction is inadequate.

In contrast, Petronio and Lillo-Martin (1997) now claim that nonmanual *wh*-marking always spreads over the entire question. In order to account for cases of optional spread such as those identified by Lillo-Martin and Fischer, they claim that examples such as (9) and (10) are not single sentences, but instead necessarily represent "multisentence discourses," involving a concatenation of a statement—in which the phrase about to be questioned is a null non-*wh* pronominal—followed by an independent question consisting only of a *wh*-phrase that refers back to and questions the null argument in the prior sentence. This approach allows them to simplify the account of the distribution of nonmanual *wh*-marking (but not without some expense); they now claim that any signs not accompanied by nonmanual *wh*-marking are not part of a question. Thus, Petronio and Lillo-Martin deny the existence of cases of optional spread, although they do so not by disputing the existence of the data presented here (and in Lillo-Martin and Fischer 1992), but by redefining what constitutes a sentence. Problems with their analysis are discussed in section 7.4.1.

7.3.5 Summary
With respect to the grammaticality of simple sentences involving *wh*-phrases that have moved to the left and right periphery of the question

clause, there is a certain amount of agreement, despite the appearance of dramatically conflicting reports in the literature. The data are consistent with the rightward-movement proposal.

There is even less disagreement about the data involving extraction from embedded clauses. Petronio and Lillo-Martin (1997) have not contested the examples we have put forward involving extraction to a right-peripheral position. However, as for the nonoccurring forms predicted by leftward movement, they (now) declare these to be "unattested" rather than "ungrammatical" (as previously characterized by Lillo-Martin (e.g., Lillo-Martin 1990, 1992)).

As we will show in section 7.4.1, Petronio and Lillo-Martin take a similar approach to the kinds of examples demonstrating rightward movement that we have claimed are grammatical. Like Petronio (1993), Petronio and Lillo-Martin (1997, 36–37) attribute to those a new status, saying that when such sentences "are presented in isolation, judgments vary—some signers accept them, but others do not."[40]

As for cases of optional spread of *wh*-marking, there is agreement about the existence of constructions involving *wh*-marking solely over a right-peripheral *wh*-phrase. The disagreement now focuses on whether those examples are (single) sentences or multisentence discourses.

Thus, although there is not total consensus about the facts that are to be explained, it is also not simply the case that the leftward and rightward *wh*-movement analyses are based on completely different claims about the ASL data. Further progress toward reconciling disagreements about the data can only come as samples of the contested data are made available for scientific scrutiny.[41]

7.4 Alternative Accounts in Terms of Leftward *Wh*-Movement

Descriptive accounts of ASL sentence structure have contained statements like the following, from Baker and Cokely 1980a, 15:

In general, 'wh-word' signs occur at the end of the question. However, they sometimes occur at both the beginning and the end. Thus, a Signer may ask:

$$\overline{\text{ARRIVE WHEN}}^{\text{wh-q}} \quad \text{or} \quad \overline{\text{WHEN ARRIVE WHEN}}^{\text{wh-q}}$$

Nonetheless, the general view in the syntactic literature (with the notable exception of Perlmutter 1991) has been, perhaps following Lillo-Martin

1990, 1991, 1992, that *wh*-phrases move leftward in ASL. Petronio (1993) and Petronio and Lillo-Martin (1997) attempt to justify a leftward *wh*-movement analysis. We have argued in detail against these proposals in NKBAM 1997 and NMLBK 1998b. In section 7.4.1, we summarize the alternative proposed in Petronio and Lillo-Martin 1997 and consider several problems with that account. Finally, in section 7.4.2, we revisit an approach, consistent with Kayne's (1994) proposed restrictions on phrase structure and directionality of movement, first discussed in NKBAM 1997. We conclude, on the basis of evidence from the distribution of nonmanual *wh*-marking, that such an approach is problematic.

7.4.1   Proposal by Petronio and Lillo-Martin (1997)

Petronio and Lillo-Martin (1997) suggest that there is a specific constraint such that [Spec, CP] (but not C) must precede IP universally. Despite Petronio and Lillo-Martin's statement that "this phenomenon remains unexplained,"[42] the rest of their paper is devoted to showing how ASL can be made to fit this supposed universal. They thus assume that *wh*-movement is leftward in ASL, and they offer an account of right-peripheral *wh*-elements in terms of other mechanisms.

Petronio and Lillo-Martin's analysis of *wh*-constructions is rather intricate, and explaining it requires some effort. In this section, we go into a fair amount of detail about what they are proposing and why it is inadequate. A shorter version of the information contained here appears as NMLBK 1998a. A longer version appears as NMLBK 1998b.

Petronio and Lillo-Martin (1997) propose that [Spec, CP] occurs to the left of TP, but C occurs to the right of TP. They claim that *wh*-phrases optionally move leftward to [Spec, CP]. *Wh*-signs appearing at the right periphery of the sentence are necessarily heads (not phrases) occurring in a focus position, C. These signs are base-generated "doubles" that are required to match an identical +F(ocus) "twin" elsewhere in the sentence, although the "twin" need not be overt.[43] Petronio and Lillo-Martin say that "the twin functions as a focus operator, and as an operator, it undergoes ... raising to Spec-CP" (p. 32).[44] Thus, the simple cases that we analyze as rightward movement of a subject *wh*-phrase to [Spec, CP], they analyze as shown in (56). They claim that such a construction contains a null *wh*-element (distinct from a *wh*-trace)[45] within TP (i.e., a null focus operator that raises to a sentence-initial [Spec, CP] by LF) plus a lexical "double" base-generated in the sentence-final C position.[46]

$$\text{(56)} \; \overline{[\; [\quad e_i \quad]_{[\text{Spec, CP}]} \; [\; [\quad t_i \quad \text{HATE JOHN} \;]_{\text{IP}} \; [\; \text{WHO}_{j=i} \;]_\text{C} \;]_{\text{C}'} \;]_{\text{CP}}}^{\text{whq}}$$

+*WH*, +*F*   +*WH*, +*F*   +*WH*, +*F*

   "twin"   "double"

   'Who hates John?'

   (as analyzed by Petronio and Lillo-Martin)

$$\text{(57)} \; \overline{[\; [\; t_i \; \text{HATE JOHN} \;]_{\text{TP}} \; \text{WHO}_i \;]_{\text{CP}}}^{\text{wh}}$$

   'Who hates John?'

   (as analyzed here)

Putting aside theoretical problems with their account,[47] we show in what follows that Petronio and Lillo-Martin's proposal cannot account for the facts. We first show that a final head position cannot account for *wh*-phrases in final position. We also argue against Petronio and Lillo-Martin's claim that there is independent motivation for such a final focus head. We next consider their treatment of constructions in which the *wh*-marking occurs solely over a *wh*-phrase, without spreading over additional material. They analyze all such cases as multisentence discourses rather than simple questions, an analysis we show to be incorrect.

7.4.1.1 Right-Peripheral "Focus" Elements in C Petronio and Lillo-Martin claim that right-peripheral *wh*-signs occur in C, the same position (on their analysis) in which other types of sentence-final elements (including modals, quantifiers, and verbs) appear, as base-generated "doubles" matching overt or nonovert "twin" focus operators elsewhere in the sentence. In this section, we present a number of arguments against this analysis. First, their account incorrectly predicts that *wh-phrases* may not occur in this right-peripheral position. Second, we show that the hypothesized sentence-final focus head position lacks independent motivation. In trying to establish independent motivation for their focus-"doubling" analysis, Petronio and Lillo-Martin conflate a variety of different constructions, including the tag construction discussed in chapter 4. Third, their analysis incorrectly predicts that post-TP *wh*-signs and modals should exhibit complementary distribution; as we will show, such elements can co-occur. Finally, their analysis cannot account for several apparent restrictions on co-occurrence possibilities of "doubles" and "twins."

Petronio and Lillo-Martin's account predicts that only lexical heads, but not phrases, should be able to appear in this final C position, which is clearly false. Consider first the question of whether *wh-phrases* can appear sentence-finally. In NKBAM 1997, examples of *wh*-phrases containing WHICH demonstrate the occurrence of post-TP *wh*-phrases.[48] Similarly, the following sentences with possessive *wh*-phrases demonstrate that there is no restriction against phrasal material in final position:[49]

$$\overline{\hspace{6.5cm}\text{wh}\hspace{0cm}}$$

(58) [[WHO POSS MOTHER] DIE]$_{TP}$
      'Whose mother died?'

$$\overline{\hspace{7.5cm}\text{wh}\hspace{0cm}}$$

(59) [t_i DIE]$_{TP}$ [WHO POSS MOTHER]$_i$
      'Whose mother died?'

$$\overline{\hspace{6.5cm}\text{wh}\hspace{0cm}}$$

(60) [t_i DIE]$_{TP}$ [WHO POSS MOTHER]$_i$
      'Whose mother died?'

$$\overline{\hspace{7.5cm}\text{wh}\hspace{0cm}}$$

(61) [[WHO POSS CAR] BREAK-DOWN]$_{TP}$
      'Whose car broke down?'

$$\overline{\hspace{8.5cm}\text{wh}\hspace{0cm}}$$

(62) [t_i BREAK-DOWN]$_{TP}$ [WHO POSS CAR]$_i$
      'Whose car broke down?'

$$\overline{\hspace{7.5cm}\text{wh}\hspace{0cm}}$$

(63) [t_i BREAK-DOWN]$_{TP}$ [WHO POSS CAR]$_i$
      'Whose car broke down?'

These examples are accounted for straightforwardly by assuming that *wh-phrases* undergo rightward *wh*-movement. The distribution of nonmanual *wh*-marking is correctly predicted by the generalizations presented earlier. These examples are incompatible with Petronio and Lillo-Martin's proposed analysis of sentence-final *wh*-elements as lexical "doubles" base-generated in C.

Not only is their analysis unable to account for *wh*-phrases at the right periphery; their claim that there is independent motivation for the sentence-final focus head position that they invoke as part of that analysis is also dubious. They claim that this position is independently needed to account for sentence-final modals. Consider the following example:[50]

(64) $\overline{\text{JOHN GO SHOULD}}^{\text{hn}}$
      'John should go.'

Petronio and Lillo-Martin generate such constructions by positing a null
focus "twin" within IP (which raises to the leftward [Spec, CP] position)
and a base-generated lexical "double" in the final C position. As pointed
out in ABKN 1992 and Aarons 1994, however, the claim that the final
SHOULD is in C incorrectly predicts the position of such a modal relative to negation in a negative construction, such as (65). (Nonmanual
markings are not indicated for the two ungrammatical examples, as they
are ungrammatical regardless of where the negative marking occurs.)

(65) JOHN GO SHOULD $\overline{\text{NOT}}^{\text{neg}}$
      'John should not go.'

(66) *JOHN NOT GO SHOULD

(67) *JOHN NOT GO SHOULD NOT

On the basis of such evidence, ABKN (1992) and Aarons (1994) suggest
that constructions such as (64) involve leftward movement of the VP (in
fact, the whole aspect phrase). This proposal is consistent with the nonmanual marking in (64), which reflects null verbal material following the
modal (see discussion in chapter 4).

    Even those cases where there is (on Petronio and Lillo-Martin's
analysis) an overt "twin" corresponding to the "double" in C do not
provide evidence for their account. Far from confirming a sentence-final
+focus C position for base-generated "doubles," such constructions correspond to ordinary tags. As discussed in chapter 4 and illustrated again
in (68), modals (occurring in the head of TP) appear frequently in tag
constructions.

(68) JOHN SHOULD GO $\overline{\text{SHOULD}}^{\text{hn}}$
      'John should go, (he) should.'

As with other tags, there may be a prosodic break before the tag portion,
although this is not required.[51] A head nod accompanies the tag portion,
which is essentially clausal but contains no overt verbal material.

    We would analyze as tags the final portion of many of the examples that
Petronio and Lillo-Martin cite, from commercially available videotapes,[52]

to support their proposal that such a focus position is independently motivated. Petronio and Lillo-Martin (1997) offer examples such as (69) and (70) (presented here with Petronio and Lillo-Martin's glosses) to support their claim that a sentence-final focus position is needed to account for ASL, independent of *wh*-constructions.

cond

(69) ... KNOW PROBLEM SITUATION, CANNOT J-U-R-Y CANNOT
'... If [you] are aware of the problem, the situation, then [you] CANNOT be on the jury.'
(Petronio and Lillo-Martin 1997, ex. (25), listed as ex. (30) in their appendix)

(70) SEEM #ALL PEOPLE DEAF SEEM
'It seems that all the people [on the program] are deaf.'
(Petronio and Lillo-Martin 1997, ex. (33), listed as ex. (38) in their appendix)

However, as actually signed on the videotape, these examples in fact provide evidence *against* Petronio and Lillo-Martin's claim that the final sign in both sentences occurs in a sentence-final C position with no prosodic break separating that sign from the preceding material. Consider first sentence (69). Consistent with our analysis of the tag construction and the predicted intensity of nonmanual markings, the negative marking exhibits two distinct peaks of maximal intensity, clearly visible on the videotape, as illustrated in (71). This follows from our analysis of such sentences as involving two negative clauses—the matrix clause and the adjoined tag—each with an independent source of negative marking. (Petronio and Lillo-Martin do not indicate the negative marking in their gloss.)

neg   neg

(71) [CAN'T J-U-R-Y] [CAN'T]
'(You) can't be on the jury, (you) can't.'

Thus, we maintain that such sentences simply involve the (independently motivated) tag construction and provide no motivation for a focus position of the kind proposed by Petronio and Lillo-Martin.

Example (70), when accurately transcribed (as in (72)), also does not support Petronio and Lillo-Martin's claim that the final SEEM occurs in a head-final C position. Petronio and Lillo-Martin claim that head nods of the kind found in this sentence can occur only over clausal domains. Moreover, as mentioned in note 51, they have eliminated from consideration constructions involving a prosodic break.

Although Petronio and Lillo-Martin are ostensibly describing the sentence from the Baker and Cokely videotape, they have glossed this sentence differently in Petronio and Lillo-Martin 1997 (see (73)) and in Petronio 1993 (see (74)). These glosses deviate in significant respects from the gloss provided by Baker and Cokely themselves, shown in (72), which indicates a prosodic break before the final element as well as a head nod over (only) the final element. (According to Baker and Cokely, the comma indicates a syntactic break; the + symbol indicates that the sign is repeated.) The videotape from which this example is drawn reveals that Baker and Cokely's description is accurate.[53]

$$\text{nodding}$$
(72) SEEM #ALL-*arc* PEOPLE DEAF, $\overline{\text{SEEM+}}$
      (as glossed in Baker and Cokely 1980b)

(73) SEEM #ALL PEOPLE DEAF SEEM
      (Petronio and Lillo-Martin 1997, ex. (33), listed as ex. (38) in their appendix)

$$\overline{\phantom{\text{SEEM #ALL PEOPLE DEAF}}\text{hn}}$$
(74) SEEM #ALL PEOPLE DEAF SEEM
      (Petronio 1993, 133, ex. (13))

In neither case is there any discussion of the fact that Petronio and Lillo-Martin's representations of the videotaped sentence differ from the gloss contained in Baker and Cokely 1980b (or any justification for such differences).

In sum, many of the constructions that Petronio and Lillo-Martin invoke in support of a focus position at the end of the sentence, housing a lexical, base-generated, "double" of a +F focus element elsewhere in the sentence, would be analyzed, on our account, in a straightforward fashion as involving a clausal tag construction. Our analysis is consistent with the distribution and intensity of nonmanual markings and the prosody in such constructions.

Furthermore, Petronio and Lillo-Martin's account would predict that at most one element from the class of focusable elements they enumerate could occur at the end of the sentence. This prediction also fails to hold. For example, sentences like the following occur:

$$\overline{\text{(75) JOHN FUTURE}_{\text{tns}} \text{ EAT "WHAT", FUTURE}_{\text{tns}} \text{ "WHAT"}}^{\text{wh}}$$
'What will John eat, what will (he)?'

Finally, Petronio and Lillo-Martin need to ensure that, in a *wh*-question, the base-generated "double" (which could otherwise be, by their analysis, a modal, for example) is restricted to being a *wh*-element. For restrictions on the "double" construction, Petronio and Lillo-Martin (1997) refer to Petronio 1993, 148–149, where the following LF filter is proposed:

(76) *Final Double Filter*
   *[α] if α is an X^0 in a [+F] C^0, and α does not agree with the constituent in C^{spec}.

There would have to be other restrictions on what can be a "double" in a given sentence, not so easily remedied by LF filters. One problem for this analysis, pointed out in Petronio 1993, 160–161, is that although a main verb can appear in this final C position, according to Petronio (and Lillo-Martin), it can do so only if the main clause does not contain a modal. Another fact not addressed by Petronio (and Lillo-Martin) is the ungrammaticality of constructions like (77), irrespective of the distribution of nonmanual negative marking.

(77) *JOHN FUTURE$_{\text{tns}}$ NOT GO FUTURE$_{\text{tns}}$

Thus, their proposal overgenerates and would require further stipulations.

We conclude that, contrary to Petronio and Lillo-Martin's claims, there is no independent motivation for the existence of a sentence-final C position for focused elements. The constructions considered by Petronio and Lillo-Martin involving right-peripheral elements are not best accounted for in a homogeneous way in terms of a single final +focus head position. Furthermore, postulating such a position cannot explain the occurrence of sentence-final wh-*phrases* in ASL, which would not be allowed in that position under their analysis.

7.4.1.2 Null Elements Distinct from *Wh*-Traces   In order to account for cases where the *wh*-element occurs only at the right periphery in terms of the structures they have proposed, Petronio and Lillo-Martin postulate two new types of null elements that are said to occupy the apparently empty position internal to TP:

• a +wh element (the "twin") that co-occurs with the right-peripheral *wh*-word claimed to be in C;[54]

• a −wh element that is found in the first part of a "multisentence discourse" (as in (78), which Petronio and Lillo-Martin would analyze as shown in (79)) when followed by an independent *wh*-question consisting solely of a *wh*-phrase that questions that prior null element.

$$\overline{\text{wh}}$$
(78) LIKE CHOCOLATE WHO
      'Who likes chocolate?'

$$\overline{\text{whq}}$$
(79) [[e_i] LIKE CHOCOLATE]$_{CP}$ [WHO$_{j=i}$]$_{CP}$
          −WH   *+WH, +F*
      '(Someone) likes chocolate. Who?'
      (as interpreted by Petronio and Lillo-Martin)

Several observations are in order:

1. This proliferation of null elements in effect renders Petronio and Lillo-Martin's hypothesis of the focus-"doubling" construction unfalsifiable, since when there is no overt evidence of two associated constituents, a null "twin" can be invoked.
2. Petronio and Lillo-Martin do not address the licensing of these null elements.
3. The empirical evidence they offer to support the syntactic distinction between a *wh*-trace and the kind of null *wh*-element that is doubled by an overt element in C is unconvincing.[55]
4. Their account of the distribution of *wh*-marking is inadequate. In order to maintain that *wh*-marking occurs obligatorily over the entire CP in direct questions, they are obliged to postulate sentence boundaries that coincide with the boundaries of *wh*-marking. As we will discuss, the resulting claims for the sentencehood of pre-*wh* material cannot be justified.

We now consider the last three of these points in greater detail.

   Petronio and Lillo-Martin's evidence for the existence of a new kind of *wh*-element that is not a *wh*-trace is based solely on the claim that sentences containing such elements are interpreted differently from sentences that have (no null "twins" but only) *wh*-traces. In the former case, the acceptability of the sentence to informants is allegedly more sensitive to the availability of contextual information.[56] Petronio and Lillo-Martin (1997, 36–37) elaborate as follows, with respect to a specific sentence of theirs (repeated within the quotation):

A signer who will reject a sentence such as 61 when it is presented in isolation will often accept it when it is in the appropriate context, as in 64.

(64) Possible context: The speaker and addressee are discussing the addressee's car, which was just sold.

$$\overline{\text{BUY CAR WHO}}^{\text{whq}}$$
'Who bought the car?'

At the very least, from the example they give of the kind of context needed for acceptability (for some informants), this would not appear to be a case where some extraordinary context is required to allow interpretation of an otherwise marginal sentence. In any case, Petronio and Lillo-Martin suggest that this particular status provides empirical evidence in support of the new kinds of null categories they posit in order to account for the data, given the structures they assume.

There are several fallacies in this line of argumentation. First, as Petronio and Lillo-Martin acknowledge, even the simplest sentences (with ordinary SVO word order) are assigned greater acceptability ratings by informants when presented in a plausible context than when presented in isolation. According to Petronio and Lillo-Martin (1997, 46), "Within sentences ASL productively uses topicalization to front constituents. Topicalization is so common that when a declarative sentence is presented in isolation, many people will reject the underlying SVO order." Thus, Petronio and Lillo-Martin are not justified in drawing the inferences they do about the presence of particular types of null elements from the observation that contextual information leads to improved judgments of acceptability of sentences by informants.

Second, reports by Petronio and Lillo-Martin of variability in judgments are not restricted to sentences (analyzed by us as) involving rightward movement; they also report "varying judgments" for sentences such as (80), with sentence-*initial* wh-objects, representing the simplest case predicted to be grammatical by their analysis.

$$\overline{\text{(80) *WHAT JOHN BUY}}^{\text{whq}}$$
'What did John buy?'
(Petronio and Lillo-Martin 1997, ex. (108a); Petronio and Lillo-Martin mark this sentence as grammatical, but note that some informants reject it.)

They do note, however, that informants who reject such sentences accept sentences such as the following:

(81) $\overline{\text{WHAT JOHN BUY WHAT}}^{\text{whq}}$
'What did John buy?'
(Petronio and Lillo-Martin 1997, ex. (110a))

Petronio and Lillo-Martin (1997, 50) attribute the reported variability, in this instance, to "individual stylistic and idiolectal differences" (see also note 56): "The literature reports differences in judgments reported for sentences that have a single, leftward, sentence-initial WH-object. To maintain a leftward analysis, we must account for the varying judgments for this type of sentence.... [W]e ... account for the different judgments by attributing them to individual stylistic preferences that are in accord with the discourse-oriented strategies of ASL discussed above."

Thus, when the variability that they report is considered, no patterns emerge supporting any particular analysis over another. Essentially, Petronio and Lillo-Martin report variability for the majority of the constructions they discuss. Some of this variability is attributed to the presence of special null elements, and some of it is considered to be idiosyncratic; no principled basis for distinguishing between the two is provided.

Finally, Petronio and Lillo-Martin offer no evidence for the claim that a sentence like (82) is anything but a single sentence.[57]

(82) *e* LOVE JOHN $\overline{\text{WHO}}^{\text{wh}}$

The suggestion that the signs in (82) that precede WHO constitute an independent sentence is untenable. Sentence (83) is uniformly reported to be ungrammatical.

(83) **e* LOVE JOHN

In fact, this sentence, as glossed, is ungrammatical in any context *except one in which the "question" WHO immediately follows*. Note that the question that immediately follows must actually contain WHO, in this case. Not even WHY, for example, makes the preceding sentence grammatical, as shown by the ungrammaticality of (84), which one might expect to be grammatical, with the meaning 'Someone loves John. Why?' according to Petronio and Lillo-Martin's analysis.

(84) **e* LOVE JOHN $\overline{\text{WHY}}^{\text{wh}}$

The ungrammaticality of (83) is to be expected, however, since there is no way for the null element that Petronio and Lillo-Martin posit to be properly licensed (as discussed in chapter 5). An overt manifestation of agreement, either manual or nonmanual, is required to license a null subject. Thus, (83) lacks an essential grammatical argument—unless that argument is provided by the *wh*-phrase that we analyze to be in [Spec, CP]. It would appear, then, that the most relevant effect of "context" on the grammaticality judgment here is the effect of the occurrence of what Petronio and Lillo-Martin analyze to be the independent question, WHO, on the grammaticality of the preceding statement.

We conclude that Petronio and Lillo-Martin's two-sentence analysis for such constructions is untenable. We maintain that (78) is a single sentence and, moreover, one for which Petronio and Lillo-Martin have no account.

Accounting for the obligatory versus (apparently) optional spread of *wh*-marking in the constructions discussed in the first part of this chapter has proven difficult for proponents of leftward *wh*-movement (e.g., Lillo-Martin and Fischer 1992, as discussed in section 7.3.4). Petronio and Lillo-Martin (1997) eliminate the problem by relabeling sentences in which it appears that spread has not occurred as multisentence discourses, and by claiming that spread is always obligatory.[58] However, the alternative analysis they propose for the relevant constructions cannot be maintained.

7.4.1.3 Summary Petronio and Lillo-Martin analyze *wh*-signs in terms of what they suggest is an independently motivated focus head position. Their proposal is inadequate in a number of respects. First, the simplest constructions that their leftward *wh*-movement analysis predicts to be grammatical are not, in fact, grammatical. As shown in section 7.3.1, sentences involving left-peripheral *wh*-objects (without an additional *wh*-phrase in the sentence corresponding to the questioned argument) are ungrammatical. Second, their analysis of the cases of right-peripheral *wh*-phrases cannot properly account for the facts about word order and the distribution of nonmanual *wh*-marking.

Petronio and Lillo-Martin's analysis conflates different constructions that should not receive a homogeneous treatment. However, even assuming that there *were* independent evidence for a sentence-final +focus C and for the null elements they postulate, their analysis does not correctly account for the distribution of *wh-phrases*, which cannot be accommodated in the head position they posit.

Finally, Petronio and Lillo-Martin do not have an adequate account for the distribution of nonmanual *wh*-marking. With respect to the cases of optional spread we have observed, their attempt to eliminate these from consideration by claiming they involve multisentence discourses is untenable.

7.4.2 Alternative Leftward-Movement Analysis Consistent with Kayne 1994

By arguing against the specific proposals put forward by Petronio and Lillo-Martin (1997), we have not addressed the possibility that the facts we have described here might still be accounted for in terms of leftward *wh*-movement. The claim that *wh*-phrases appear, at the surface, in a sentence-final [Spec, CP] position does not preclude an analysis involving leftward movement and an underlying specifier-head-complement order for CP. In fact, NKBAM (1997) consider an alternative approach, consistent with Kayne's (1994) antisymmetry framework, according to which the *wh*-phrase first moves leftward to a *clause-initial* [Spec, CP] position, after which the remainder of the clause moves to some even higher position(s). It might appear at first that such an approach could be made to work. However, NKBAM (1997) show that this kind of analysis runs into difficulty in accounting for the distribution of nonmanual *wh*-marking. In particular, they show that the optionality of the spread of *wh*-marking cannot be accounted for given the structure that would result from such movements.

NKBAM actually consider several leftward-movement alternatives (such as the fronting of TP to a specifier position higher than CP, or the further raising of both C and TP). Although such alternatives can capture the word order facts, NKBAM show that it is not possible, under any single structure, to account for the spread of *wh*-marking over TP that optionally occurs when the *wh*-phrase appears in final position. That is, the alternatives they consider predict either that spread should be obligatory or that spread should not be possible at all. In what follows, we show how one might account for the ASL facts under a leftward-movement approach, although such an account has several undesirable properties.

In order to accommodate the ASL data within the antisymmetry framework, one would have to propose that the cases where *wh*-marking does and does not spread are a reflection of different structures (in essence, combining the alternatives considered by NKBAM). Consider first the structure shown in (85).

(85)
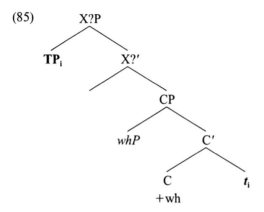

The sentence-final positioning of the *wh*-phrase is the result of the fronting of TP to some higher position. In this case, the nonmanual *wh*-marking is predicted to occur only over the *wh*-phrase, as there is no other material within the c-command domain of C over which the marking can spread. As we have shown, however, it is also possible to find *wh*-marking over the entire question; the structure in (85) cannot accommodate this possibility. In order for *wh*-marking to occur over TP, TP would have to be within the c-command domain of C. To achieve this, one could propose that sentences where the *wh*-phrase occurs in final position and where *wh*-marking occurs over the entire question involve further raising of C (and hence of the +wh feature, assuming such a feature is interpretable and hence was not deleted after checking occurred within CP) to a higher functional head, as depicted in (86).

(86)
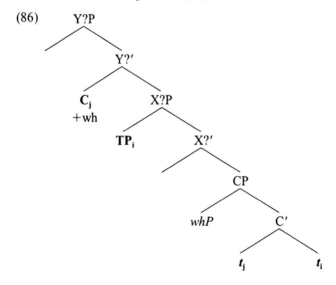

In this case, nonmanual marking associated with the +wh feature in C would spread obligatorily over its c-command domain, and hence would occur over both TP and the *wh*-phrase.

Thus, by proposing distinct structures for the spread and nonspread cases, one could account for the ASL *wh*-data within the antisymmetry framework. Such an account, although offering no new insights,[59] poses several new problems.

• What is the identity of X?P, and what drives movement of TP? The head of X?P does not appear to have any semantic or phonetic content. Assuming that movement is driven by the need to check some syntactic feature, it is not clear what feature would force the raising of TP.
• Similarly, what is the identity of Y?P, and what drives the raising of C? Again, the head of Y?P does not appear to have any semantic or phonetic content of its own. The +wh features in C and in the *wh*-phrase have already been checked within CP, so this feature cannot be responsible for the movement of C.

Unless such issues can be resolved satisfactorily, we feel this kind of analysis remains problematic.

Such a restatement of a simple analysis involving rightward movement in terms of the constraints imposed by Kayne's antisymmetry framework requires postulating additional functional projections and movements that are apparently otherwise unmotivated. This would seem to conflict with the minimalist approach to syntax, where movement is driven by the need to check features, and where projections are postulated only if justified (cf. Chomsky's desire to eliminate AgrP).

In sum, it is difficult to reconcile the ASL data with a framework that allows only leftward movement. Thus, we maintain that the ASL *wh*-facts are most straightforwardly accounted for by rightward *wh*-movement to a sentence-final [Spec, CP] position.

7.5   Conclusions

The analysis proposed here has theoretical significance for evaluating proposals such as Kayne's (1994) that would place restrictions on phrase structure and on directionality of movement. Clearly, Universal Grammar must provide a space in which the options instantiated by signed languages may be accommodated. It is certainly possible that modality-specific aspects of signed languages might account for particular differences between signed and spoken languages. Further crosslinguistic research on signed languages would be needed to investigate such possibilities. In any event, the evidence demonstrates that rightward *wh*-movement is attested in ASL.

An important source of evidence for the analysis proposed in this chapter is the distribution of nonmanual marking associated with the +wh feature. The distribution and intensity of nonmanual *wh*-marking provide evidence for the existence of a +wh feature not only within *wh*-phrases (by virtue of lexical features of *wh*-signs that head such phrases) but also in C. Thus, the distribution and intensity of *wh*-marking in ASL support the existence of a +wh feature in more than one location, consistent with a feature-checking approach of the kind suggested in, for example, Chomsky 1993.

Chapter 8
Conclusions

In this book, we have examined the structure of ASL clauses and noun phrases, on the basis of data collection conducted with an acute awareness of the sociolinguistic characteristics of the use of this language, as described in chapter 2. As has no doubt become apparent, the literature is replete with disputed claims about the grammaticality of even simple constructions. The underlying reasons for differences in reported judgments are, in many cases, unclear. There are surely interesting kinds of dialectal and idiolectal variation yet to be documented. It is also likely that some of the disagreements stem from the methodological difficulties related to the challenge of isolating, in an experimental setting (often with non-Deaf researchers), the language used by native signers among themselves. It is difficult to evaluate claims about data in the absence of video exemplars of the sentences under discussion, in part because the gloss representations used here and elsewhere provide at best partial information about what was actually signed. For this reason, we have made QuickTime video examples available over the Internet and on CD-ROM in conjunction with this book. We hope that other researchers will similarly make video samples of constructions under discussion publicly accessible in this way.

Specifically, we have examined the manual and nonmanual instantiations of several major syntactic features in ASL, with particular attention to the evidence they provide about the syntactic organization of the language. In differing degrees of detail, we have considered negation, tense, agreement, definiteness, and question features within the clause and the noun phrase.

8.1   Findings Counter to Prior Claims about ASL

We have been able to correct the record with respect to several prior claims about the syntactic organization of ASL. In particular, contrary to prior claims, we have demonstrated

- **the existence of tense in ASL**

ASL has grammatical tense. There are lexical tense markers that are distinguishable from related adverbials.

- **the existence of determiners in ASL**

ASL has both definite and indefinite determiners.

- **the existence of a uniform mechanism for licensing null arguments**

Null subjects and objects are uniformly licensed by an overt expression (either manual or nonmanual) of syntactic agreement. Verbs of all morphological classes occur in syntactic structures of a single type (namely, clauses containing syntactic agreement).

- **the permissibility of extraction out of embedded clauses**

Wh-phrases can be extracted out of embedded clauses.

- **the existence of a basic hierarchical word order**

Deviations from the basic SVO word order are explained in terms of material occurring in positions that precede or follow TP. Careful examination of topics, tags, and right dislocations, for example, and of the associated prosody and nonmanual markings found in such constructions, reveals that claims of free word order are without foundation. Further support for the existence of hierarchically grouped constituents comes from the distribution of nonmanual syntactic markings that spread over c-command domains. Thus, on the issue of basic underlying word order, we share the consensus in the literature that it is SVO.

8.2   Findings Consistent with Other Theoretical Results

The findings presented here have significance for an understanding of the syntactic organization of ASL and for syntactic theory generally. Languages in the visual-spatial modality yield interesting new types of evidence that provide further support for theoretical results that have been based primarily on data from spoken languages, with respect to

- **functional projections**

The visible correlates of syntactic features, spreading as they do over c-command domains, provide evidence of hierarchical structure and confirm an articulated phrase structure involving multiple functional projections within both the clause and the noun phrase.

- **existence of abstract syntactic features**

The fact that, in ASL, features such as +neg, +wh, and φ-features—which have been posited independently to account for various phenomena in spoken languages—are expressed nonmanually provides evidence for the existence of such features. The fact that the distribution of these nonmanual expressions can be captured by a single set of generalizations supports treating these features in a uniform manner.

- **feature checking**

Interesting new evidence to support recent approaches involving feature checking comes from the expression of particular features in ASL in more than one syntactic position, thus indicating that the feature is present both as part of an inflected lexical item and as part of a functional head. This was demonstrated with respect to agreement and +wh features. In particular, such evidence argues against older approaches in which lexical items acquired their inflections in the course of the syntactic derivation. This is a particularly interesting result, since such differences in theoretical approaches have been difficult to distinguish empirically.

- **the role of agreement in TP and DP**

In recent literature, the clause has been argued to involve agreement projections, and this type of analysis has also been extended to determiner phrases. Support for the claim that agreement projections are fundamental to both domains comes from the nonmanual expressions of agreement discussed in chapters 5 and 6. Furthermore, the parallels between transitive clauses and possessive noun phrases on the one hand, and between intransitive clauses and possessorless noun phrases on the other, observed in many spoken languages, are brought to light in an interesting new way by the parallel manifestations of agreement marking in these ASL constructions.

8.3   Findings That Shed Light on Current Theoretical Debates

Languages in the visual-spatial modality provide evidence of a kind not available in spoken languages. Such evidence can be especially useful in resolving open questions about syntactic structure. In particular, we have argued that data from ASL may help to resolve current debates over

- **the existence of agreement projections**

The distribution of nonmanual correlates of syntactic agreement supports postulating independent agreement projections, both in the clause and in the noun phrase.

- **the relative position of agreement and tense projections**

The distribution of nonmanual correlates of agreement also makes it possible to determine that, at least in ASL, the tense projection dominates the agreement projections.

- **universal restrictions on the directionality of syntactic movement**

Wh-questions in ASL are best analyzed in terms of rightward *wh*-movement. This would suggest that Kayne's (1994) proposed restrictions on phrase structure and the directionality of syntactic movement do not hold universally.

8.4   Closing Thoughts

As we hope this book has demonstrated, data from languages in the visual-spatial modality can offer new insights into the nature of language. Much research remains to be done for a better understanding of ASL and other signed languages. Such crosslinguistic research will also help to define which phenomena may be characteristic of languages in the visual-spatial modality.

Appendix

Notational Conventions

This appendix details the conventions that we employ throughout the book for presenting ASL examples in gloss format. Note that where we cite examples from published works, the cited gloss generally preserves the original notation, which may differ slightly from what we use for our data.

English translations are provided for the grammatical ASL examples. However, these translations are only approximate. In some cases, different readings of the same sequence of signs (perhaps with slightly different prosody or nonmanual markings) may be possible.

A.1 Representation of Manual Signs

Manual signs are glossed using English words, in capital letters, which represent a close equivalent to the meaning conveyed by the sign.

ARRIVE
> Glosses of signs are written with capital letters.

fs-TULIPS
> The "fs" prefix before a sign indicates that the sign is fingerspelled. (Note that although names in our examples are fingerspelled, this is not explicitly noted in the glosses.)

SHOW-UP
> Hyphenation is used when more than one English word is needed to gloss the ASL sign.

REAL/TRUE
> A slash is used when a single ASL sign has two different English equivalents.

(1h)

This prefix indicates that a sign, normally articulated with two hands, was articulated with one hand. Example: (1h)LOVE.

#

This symbol is used at the beginning of a gloss for a fingerspelled loan sign. Examples: #CAR, #WHAT, #EX.

SHOULD^NOT

The ^ character is used between parts of a contracted sign.

+

When this diacritic occurs between two glosses, it indicates a morpheme boundary. Example: #EX+PRESIDENT. When the diacritic appears at the end of a gloss, it indicates a repetition in the articulation of a sign. For example, POSS+ indicates a possessive sign that receives a double articulation.

"..."

Quotation marks are used in glosses to describe in further detail what is being conveyed by the sign in question. Such markings are often used with indexes, for example, IX_{adv_i} "way over there".

$FUTURE_{adv}$, $FUTURE_{tns}$

Subscripted category or function labels are used to disambiguate similar related signs that have different grammatical functions. For example, $FUTURE_{adv}$ is an adverbial with the meaning 'in the future', whereas $FUTURE_{tns}$ is a future tense marker.

,

Commas are used to mark major constituent boundaries; they are frequently used to set off TP-external elements, such as topics and tags, from the main clause. Commas do not (necessarily) indicate the presence of a pause.

A.2   Use of Indices and Related Diacritics

Subscripted indices are employed to convey information about the spatial and referential properties associated with an utterance. The different uses of subscripts are first described and then illustrated by examples.

1. Subscripted indices used with indexical signs such as IX or POSS or on labels of nonmanual markings like head tilt and eye gaze refer to the location in space where the sign is produced or to which the sign or marking points.

2. On verbs, subscripted indices, as well as annotations like "neu" or "indef," appended to the beginning and/or end of the verb, indicate characteristics of the spatial start and end points of the verb.

3. Indices on noun phrases and other signs do not indicate (necessarily) that those signs were produced in a particular location. Such indices indicate that there is a relation between that element and one or more other elements in the utterance. For example, a noun phrase and a verb that are marked with the same subscripted index participate in an agreement relation. A noun phrase and a pronoun with the same index are coreferential.

IX_i

This index sign points to location i.

$_iGIVE_j$

The sign begins at location i and ends at location j.

$_{neu}GIVE_{indef}$

The sign begins at a neutral location and ends with an open handshape.

$JOHN_i$ ARRIVE EARLY, IX_{pro_i}

JOHN and the pronominal index (articulated at location i) are coreferential.

$\overline{\text{t1-mv}}$

$JOHN_i$, $MARY_j$ $_jGIVE_i$ t_i BOOK

In this example, MARY is associated with the location where GIVE begins and JOHN is associated with the location where GIVE ends. That is, MARY is linked to the subject agreement marking on GIVE and JOHN is linked to the object agreement marking. The notation does not imply that the signs JOHN and MARY were produced at locations i and j, respectively, although they could have been. In addition, JOHN is the antecedent of the coindexed trace.

A.3 Specific Manual Signs Important to This Work

Index signs are pointing signs that are generally articulated with the index finger. The index sign references a particular location in space, which is indicated by a subscript. Such signs are normally glossed as IX_i (where the subscript indicates the spatial location pointed to). Sometimes it is useful to provide more information about the function of that index, as shown here:

IX_{det}

An index sign functioning as a determiner. (Illustrated in figures 3.5 and 6.1.)

IX_{pro}, $IX_{pro_{1p}}$

An index sign functioning as a pronominal. A first person pronominal, which is articulated by pointing to the signer's body, is glossed as $IX_{pro_{1p}}$.

IX_{adv}

An index sign functioning as an adverbial. Adverbial index signs can vary in their articulation, in order to convey more detailed information about the location (such as distance information). One of these variations is described below.

IX_{adv}"far"

An adverbial index sign, expressing a location far away. (Illustrated in figure 6.3)

The sign SOMETHING/ONE is articulated with the index finger pointing upward. The forearm moves in a circular, tremoring motion. Subscripted labels may be used to provide more information about the function of this sign.

$SOMETHING/ONE_{det}$

SOMETHING/ONE functioning as an indefinite determiner. (Illustrated in figure 6.2.)

$SOMETHING/ONE_{pro}$

SOMETHING/ONE functioning as a pronoun (meaning 'something' or 'someone').

The possessive marker sign is glossed as POSS. It is articulated with an open handshape. POSS can either reference a particular spatial location or be produced in a neutral location that does not carry referential meaning.

$POSS_i$, $POSS_{1p}$

POSS references a specific spatial location. The sign is articulated at spatial location i, with the palm oriented toward that location. The first person possessive, articulated such that the hand makes contact with the signer's chest, palm oriented inward, is glossed as $POSS_{1p}$. (Illustrated in figures 3.6 and 6.4.)

$POSS_{neu}$

POSS is produced in a neutral (nonreferential) location. The sign is generally articulated higher than $POSS_i$, slightly toward the dominant side, with the palm oriented forward or toward neutral space. (Illustrated in figure 6.5.)

Other manual signs used in this work include the following:

"WHAT"
    A generic *wh*-sign produced with both hands extended and moving
    slightly from side to side. (Illustrated in figure 7.1.)

QMwg
    A question sign produced with a bent, wiggling index finger.

A.4 Nonmanual Markings

Nonmanual markings are indicated by a labeled line extending over the
manual material with which the marking co-occurs. The label identifies
the marking. The nonmanual markings used in this work are listed below.

y-n
    Yes-no question marking. (Illustrated in figure 7.3.)

wh
    Wh-question marking (other cited works notate this marking as "whq"
    or "wh-q"). (Illustrated in figure 7.1.)

rh/wh
    Rhetorical *wh*-question marking (other cited works notate this marking
    as "rhq"). (Illustrated in figure 7.4.)

neg
    Negative marking. (Illustrated in figure 3.21.)

t1-mv, t2-bg, t3-bg
    Topic markings are described in table A.1 (Illustrated in figures 4.1,
    4.2, 4.3.)

top/wh
    A combination of *wh*- and topic marking, found with *wh*-topics. (Illus-
    trated in figure 7.2.)

cond
    Conditional marking.

hn
    Repeated head nod (other researchers may notate this as "nodding").

hs
    Head shake.

head position$_i$
    Head (and upper body) positioned toward location i, occurring as part
    of the nonmanual markings that characterize a role shift construction.

Table A.1
ASL topic markings

	Nonmanual realization	Moved versus base-generated	Example
t1-mv	Raised brows, head tilted slightly back, eyes wide	Moved	<u>t1-mv</u> ELEANOR$_i$, JIM LIKE t_i 'Eleanor, Jim likes.'
t2-bg	Raised brows, large movement of head back, eyes wide, head moves down as topic is signed	Base-generated	<u>t2-bg</u> FLOWER, NANCY PREFER fs-TULIPS 'As for flowers, Nancy prefers tulips.'
t3-bg	Raised brows, upper lip raised, slight rapid head nod, eyes wide, fixed gaze	Base-generated	<u>t3-bg</u> MARY$_i$, RICHARD LOVE IX$_{pro_i}$ 'You know Mary, Richard loves her.'

<u>head tilt$_i$</u>
   Head tilt (also sometimes notated as "ht") toward location i.

<u>eye gaze$_i$</u>
   Eye gaze (also sometimes notated as "eg") to location i.

<u>indefinite gaze$_i$</u>
   A form of eye gaze (to location i) that is found with indefinite DPs. The eyes may gaze toward an area or may take on an unfocused stare.

<u>far</u>
   A cluster of markings (generally including an open mouth, eye gaze, and head tilted backward) that accompanies adverbial index signs indicating a location far away.

<u>th</u>
   An adverbial marking, articulated with a slightly protruding tongue, as if making a "th" sound.

<u>mm</u>
An adverbial marking, articulated with pursed lips, as if making a "mm" sound.

<u>cs</u>
An adverbial marking indicating proximity in time or space. (Illustrated in figure 3.20.)

A.5   Dominant versus Nondominant Hand and Marking of Perseveration

In some cases, where the behavior of both the dominant hand ("dh") and the nondominant hand ("ndh") is significant, a gloss line for each is provided, as shown in the following example. The dashed lines on the nondominant gloss tier and on the labeled nonmanual line in this example indicate perseveration (i.e., that the handshape of "WHAT" and the brow position of the nonmanual *wh*-marking are held).

<u>wh- -wh</u>
"WHAT" [[JOHN BUY t_i YESTERDAY]$_{TP}$ [+wh]$_C$ "WHAT"$_i$]$_{CP}$ [dh]
"WHAT"- -"WHAT"   [ndh]
'What, what did John buy yesterday?'

Notes

Chapter 1

1. A distinction is made between "lexical projections," such as NP and VP, headed by lexical elements such as nouns and verbs, and "functional projections," headed by grammatical categories such as T, Agr, and Neg, which house abstract syntactic features. Both types of categories project phrases that conform to the rules of X-bar theory.

2. Throughout this work, following Woodward 1973, the term "Deaf" is used to refer to those individuals who are linguistically and culturally deaf (i.e., those who are members of the "Deaf-World"; Lane, Hoffmeister, and Bahan 1996). The term "deaf" is used to refer descriptively to those who are regarded audiologically as having some degree of hearing loss.

3. Nonmanual markings appear to play a role in all primary signed languages that have been studied to date.

4. This differs from the syntactic tree presented in ABKN 1992 and 1994 in several respects, which will be explained in chapter 5. A better understanding of syntactic agreement allowed us to reanalyze phenomena that Kegl (1976a,b, 1985a) had previously treated as "role prominence marking" in terms of agreement.

5. For information on the Minimalist Program, see Haegeman 1997 or the appendix of MacLaughlin 1997 for a brief overview, or, for more detail, Webelhuth 1995 or the introduction to Abraham et al. 1996.

6. The basic idea of c-command dates back at least as far as Reinhart 1976— which in turn built upon work by Klima (1964), Langacker (1969), and others— although many variations on the definition of command relations have been proposed over the years. Here we adopt the simple definition of c-command that α c-commands β iff every node that dominates α also dominates β and α does not dominate β (as formulated in Chomsky 1986). We do not have enough evidence to determine whether this definition or the updated definition suggested in Chomsky 1986 (termed "m-command") is relevant to the spread of nonmanual markings in ASL.

7. In Chomsky 1995a, it is suggested that φ-features are not contained within Agr projections. Evidence from ASL argues against this.

8. To date, there have been relatively few accounts of the syntax of ASL within other syntactic frameworks. Some of the early work on ASL was undertaken in the framework of Relational Grammar (e.g., Padden 1983, 1988; also Kegl 1976b). More recently, Cormier (1998) and Cormier, Wechsler, and Meier (1999) analyze agreement within the context of Head-Driven Phrase Structure Grammar; however, their analysis does not account for the range of data presented here.

Chapter 2

1. Lexical variants have been noted. The grammatical variations among dialects have not been fully explored. See, however, Woodward 1974, 1976 and Woodward and Erting 1975.

2. The characteristics of a minority language include the following, listed by Simpson (1981, 235–236, a, b, and c):

• It is not the language of all areas of activity indulged in by its speakers: for example, it may be excluded from administration or education, being confined to home, religious life or literature.
• It may live in the shadow of a culturally dominant language, dominant because of political, educational, social or religious factors.
• Bilingualism is a characteristic of its speakers.

3. These artificial systems have been shown to be acquired poorly by children (Schick and Moeller 1992; Supalla 1991).

4. The propensity to use code-switching and the nature of that code-switching depend in part on the signer's degree of proficiency in both the primary language and the dominant language (both of which are somewhat variable, for reasons that will be discussed), and the attitude that the signer has toward both languages.

5. See, for example, Lucas and Valli 1989, 1990a for discussion of how signing may be influenced by contact with English.

6. See Kegl 1975 for a study of code-switching by Slovene-English bilinguals. See also Eastman 1992, Fishman 1971, 1972, Grosjean 1982, Gumperz 1971, 1982a,b, Heller 1988, and Milroy and Muysken 1995 on code-switching in general.

7. For in-depth discussion of the power dynamics between Deaf people and the dominant culture, see, for example, Lane 1992, Lane, Hoffmeister, and Bahan 1996, and other references listed there.

8. In the United States, it is, in fact, Deaf children of Deaf parents who are likely to achieve the best mastery of English, because such children come to second language learning with a first language (ASL) firmly in place (Charrow 1974; Mayberry and Eichen 1991).

9. Non-Deaf people who work professionally with deaf children often learn one of the artificial sign systems mentioned earlier. For this reason, hearing parents (and some deaf parents) of deaf children often use one of these systems in the

home. Thus, some deaf children are exposed to such artificial, coded sign systems before they are in a position to learn a signed language.

Interestingly, even when the main input to deaf children is primarily such invented systems, the children's *output* tends to have many features of a natural sign language (Singleton 1989; Supalla 1991).

10. For an overview of educational options for deaf children, see Moores 1987.

11. Frequently, students were even forbidden from signing in class.

12. There are certain dialectal differences that can be traced back to particular residential schools.

13. For discussion of the linguistic effects of age of acquisition, see Emmorey et al. 1995, Mayberry 1993, 1994, Mayberry and Eichen 1991, Mayberry and Fischer 1989, Newport 1988, 1990.

14. The language produced by the interpreter in these cases is not typically ASL; frequently, it is some form of manually coded English, as mentioned earlier. A further complication is that the input that the child is receiving is a product of interpretation, which may, even under the best of circumstances, differ from natural language (Nover 1993; Patrie 1994).

15. Within this community, there is also a rich literary tradition, and artful use of language (story telling, poetry, theater) is highly valued. For more on this, see, for example, Lane, Hoffmeister, and Bahan 1996.

16. For other discussions of methodological considerations relevant to the study of ASL, see Baker-Shenk 1983, chap. 1 and Aarons 1994, chap. 1. For general discussion of grammaticality judgment tasks, see also Carroll, Bever, and Pollack 1981, Cowart 1997, Labov 1972, 1975, Schütze 1996.

17. Metalinguistic skills (in ASL) are not normally cultivated in the course of a deaf person's education. Many hearing people learn about their native language, and learn to reflect on it, in school; but it is rather uncommon for ASL to be the medium of instruction, much less the subject of instruction, in schools for the deaf (although this is starting to change in a few places).

18. This is not to suggest that there are not many other interesting but different research questions that may be posed about the use of language by deaf people with diverse backgrounds in different situations. Other researchers do focus on such issues, of course.

19. Kegl (1976b) reports one case where two impeccable native signing informants at first accepted three particular sentences as grammatical. However, when asked to actually sign the examples, both stated that they would never sign them that way, but that if a hearing person were to do so, they would understand what that person meant. These two informants, who were linguistically sophisticated, exhibited a clear difference between what they would accept as an ASL sentence and what they would sign themselves. This response is not atypical. See also Kegl, Lentz, and Philip 1976.

20. As we will show in later chapters, like English, ASL is underlyingly SVO (subject-verb-object), although unlike English, it is a null argument language and

makes productive use of topics, tags, and right dislocations, resulting in a variety of surface word orders. Subjects have been known to reject grammatical SVO sentences, as pointed out by Petronio and Lillo-Martin (1997, 46).

21. There is some disagreement about whether or not it is acceptable to use an interpreter in elicitation. We feel strongly that it is better to use an interpreter with near-native proficiency than to have elicitation conducted by a researcher with anything less.

22. The practice of pooling judgments has been acknowledged by several researchers in the field. Even more troubling than pooling of judgments of one's own informants is pooling of data reported in the literature via printed glosses. This is problematic for some reasons that are obvious and others that relate to the inadequacy of gloss notation, to be addressed in section 2.4.

Another example of pooling of judgments is found in Petronio 1993 (and subsequent work, e.g., Petronio and Lillo-Martin 1997), where native and nonnative judgments from Petronio 1991 appear to have been pooled, as discussed in chapter 7.

23. Several other transcription systems exist. For example, several systems are in use for phonological representation and computer coding of signing (Blees et al. 1996; Hanke and Prillwitz 1995; Prillwitz et al. 1989) and for coding facial expressions (Ekman and Friesen 1978). For information about attempts to develop a writing system for ASL, see McIntire et al. 1987, Newkirk 1976, 1981, Stokoe, Casterline, and Croneberg 1965, Sutton 1981. However, there is no general written system for ASL used throughout the Deaf community at this point in time.

24. In other words, the names in these examples are not expressed by a single ASL sign but are instead spelled out by letters of the ASL manual alphabet. The manual alphabet is used primarily for names and words borrowed from English.

25. We do, however, notate fingerspelling in our examples when used with signs other than names.

26. In the early ASL literature, nonmanual behaviors were often not marked at all in the transcriptions. Such transcriptions, as presented, are thus of limited usefulness.

27. Bouchard and Dubuisson (1995), for example, relied upon written glosses in prior ASL literature and drew conclusions about the absence of particular nonmanual markings from the fact that they had not been transcribed. This practice is problematic, particularly in the light of note 26. Even when referencing more recent literature in which nonmanual markings in an utterance are transcribed, one cannot conclude that everything that occurred is represented in the transcription. See also note 22.

28. Links to information accessible over the World Wide Web about tools of this kind may be found at our Web site: http://www.bu.edu/asllrp/.

29. For more information about SignStream, see MNL 1996, MNLG 1998, NM 1998, NMLBK 1997, and http://www.bu.edu/asllrp/SignStream.

30. There are anecdotal incidents where researchers presenting their findings have shown videotaped examples and where native Deaf signers in the audience were able to see that the data had been misanalyzed. Ideally, such contributions from native signers should come at an earlier stage, in the course of the linguistic analysis itself.

31. This is another frequent complaint by Deaf conference participants.

32. Unfortunately, there has been a long tradition within signed language research of treating the data as confidential and proprietary. One of the reasons given for not displaying examplars of sentences under discussion is that distribution of data necessarily reveals the identity of the informants consulted in the collection of those data. There is a distinction, however, between revealing the work product of elicitation with individual informants who may wish to remain anonymous and providing a signed model of a construction being offered to support a particular linguistic proposal. It is hard to believe that, for a given sentence a researcher believes to be grammatical, no native signer can be found who would be willing to sign the sentence for demonstration purposes. The data that we make publicly accessible are the end product of research conducted with a variety of informants (not all of whom have been shown publicly). The sign model in our displayed video examples is merely illustrating the grammatical construction under discussion (which has previously been tested with multiple informants).

33. For example, a data repository has been established, in association with the SignStream project, to facilitate shared access to video data and associated transcriptions.

Chapter 3

1. The location in which a sign is produced may or may not provide additional linguistic information. For example, a sign like HOUSE may be articulated in front of a signer's body (an area that has often been referred to as "neutral space" (Klima and Bellugi 1979; Stokoe, Casterline, and Croneberg 1965)), but the location of the sign provides no additional meaning; it is merely where the sign is articulated. In contrast, some signs (including HOUSE) may also be produced in a spatial location that is used to convey information about the referent. The specifics of this and other linguistic uses of space are discussed in section 3.3.

2. Even though signs may be underlyingly one- or two-handed, variations in production may occur as a result of different factors (Battison 1978).

3. Signs were first decomposed into distinctive units (specifically, handshape, location, and movement) by Stokoe and his colleagues (Stokoe 1960; Stokoe, Casterline, and Croneberg 1965), although they used different terminology: "cherology" (phonology), "chereme" (phoneme), and "allocher" (allophone). The parameter of palm orientation was introduced by Battison (1978). For additional information about ASL phonology, see, for example, Ann 1993, Boyes Braem 1981, Brentari 1990, 1998, Coulter 1990, Friedman 1976b, 1977, Kegl and Wilbur 1976, Lane, Boyes Braem, and Bellugi 1976, Meier 1993, Perlmutter 1992,

Sandler 1987, 1989, Uyechi 1996, as well as papers in Coulter 1993 and a brief summary in Bahan 1996, 10–19.

4. We use the term "coarticulation" to describe items that are articulated simultaneously.

5. The pair in figure 3.1 is an unusual example, in that the English translations of these two signs, by pure coincidence, also constitute a minimal pair in English.

6. For more about derivational and inflectional morphology in ASL, see, for example, Bahan 1996, Bellugi 1980, Klima and Bellugi 1979, Newkirk 1979, Padden 1983, 1988, Padden and Perlmutter 1987, Supalla and Newport 1978.

7. For discussion of classifiers, see, for example, Allan 1977, Boyes Braem 1981, Kegl 1985b, Kegl and Wilbur 1976, McDonald 1982, Schick 1987, 1990, S. Supalla 1986, T. Supalla 1982.

8. In addition to the semantic classifiers, of which the vehicle classifier is one example, there are two other classifier types: size and shape specifiers (SASSs) and handling or instrument classifiers (HCLs or ICLs). SASSs interact with movement roots to trace the size and shape of objects (Klima and Bellugi 1979). HCLs use handshapes to represent how objects are handled and play a role in marking causation and agency (Forman and McDonald 1978; Kegl 1985a).

9. For more information about verbs of motion and location, see Lucas and Valli 1990c, Supalla 1982, 1990.

10. Much has been written about the use of space in ASL to represent discourse entities (see, e.g., Bahan and Petitto 1980; Fischer and Gough 1978; Friedman 1975; Gee and Kegl 1982; Hoffmeister 1978; Johnson and Liddell 1987; Kegl 1976a, 1985b; Klima and Bellugi 1979; Lacy 1974; Loew 1984; Padden 1983, 1988; Winston 1991). There has been some controversy about whether such use of space is or is not strictly linguistic. For an alternative view to the one presented here, see Liddell 1995.

11. If two referents are being distinguished, for example, one to the signer's left and one to the signer's right, great precision is not required in order to make it clear which referent is being pointed to. Thus, the signer will point to essentially the same location (but obviously not exactly the same point in space) for subsequent reference. This is comparable to any linguistic articulation, where multiple articulations of the same linguistic unit are never absolutely identical.

12. The use of a point to designate a referent that, in fact, occupies much more space than a single point, gives rise to many interesting spatial phenomena, beyond the scope of this discussion. See, for example, Liddell 1996, in press.

13. Note that ASL does not grammatically encode gender features. Number may be expressed in the nominal, adjectival, and verbal systems (see, e.g., Chinchor 1981; Klima and Bellugi 1979; Liddell 1986; Metlay and Supalla 1995; Padden 1990; Wilbur 1979); such expressions are complex and have yet to be fully analyzed. Throughout this book, we focus specifically on person features.

14. Various claims have been made about person distinctions in ASL. Friedman (1975) suggested that there are grammatical distinctions among first, second, and

third person reference. Conversely, Lillo-Martin and Klima (1990), who examine only singular pronoun forms, claim, "There are no contrasts for person in ASL" (p. 198). Meier (1990) examines the full system (including plural and possessive forms) and makes a strong case for a grammatical distinction between first person and nonfirst person. (Lillo-Martin (1995) rejects the view taken in Lillo-Martin and Klima 1990 in favor of Meier's view.) Here we propose that, although (consistent with Meier's claim) there is a primary distinction between first and nonfirst persons, nonfirst person can be further subclassified into many distinct person values.

15. Pointing may sometimes be performed instead by the thumb or, in the case of honorifics, by an open B handshape moving downward, with the palm up. In the latter case, it is the tips of the fingers that can be considered to be "pointing."

16. Lexical numerals can be incorporated into the articulation of a pronoun (giving a form meaning, for example, 'the three of us'). In such cases, the hand (with the numeral handshape) moves among the points in space associated with the included referents.

17. However, see Janis 1995 for a different perspective. Janis suggests that the agreement properties of different types of verbs can be made to follow from other considerations.

18. As explained in the appendix, subscripted indices used with indexical signs such as IX or POSS refer to the location in space where the sign is produced (a reflection, we argue, of the ϕ-features that are being expressed). In the case of verbs, the subscripted indices appended to the beginning and end of the verb indicate the spatial start and end points of the verb.

Indices on noun phrases and other signs, however, do not indicate (necessarily) that those signs were produced in a particular location. In (1), they indicate agreement relations. That is, the verb's start point corresponds to the point in space associated with JOHN's ϕ-features. (In other contexts, subscripted indices may serve to mark coreference, or to indicate that an XP and its trace form a syntactic chain.)

19. With a few verbs, the "backward verbs" like INVITE (see Brentari 1988; Friedman 1976a; Padden 1988), subject agreement is expressed by a suffix and object agreement is expressed by a prefix.

20. When one of the arguments is nonreferential, expressing the idea of "nobody" or "nothing," there is no referential use of space associated with it. Instead, as mentioned in note 1, the sign requires some spatial articulation, but the location used is not interpreted referentially.

21. Whereas many other languages use third person as the unmarked form, ASL seems to use a first person form systematically. This could be due to the fact that signers articulate signs using their own body; first person is the most "unmarked" form since it is the form that is articulated closest to the signer's body. Furthermore, the grammatical person system of ASL affords no other form to serve as a default. As discussed in note 14, ASL distinguishes grammatically between first and nonfirst person. Within such a system, it is not surprising that first person

would serve as the default form. Aikhenvald and Dixon (1998) note that in (spoken) languages having only first and second person pronouns (third person reference being accomplished via the use of deictics), if there is an unmarked person form, it will generally be first person.

22. For discussion of the notion of identifiability, see Lambrecht 1994. A referent may be more or less identifiable, as the speaker may possess more or less knowledge about the referent.

23. Other manifestations of agreement in ASL show sensitivity to definiteness features as well, including nonmanual marking of object agreement in the clause (chapter 5) and expressions of agreement in DP (chapter 6). Notably, expressions of subject agreement do not manifest such distinctions.

24. Benjamin Bahan has observed an interesting and creative way in which one signer, his father, may access the locations in space associated with φ-features. Bahan (1996, 85, fn. 5) observed that James Bahan "makes productive use, in his own idiolect, of a process borrowed from Puerto Rican gestures that involves pursing the lips to point to a location in space. James Bahan has generalized that use for linguistic purposes, and he uses such lip pointing for pronominal reference and so on."

25. This systematicity provides strong evidence that space is being used linguistically for expression of φ-features, rather than in a gestural fashion (Liddell in press). Further support for the linguistic nature of the pronominal system in ASL comes from errors made in the course of first language acquisition, which parallel spoken language pronominal development (see Petitto 1983 and discussion in Newport and Meier 1985).

26. This, in turn, has several further consequences for the use of pronominals in relation to full noun phrases. For example, backward anaphora does not occur and right dislocation is restricted to pronominals.

27. Although it was long thought that ASL expresses tense information exclusively through temporal adverbials, ASL does make use of lexical tense markers. See chapter 5 for discussion. See also Shepard-Kegl, Neidle, and Kegl 1995 for the ramifications of such misconceptions with respect to miscommunication by interpreters in a legal setting.

28. Some lexical tense markers have forms related to temporal adverbials. The articulation of such tense markers does not vary. See chapter 5.

29. There is another variant of this sign where both hands move simultaneously to represent the change in time.

30. In addition, NOT-YET, like other negative signs, such as NOT and NEVER, is accompanied by a distinct nonmanual negative marking, which is discussed in section 3.4.4.

31. It is, of course, not always the case that eliminating a lexically associated nonmanual marking gives rise to an existing sign with a different meaning.

32. The proper analysis of this kind of coarticulation of verbal and adverbial information in ASL, involving manual and/or nonmanual adverbial modifications to a verb, awaits further research.

33. In fact, closer examination of the relatively few attested cases of "lexical" nonmanual markings may reveal that they have adverbial content and/or express syntactic features of the kind to be discussed in the next section. Several cases of lexically associated nonmanual markings described in Baker 1976a have been reanalyzed by Bahan (1996) as involving syntactic agreement marking of the kind discussed in chapter 5.

34. Adverbial facial expressions and those associated with syntactic features may also be differentially impaired (Kegl and Poizner 1997).

35. In addition, lexical items that are invariably associated with a syntactic feature (such as the negative sign, NOT-YET, discussed in note 30) are marked with the associated nonmanual expression even when signed in isolation.

36. The characteristics of the nonmanual negative expression have been described by many researchers (see, e.g., Baker 1976b, 1980; Baker-Shenk 1983; Baker and Cokely 1980d; Baker and Padden 1978; Bellugi and Fischer 1972; Liddell 1980; Stokoe 1960; Veinberg and Wilbur 1990).

37. The physical realizations of the nonmanual markings for negation and questions have been well described in the literature. Here we do not focus on their articulatory characteristics, or on the extent to which the articulatory components of those expressions may be further analyzable semantically. For an interesting approach along those lines, see Coulter 1979. (See also Wilbur 1995, where a structural basis for determining eyebrow position is suggested.)

38. The relation of optional versus obligatory spread to the availability of manual material was first noted for wh-questions by Lillo-Martin and Fischer (1992) (although their generalization did not take this form and Lillo-Martin has since abandoned the position that spread is ever optional; this will be discussed in detail in chapter 7).

39. The observation that c-command relations are relevant to the spread of nonmanual negative marking is due to Liddell (1980). The general account here of the spread of nonmanual grammatical markings over c-command domains follows the formulation in ABKN 1992. Lillo-Martin and Fischer (1992) and Petronio (1993) also make use of c-command to explain the distribution of nonmanual marking, but their accounts differ significantly from what is presented here.

40. Petronio (1993) and Petronio and Lillo-Martin (1995, 1997) have claimed that the nonmanual marking associated with IP-internal negation must spread over the entire sentence. Thus, they dispute the grammaticality of examples such as (5), (6), and (9), while offering examples like the following as grammatical:

$$\overline{\qquad\qquad\qquad\text{neg}\qquad\qquad\qquad}$$
(i) JOHN NOT BUY HOUSE
    'John did not buy the house.'

Our informants find sentences such as (i) ungrammatical on the reading in question. (Such sentences can only be interpreted as having the reading 'No, John didn't buy the house'. In such cases, there are multiple sources of the negative marking, and the spread over the subject is a result of perseveration, which will be discussed shortly.) The spread reported in examples (5), (6), and (9) is consistent with previous claims in the literature (see McIntire, Reilly, and Anderson 1994; Veinberg and Wilbur 1990). Braze (1997, 34, ex. (29)) also reports such examples as grammatical.

It is possible that Petronio and Lillo-Martin are misinterpreting the anticipatory movement of the head in cases where we claim that the negative marking begins with the sign NOT. This may be a consequence of their use of pronominal subjects or other subjects of short articulatory duration.

Head movements like the negative head shake and the affirmative head nod are generally characterized by an anticipatory motion to a starting position that will allow a maximal initial movement. Thus, the head normally raises prior to a head nod and moves sideward prior to a head shake. The anticipatory nature of this movement is particularly evident in examples where manual material intervenes between the subject and the negative sign, as shown in (ii), where it is apparent that the negative marking does not occur over the subject.

                                          neg
(ii) JOHN MAYBE NOT BUY HOUSE
     'John might not buy a house.'

41. There are two basic types of nonmanual markings, distinguished by their articulatory characteristics. Certain markings, such as brow position or eye gaze, involve essentially the holding of a given position. When such markings persever-ate (i.e., when there are two separate syntactic positions in which the feature associated with the marking appears), the maximal intensity is held between the two positions. In contrast, head nods and shakes, involving repeated movements, exhibit discernible intensity peaks at each of their sources, although the general movement (whether nod or shake) continues between the two positions.

42. Characteristics of intensity and perseveration of nonmanual markings have received little attention to date (with the notable exception of Baker-Shenk's (1983, e.g.) descriptions of intensity). These issues are discussed in more detail in Bahan 1996, NKBAM 1997, and NMLBK 1998b, and in chapter 7.

43. Crucially, nonmanual spread reflects c-command relations that hold at Spell-Out (within the model of Chomsky 1993 or 1995a) or at S-Structure (within earlier models), but neither *before* nor *after*. We are not adopting recent proposals that features that must be checked have moved by Spell-Out. For example, proposals such as those made by Bobaljik (1995), Brody (1995), Groat and O'Neil (1996), and Pesetsky (1997) would eliminate the need for covert movement after Spell-Out. We assume, with Chomsky (1993, 1995a), that features (at least) do move covertly after Spell-Out. Evidence for distinguishing among these possibilities is hard to come by. We will argue, however, that in particular constructions, the nonmanual markings associated, for example, with the +wh feature constitute evidence that such features are present in two different locations at Spell-Out and thus that feature movement and checking have not yet occurred.

44. As proposed by Kitagawa (1986), Koopman and Sportiche (1991), Kuroda (1988), Rosen (1989), Speas (1986), Woolford (1991), Zagona (1982); see McCloskey 1997 for discussion of the various proposals that have been made.

45. There are, in addition, other uses of nonmanual markings that we have not discussed: for example, to convey prosodic information, such as stress (Wilbur 1990; Wilbur and Patschke 1998; Wilbur and Schick 1987).

Chapter 4

1. Although we have suggested that these occur in adjoined positions, other analyses are possible. For example, Kayne (1994), who disallows right adjunction, suggests alternative analyses of tag and right dislocation constructions.

2. This is linguistic evidence of the usual type relevant to establishing constituency. We certainly do not mean to suggest that there is necessarily a one-to-one correspondence between any particular prosodic signal and a particular syntactic structure. Evidence of this type, however, taken as a whole, provides essential information about constituency.

3. For further explanation of the discourse conditions under which these types of topics are used, see Aarons 1994.

4. An example of the other kind of base-generated topic preceding a moved topic is illustrated in (i).

Context: You are planning a dinner party for some friends with finicky tastes. You have decided on a tentative menu, but you want to make sure that everyone will find something they like. The menu includes both fish and chicken. Person 1 says that John and Mary don't eat fish. Person 2 replies that Mary does like fish and . . .

$$\text{t2-bg} \quad \text{t1-mv}$$
(i) $\overline{\text{JOHN}_i, \text{ FISH}_j,}$ IX_i WON'T EAT t_j BUT IX_i CAN EAT CHICKEN
    'As for John, fish he won't eat, but he can eat chicken.'

The moved topic cannot precede the base-generated topic.

5. There are, however, some restrictions. See Aarons 1994 for discussion.

6. Wilbur (1995) assumes that moved topics occur in [Spec, CP], the same position to which *wh*-phrases move, and that [Spec, CP] is on the left. Although she does not present an analysis of ASL *wh*-questions, the structure of CP that she assumes cannot account for the *wh*-data discussed in chapter 7.

7. For example, Lillo-Martin (1992), apparently assuming that all topic constructions necessarily involve movement, interprets any overt pronoun that refers back to a topic in the same sentence as a "resumptive pronoun." She goes on to propose that movement in ASL is more highly constrained than in English (for example), basing the proposal on the distribution of what she analyzes to be resumptive pronouns. A very different analysis would emerge if one recognized the existence of base-generated topics.

8. Padden (1983, 1988) describes a phenomenon that she calls "subject pronoun copy," where "a pronoun copy of the subject is tagged onto the end of the sentence" (Padden 1988, 86). We suggest that many of the cases that Padden identifies as involving subject pronoun copy are actually instances of right dislocation (some may involve tag constructions, described below), although pronominal right

dislocation in ASL is not restricted to subjects. In addition, it is possible, under certain circumstances, to find two right-dislocated pronominals at the end of a sentence, as shown in (i).

(i) JOHN$_i$ LIKE IX$_j$, IX$_i$, IX$_j$
    'John likes her, him, her.'

9. The traditional term "dislocation" is misleading, in this respect. Note that we are not proposing any specific analysis for right dislocation, although we have generally assumed that, in such constructions, the pronominal is right-adjoined to CP. Rightward adjunction is inconsistent with Kayne 1994; we have not adopted Kayne's framework for reasons we will present in chapter 7. Kayne (1994, 78–83) proposes an alternative analysis of right dislocation; however, it is not clear that his account allows for the distinction, important in ASL, between tags and right dislocations, since he treats them as essentially the same construction.

10. For some discussion of right dislocation in Norwegian, see Fretheim 1995. Fretheim (1996) has investigated interesting interactions between Norwegian intonation and right dislocation in relation to the appropriateness of given constructions in particular discourse contexts. From preliminary investigation, many of his findings for Norwegian, in terms of both the discourse functions of pronominal right dislocation and the cognitive status of the NP that is referred back to by a right-dislocated pronoun, appear to extend to both French and ASL. Further research on these issues is warranted.

11. Many of the examples that we analyze as involving sentence-final tags are treated quite differently by Petronio and Lillo-Martin (1997) (see also an earlier proposal in Petronio 1993). These authors identify a variety of lexical items that they analyze as occurring in clause-final position, including pronouns, modals, quantifiers, verbs, and *wh*-words. They claim that these elements occur in C and function as focus words that "double" a (possibly null) element elsewhere in the clause. This analysis is addressed in detail in chapter 7.

Petronio and Lillo-Martin (1997) explicitly exclude from their account any cases where there is a pause before the final element, suggesting that when a pause is present, "the construction has different syntactic properties" (fn. 12), although they do not specify what those properties might be. Petronio and Lillo-Martin provide no justification for excluding such cases. In our view, just like tag constructions in other languages, the tag in ASL may or may not be preceded by a pause.

12. As mentioned in ABKN 1995, this head nod seems to be the counterpart of the kind of phonological compensatory lengthening found before null categories in English, as in the following examples, with stress on the italicized words:

(i)   John will leave, and then Bill *will* [e]$_{VP}$.

(ii) John is taller than Mary *is* [e]$_{AP}$.

(iii) John can bring bread and Mary *can* [e]$_V$ wine.

(iv) John left. He *did* [e]$_{VP}$.

13. Liddell shows that, although the affirmative head nod may occur optionally in clauses that contain overt verbal material, the head nod is obligatory when no overt verb is present (as in the tag construction, illustrated in (17) through (19)). Although this head nod warrants further study, its co-occurrence with a post-clausal element provides evidence that this final element occurs as part of a clausal tag construction.

Petronio and Lillo-Martin (1997) make claims about the affirmative head nod that contradict both Liddell's work and our own findings. Petronio and Lillo-Martin claim that the head nod, when present, obligatorily occurs over the whole clause (including the subject). For discussion, see NMLBK 1998b and chapter 7.

14. We focus here on affirmative declarative tags. However, tags are also found with negative, yes-no question, and *wh*-question constructions. In chapter 7, we will consider tag constructions again, particularly in relation to *wh*-questions.

15. If the main clause is relatively brief, then the affirmative head nod over the clause may not have time to damp significantly prior to the articulation of the tag. In such cases, it may be difficult to discern two distinct peaks of intensity in the head movement.

16. The analysis of (22) as involving right dislocation supersedes the suggestion in ABKN 1992 that the subject occurs in clause-final position within the tag.

17. Early descriptions of ASL sentence structure included examples with word orders other than SVO. (For example, Fischer (1975), although arguing that the basic word order for ASL is SVO, noted deviations from that order in certain cases; see also Kegl 1976b, 1977.) Some of the non-SVO examples may, in fact, involve sentence-initial topics, accounting for instances of OSV word order. Others, however, are likely to involve other types of movement processes that have yet to be carefully studied and analyzed. For example, Braze (1997) and Matsuoka (1997) have proposed a process of object shift. We have found evidence of another fronting process that appears to involve movement of the aspect phrase (as will be discussed later). These constructions are in need of further study.

18. In support of their proposal, Bouchard and Dubuisson (1995, 121) state, "This leads the Deaf signers consulted to propose that, in context, the signer makes a choice on essentially articulatory grounds. This choice concerns the fluidity of movement between adjacent signs: they hypothesize that this is not a constraint but rather a tendency." It is not clear how this differs from a spoken language informant's explaining a particular choice of construction by saying that it sounded better than the alternative or was easier to say.

19. It is not clear whether Bouchard and Dubuisson are suggesting that all signed languages have a "default" SVO order. There are signed languages that have been reported to have SOV order (Fischer (1975) has made this claim for old LSF (French Sign Language), for example).

20. In an attempt to explain the generalizations presented in ABKN 1992 without reliance on hierarchical structure, Bouchard and Dubuisson (1995) suggest several

alternative generalizations that might hold within ASL. However, they do not verify those generalizations against the facts of ASL (or even against the full range of data presented in ABKN 1992).

Chapter 5

1. Various interpretations of head and eye movements are found in the literature. For example, Kegl (1985b) interpreted what we now analyze as nonmanual markings of subject agreement as instead marking "role prominence." The existence of such role prominence marking was also assumed in ABKN 1992, 1994 (following Kegl). The analysis presented here supersedes the analysis in those works.

2. Bahan (1996) discusses interactions between the manual and nonmanual expressions of agreement. For example, he observes that when subject agreement is expressed overtly both through nonmanual marking and through verbal morphology, the manual expression may be somewhat reduced (i.e., articulated closer to the body). When object agreement is expressed both manually and nonmanually, eye gaze tends to be reduced in duration.

3. There is one exceptional case where the associations between head tilt and eye gaze, on the one hand, and subject and object agreement, on the other, are reversed: when the object is first person. See Bahan 1996 for details.

4. Several factors may contribute to what may appear to be an early termination of the nonmanual agreement markings in many cases. Bahan (1996) notes that interactions between manual and nonmanual expressions of agreement may result in early termination of eye gaze, as mentioned in note 2.

In addition, eye gaze serves a variety of other functions in ASL (e.g., it is used to regulate discourse turn-taking, and it is a major signal of "role shift" (as is head positioning); see Bahan 1996 and references therein for further discussion), which may override its use as an expression of syntactic agreement.

With respect to head tilt, because the head moves relatively slowly, it must begin repositioning itself in anticipation of its next function; this anticipatory movement often overrides the prior head positioning, resulting in the appearance of an early termination of the prior head position.

5. The verb does not raise overtly to Agr heads in ASL. Simple word order facts (such as the negation data presented in chapter 3) suffice to show that the verb does not raise past negation, nor past adverbials such as ALWAYS. The fact that the nonmanual expressions of agreement begin prior to the articulation of the verb and spread obligatorily over the VP provides evidence that the verb does not raise (overtly) to Agr. Given that the agreement projections immediately dominate the VP (as shown in section 5.4), the verb could not raise to aspect or tense (in nonnegative sentences) without violating the Head Movement Constraint (Baker 1988; Chomsky 1986; Travis 1984) (or its current theoretical equivalent).

Some ASL researchers have presented analyses involving verb raising (Fischer and Janis 1992; Matsuoka 1997; Romano 1991). To account for "verb sandwich" constructions such as (i), Romano (1991, 251) proposes a head-final I position, to which "heavy verbs" raise; when they raise, they, "of course, leave a dummy verb behind, which is optionally phonetically realized."

(i) HAROLD SWEEP FLOOR SWEEP-CL:S(2h)
    (Romano, 1991, ex. (26))

Such "doubling" constructions, which form the basis for a number of claims about the syntactic structure of ASL in the literature (see also Petronio and Lillo-Martin 1997), are at best compatible with analyses that do not involve the assumption that the sentence-final element occurs in a post-VP functional head (whether raised or base-generated, according to different proposals). Each of these proposals is fraught with theoretical and empirical problems.

For example, Matsuoka (1997) explains the "verb doubling" in terms of right-ward raising of the verb to a head-final I, the trace being a copy of the moved element that is optionally pronounced. Although her proposal requires head-final Agr projections, she concludes that, in ASL, "verb agreement is not licensed by AgrS or AgrO" (p. 148). Nonetheless, she argues that AgrsP occurs in a higher position than TP. In order to account for verb doubling, she assumes (p. 133) "the Copy Theory of Movement (Chomsky, 1995[b]). This theory states that a trace is a copy of the moved element, which is deleted at the PF component. The Verb Sandwich construction indicates that the PF-deletion rule is optional in ASL, which allows a copy of the verb to remain in PF representation." She also discusses some ASL constructions that she treats as involving object shift. She notes, "Unlike verbs in ASL, an object NP does not have the option of leaving an overt copy in its original position ... [so] I assume that A-movement does not leave a trace" (p. 139). She claims that her proposal is superior to that of ABKN (1992), since "Aarons et al. had to postulate various language-specific stipulations and non-standard reinterpretations of notions previously proposed in linguistic theory" (p. 144).

We maintain that the verb does not raise overtly to the Agr heads in ASL.

6. The neutral head tilt can be distinguished from a lack of nonmanual marking in part on the basis of its interactions with other manual and nonmanual expressions. For example, this neutral form of head position very often co-occurs with a body lean. For discussion of these issues, see Bahan 1996. (Wilbur and Patschke (1998) also describe other uses of body lean.)

7. The issue of whether it is the features in the functional head or the features associated with verbal inflection that trigger movement has not been resolved. Both positions have been taken in recent work by Chomsky, although most recently (e.g., Chomsky 1995a), it is the features in the functional head that are said to "attract" matching features. The formulation presented here assumes that it is the inflectional features on the verb that require checking.

8. As described in Bahan 1996 (see also MacLaughlin 1997), the wandering eye gaze is often accompanied by a slight but rapid head shake (which contributes to the perception of a wandering gaze).

9. In classifier predicate constructions (mentioned in chapter 3), where a specific classifier handshape is used to represent a nominal argument, which then moves

along a trajectory, the position in space associated with the referent's ϕ-features is constantly changing (as reflected by the moving hand position). The eye gaze follows the manual movement, pointing to the successively changing locations in space associated with the referent's ϕ-features. A similar kind of eye gaze occurs with verbs that allow object incorporation via use of a classifier handshape. In such cases, the eye gaze may express agreement with the incorporated argument, by following the movement of the (classifier within the) verb. (See discussion in Bahan 1996, 203–207.)

10. Interestingly, the same nonmanual markings of agreement that occur within the clause are also used at the discourse level to express discourse relations among referents in a particular construction referred to as "role shift" or "referential shift." In a role shift construction, a signer attributes a thought, idea, or quotation to another by shifting the head and/or shoulders toward the location in space associated with the intended referent. All utterances articulated from this shifted position are interpreted as being expressed by this referent, not the signer. (It is also possible for a signer to use role shift to shift into a position associated with himself or herself in a nonpresent time context.)

An example of a role shift direct speech construction is shown in (i). In such an example, the signer shifts into the location associated with JOHN, and the signer's eyes gaze toward the location associated with MARY. Thus, head position marks the identity of the utterer and eye gaze marks the addressee (of the related discourse).

$$\begin{array}{c} \overline{\text{head position}_i} \\ \overline{\text{eye gaze}_j} \end{array}$$

(i) JOHN$_i$ TELL$_j$ MARY$_j$ IX$_{1p_i}$ BUY HOUSE
    'John told Mary, "I am buying a house."' (I = John)

Although the use of head position and eye gaze is characteristic of role shift, other nonmanual behaviors have also been associated with such constructions (Bahan and Petitto 1980; Loew, Kegl, and Poizner 1997; Padden 1983). For syntactic treatments of such constructions, see Lillo-Martin 1995 and LNMBK 1997.

11. There appears to be a subclass of intransitive verbs for which eye gaze points to a location that is different from the spatial location associated with the subject argument. For example, with the verb DREAM, the eyes gaze upward. Baker (1976a) suggests that eye gaze in such cases is lexically determined. However, as suggested in Bahan 1996, it might be possible to analyze such verbs as involving an implicit argument that is not syntactically realized, along the lines of the approach taken by Hale and Keyser (1991, 1993). The eye gaze found in these cases could be an expression of agreement with an implicit argument.

12. Because of space limitations, we have restricted discussion to the basic agreement facts. For further discussion and analysis of the ASL agreement system (e.g., how agreement is manifested in embedded clauses and interactions with DP agreement), see Bahan 1996.

13. As argued by Rizzi (1986) and others (see, e.g., Jaeggli and Safir 1989), there is an important distinction between *licensing* and *identification*. Here, we discuss only licensing conditions of null arguments.

14. Note that the null pronominal is inherently definite. One consequence of this fact is that a null object can be licensed only by the definite form of nonmanual object agreement marking.

15. For a different proposal, see Poulin 1994, where it is claimed that all empty categories in ASL are variables.

16. Lillo-Martin (1986, 430), closely following Huang's (1984) proposals for Chinese, states that in most configurations, a null argument of a nonagreeing verb is a variable rather than an empty pronoun. One exception, however, is the null subject of an embedded nonagreeing verb, as in (i), which Lillo-Martin says may be either a pronominal or a variable.

(i) JOHN SAY *e* LIKE BILL
    'John said [he] likes Bill.'
    (Lillo-Martin 1986, 432, ex. (32d))

17. Although Lillo-Martin (1986) cites Kegl (1985b, 480–491) (albeit as 1986), she does not address Kegl's counterexamples.

18. ABKN did not themselves note any nonmanual markings of agreement, as these markings were not recognized as such until Bahan 1996. ABKN's example demonstrates that Topic cannot be responsible for licensing the null argument in this case. The authors suggest that Agr is present, even though it does not appear to be expressed overtly, and that Agr licenses the null argument. In fact, the sentence requires a head tilt (either neutral or fully specified) expressing agreement with the null subject. Thus, even in this case, an overt expression of agreement has now been identified, lending further support to ABKN's original claim that Agr is present in such constructions.

19. In other words, such examples are comparable to the following sentence from Italian:

(i) *Italian*
    [*Il tuo libro*]$_i$ ho letto t_i (, non il suo).
    '*Your book* I read (, not his).'
    (from Rizzi 1997)

Therefore, ASL is not unlike Italian in having both null subjects licensed by agreement and traces not requiring such licensing.

20. It has also been proposed that some languages may have (distinct) agreement projections whereas others may not (see, e.g., Bobaljik 1995 and Thráinsson 1996, where it is argued that English and Mainland Scandinavian do not have separate agreement projections, but Icelandic does). Campbell (1991) has suggested that even within a language, there may be differences in the functional projections that occur in various structures. Obviously, the data from ASL suggest only that distinct agreement projections are present in ASL, and thus, that at least some languages have such projections.

21. The variability in distance in time may also be expressed nonmanually. Again, such nonmanual expressions may co-occur only with time adverbials, not with tense markers.

22. The #EX marker clearly surfaces in the tense position, not the aspect position: it is in complementary distribution with modals and other tense markers, and it precedes negation (aspect markers follow negation; see section 5.4). One could suggest that #EX is base-generated in Aspect and then raises to T (potentially crossing elements in Neg); however, this would be speculation, as there is no empirical evidence to support such a hypothesis.

Although the ASL data clearly support an analysis of the clause involving two different positions for housing tense and aspect markers, there nonetheless appears to be a tight relationship between expressions of tense and aspect in ASL that has not yet been fully investigated. In addition to markers like #EX that combine tense and aspectual information, there are tense markers that may be restricted to particular aspectual contexts (e.g., there is evidence to suggest that $PAST_{tns}$ may be restricted to atelic verbs). In addition, the nonmanual markings identified by ABKN (1992, 1995) as co-occurring with tense markers and modals may be expressions of aspectual information, rather than tense, as these authors originally suggested.

23. In ASL, a clause cannot contain both a modal and a lexical tense marker. We are assuming that there is a single head housing tense features (T). In a more elaborate system with multiple tense (and aspect) projections, such as that proposed by Cinque (1999), a different explanation for the co-occurrence restrictions between tense markers and modals would be required.

24. A temporal adverbial, used parenthetically, may superficially appear in what seems to be the same linear position as a tense marker. However, semantic and prosodic evidence supports analyzing such cases as parentheticals, not as variably articulated forms occurring in T. Note that an adverbial parenthetical may be followed by an overt tense marker.

$$\overline{\hspace{3cm}\text{neg}\hspace{3cm}}$$
(i) JOHN, $FUTURE_{adv}$, NOT BUY HOUSE
     'John, in the future, is not buying a house.'

$$\overline{\hspace{4.5cm}\text{neg}\hspace{1.5cm}}$$
(ii) JOHN, $FUTURE_{adv}$, $FUTURE_{tns}$ ^ NOT BUY HOUSE
     'John, in the future, won't buy a house.'

25. In ASL, aspect may be expressed through morphological verbal inflection or through a limited set of lexical aspect markers. Although the morphology of aspect has been studied to some extent (see, e.g., Klima and Bellugi 1979; Newkirk 1979), the distributional properties of aspect markers have received little attention. The most well known aspect marker (among ASL linguists) is the sign FINISH. Analysis of this sign is complicated by the fact that there is also a main verb FINISH, and other similar signs with different functions. These signs, similar in articulation, have yet to be carefully distinguished and analyzed. It is as yet unknown what other signs may function as aspect markers in the language.

26. Infinitival clauses in ASL do allow expressions of agreement (see Bahan 1996), and tensed clauses may have null subjects. Thus, infinitival clauses are most readily detectable by their inability to contain lexical tense markers. However, it is

essentially the same semantic class of verbs (e.g., PREFER, TRY) that sub-categorize for infinitival complements crosslinguistically that disallow tense markers and modals in their complement clauses in ASL.

27. Note that, in examples (34) through (41), the adverbial form of FUTURE is distinguishable from the tense marker in the potential variability of its pathlength, as previously described.

28. There are, however, constructions in which the tense or modal may surface following the verb phrase, as illustrated in (i) and (ii).

$$\overline{\qquad \text{hn} \qquad}$$
(i) JOHN BUY CAR FUTURE$_{tns}$
'John *will* buy a car.'

$$\overline{\qquad \text{hn} \qquad}$$
(ii) JOHN BUY CAR SHOULD
'John *should* buy a car.'

We suggest that such cases involve fronting of the aspect phrase (containing the VP) to an as yet unidentified clause-internal position (see ABKN 1995).

$$\overline{\qquad \text{hn} \qquad}$$
(iii) JOHN [$_{XP}$ [BUY CAR]$_{VP_i}$ [FUTURE$_{tns}$ t_i]]

Although the exact analysis of this construction remains to be worked out, several pieces of evidence suggest that what is involved is leftward movement of the aspect phrase, rather than rightward movement of tense:

• the obligatory occurrence of a head nod over the modal or tense marker (pro-viding evidence of null verbal structure),
• the position of the negative element in negative constructions (necessarily occurring to the right of the modal or tense marker, possibly contracting with it),
• the distribution of nonmanual negative marking (which does not extend over VP, indicating that Neg does not c-command the VP material at Spell-Out).

These facts are illustrated by the following examples. (Examples (viii) and (ix) are unacceptable regardless of the distribution of nonmanual negative marking.)

$$\overline{\qquad\qquad\qquad\qquad \text{neg} \quad}$$
(iv)   JOHN BUY CAR FUTURE$_{tns}$ ^ NOT
'John won't buy a car.'

$$\overline{\qquad\qquad\qquad \text{neg} \quad}$$
(v)   JOHN BUY CAR SHOULD NOT
'John should not buy a car.'

$$\overline{\qquad\qquad\qquad\qquad\qquad\qquad \text{neg} \quad}$$
(vi)   *JOHN BUY CAR FUTURE$_{tns}$ ^ NOT
'John won't buy a car.'

$$\overline{\qquad\qquad\qquad\qquad\qquad \text{neg} \quad}$$
(vii) *JOHN BUY CAR SHOULD NOT
'John should not buy a car.'

$$\text{(viii)} \quad \text{*JOHN } \overline{\text{NOT BUY CAR FUTURE}_{\text{tns}}}^{\text{neg}}$$

$$\text{(ix)} \quad \text{*JOHN } \overline{\text{NOT BUY CAR SHOULD}}^{\text{neg}}$$

29. Still others have proposed that this order may differ from one language to the next (e.g., Ouhalla 1991a). Haverkort (1998) suggests that languages may not have a parametric choice about whether Agr is above T or vice versa (as Ouhalla proposes); rather, he suggests, T must always be hierarchically higher than Agr, as in ASL.

30. Bahan (1996, 186–188) identifies cases where the nonmanual agreement markings begin early, apparently extending outside their c-command domain, as in the following examples:

(i) $\text{JOHN } \overline{\text{DECIDE VISIT}_i \text{ MARY}_i}^{\text{eye gaze}_i}$
   'John decided to visit Mary.'

(ii) $\text{JOHN FUTURE}_{\text{tns}} \overline{\text{FINISH SEE}_i \text{ MARY}_i}^{\text{eye gaze}_i}$
   'John will have seen Mary.'

In (i), eye gaze marking agreement with the embedded object begins (unexpectedly) prior to the articulation of the main verb, whereas in (ii), the eye gaze begins prior to the tense and aspect markers. Bahan argues that such cases should be analyzed as involving "feature climbing," analogous to clitic climbing, where the agreement features have climbed to a higher head position. He observes that this "climbing" is blocked in the same kinds of constructions where clitic climbing is prohibited crosslinguistically, such as when there is an object intervening between the main verb and the infinitival complement clause, or when the complement clause is finite.

31. This tree differs in two significant respects from earlier proposals in ABKN 1992 and 1994. As mentioned in note 1, we have reanalyzed as nonmanual manifestations of agreement head movements previously analyzed by Kegl (and assumed in early work by ABKN) to be role prominence markings. Furthermore, our current understanding of head movement and eye gaze has enabled us to determine the relative order of aspect and subject agreement projections, as shown in (56).

32. Additional evidence that TP dominates AgrP comes from research on language breakdown. For example, Cahana-Amitay (1997) has found that Dutch- and English-speaking aphasics produce either mixed tense and agreement errors or pure tense errors, but not pure agreement errors. On the basis of these findings, she argues not only that tense and agreement are in distinct projections, but also that the tense projection dominates the agreement projection(s).

Chapter 6

1. See, among many others, Abney 1987, Bernstein 1993, Carstens 1991, Cinque 1994, Delsing 1993, Giorgi and Longobardi 1991, Radford 1993, Ritter 1991, Stowell 1991, Szabolcsi 1987, Taraldsen 1990, Valois 1991, Zamparelli 1995.

2. The term "noun phrase" will continue to be used as a general term for a nominal phrase, analogous to the use of "clause" in the verbal domain. "NP" refers to the specific NP projection within the noun phrase.

3. As in chapter 5, discussion of agreement focuses on person (not number) agreement.

4. ASL does not have deverbal nominal argument-taking structures; constructions like *the destruction of the city* in English are expressed through verbal structures in ASL. For descriptions and analyses of other aspects of nominal structure in ASL, see, for example, Baker and Cokely 1980d, Boster 1996, Chinchor 1978, Kegl 1977, Klima and Bellugi 1979, Padden 1988, Wilbur 1979.

5. In fact, the definite determiner may receive either a definite or a demonstrative interpretation.

6. Those researchers who have suggested the existence of determiners in ASL have made several different claims about the associated semantics. Wilbur (1979) suggests that a noun phrase is interpreted as definite if an index is present (either prenominally or postnominally) and indefinite otherwise. As the examples presented in this chapter show, Wilbur's suggestion is not correct. Zimmer and Patschke (1990) observe that the presence of an index sign, which they assume to be a determiner whether it occurs prenominally or postnominally, does not correlate with any particular semantic interpretation, concluding that "[a]s yet, we have identified no process marking the definite/indefinite distinction" (p. 207). They also claim that postnominal indexes are not possible in generic or abstract noun phrases, which is not correct (see also Baker and Cokely 1980d, 223, where it is stated that an abstract noun can be assigned a location in space).

7. The construction in which two index signs are contained within a single noun phrase, as in (3), had not been analyzed prior to BKMN 1995. This "double index" construction, we suggest, is analogous to the following cases, from French and Norwegian:

(i) *French*
     cet homme-là
     'that man there'

(ii) *Norwegian*
     den mannen der
     'that man there'

8. The issue of the apparent optionality of definite determiners requires further investigation. For example, it is possible that in many instances, semantically definite noun phrases with no overt determiner sign may contain a nonmanual expression of definite agreement (see section 6.4.2). However, there are cases (particularly with inanimate objects) where a definite noun phrase appears to have no manual or nonmanual expression of definiteness.

9. The sign SOMETHING/ONE can be found following a DP, where it functions as a pronominal appositive.

(i) ONE STUDENT, SOMETHING/ONE_{pro}, BORROW VIDEOTAPE
'A student, someone, borrowed a videotape.'

10. This nonmanual expression may occur with various types of signs (nouns, verbs, etc.) and may also occur over stretches of discourse. Thus, it is likely that, although this expression conveys information about uncertainty, its distribution is not determined by sentence-level grammar; therefore, it will not be marked in the examples here.

11. This is illustrated in the example in note 9. Differences between the numeral ONE and the indefinite determiner form that resembles the numeral ONE are discussed in MacLaughlin 1997.

12. Several authors have suggested that definite and indefinite determiners occur in different syntactic positions (see Campbell 1994; Stowell 1991; Zamparelli 1995). Although it might be possible to analyze the ASL determiner system along similar lines, we have not found evidence to support this kind of syntactic difference between definite and indefinite determiners in ASL.

13. Such variably articulated indexes do not normally immediately precede definite determiners or pronouns. This restriction might only be apparent. If two such signs were to co-occur, it is possible that they would be articulated as a single index (with a variable articulation). Thus, the following constructions may actually consist of an adverbial immediately adjacent to a determiner or pronoun:

```
                      t1-mv
             far
(i)  IXadv, "far" WOMAN HAVE BOOK
     'That woman way over there has a book.'

           t1-mv
           far
(ii) IXadv, "far" HAVE BOOK
     'He/She over there has a book.'
```

14. There is an alternative possessive construction that exhibits the order [Possessive-Marker PossessorDP NP]_{DP}, as in [POSS JOHN FRIEND]. The proper analysis of this construction remains something of a mystery; see MacLaughlin 1997, 274–275, n. 25, for discussion.

15. In phrase-final position, the possessive marker is articulated with a double movement; in such cases, it is generally glossed as POSS+.

```
           t1-mv
(i)  IXdet, BOOK [POSS+j]DP
     'That book is his/hers.'
```

This articulation is a reflection of the general phenomenon of constituent-final lengthening in ASL (for discussion of lengthening in ASL, see, e.g., Coulter 1993 and Grosjean 1979; for phrase-final lengthening in spoken languages, see, e.g., Cooper and Paccia-Cooper 1980 and Selkirk 1984).

16. It is not clear whether these are true possessive constructions. Such constructions seem to be possible only with relational nouns.

17. One case where such a sequence of signs may be used is as an echo question. For example, if one person signed sentence (i), and the addressee missed the first sign, sentence (ii) would be an acceptable way to elicit clarification.

(i) JOHN MOTHER ARRIVE
   'John's mother arrived.'

$$\overline{\hspace{6cm}\text{wh}}$$
(ii) WHO MOTHER ARRIVE
   '*Whose* mother arrived?'

In a sentence like (ii), WHO receives a stressed articulation (manifested, in particular, by intense nonmanual marking).

18. The discussion in the text focuses on manual expression of agreement with D elements. The spatial location in which a noun or adjective is produced may or may not carry referential information. Some nouns and adjectives may *optionally* express agreement manually by being produced at, or oriented toward, the spatial location associated with the agreement features. This optionality distinguishes the nominal system from the verbal system, where verbs that can agree must agree (e.g., object agreement marking on an agreeing verb is not optional). See MacLaughlin 1997 and references therein for further discussion of noun and adjective agreement.

19. See MacLaughlin 1997 for discussion of interactions between this head tilt, marking agreement in possessive and nonpossessive DPs, and other head movements that may occur over a DP, such as the constituent-final head nod and the adverbial head movement associated with postnominal adverbial indexes.

20. Eye gaze and head tilt do not spread independently of one another in a nonpossessive DP. As noted in Baker-Shenk 1983, 104, when two or more nonmanual markings express the same linguistic information, they have the same duration.

21. The sentence in (24a) is possible in the "whisper" register, which is characterized by a reduction in the signing space. In this register, eye gaze and head movement can actually substitute for some manual indexical signs, such as determiners, pronominals, and adverbials.

22. The relation between head tilt and definiteness is specific to the nominal domain. In the clause, there is no analogous restriction on head tilt; as long as there is a location in space to tilt toward, subject agreement in the clause may be expressed by head tilt, whether the subject is definite or indefinite. This is not surprising, given that the clause also differs from DP in containing no functional projection that houses definiteness features. The restriction shown by head tilt in the DP domain, then, may be related to the fact that definiteness features play an important role within DP, but not in the clause.

23. The ASL data support the claim that definiteness and agreement features are fused within a single functional head by Spell-Out. Parallelism with clausal structure, where agreement features occur in distinct functional projections, might suggest that the agreement features in DP begin in a distinct Agr head and then raise to D. However, we have found no evidence to determine whether or not this is the case.

24. In possessive DPs, head tilt, when present, necessarily involves tilting toward the spatial location associated with the possessor. We have not found any evidence to suggest that there is a neutral form of head tilt within DP.

25. There may be some anticipatory head movement during the articulation of the possessor DP. As noted in earlier chapters, head movements, in particular, typically display some anticipatory movement prior to the significant portion of their articulation.

26. There is another kind of eye gaze that may be found in a possessive DP: the eyes may gaze to the location associated with the possessor during the articulation of POSS, as shown in (i).

$$\overline{\textbf{head tilt}_i}$$

$$\overline{\mathit{eg}_i\textbf{eg}_j}$$

(i) [JOHN$_i$ POSS$_i$ FRIEND$_j$]$_{DP}$ HAVE CANDY
    'John's friend has candy.'

This is the same kind of eye gaze that is found with manual indexical signs generally, such as determiners, pronouns, adverbials, and reflexives, as mentioned in chapter 4. We believe that in addition to being used as a direct expression of agreement features, eye gaze may be used to reinforce manual pointing gestures to locations in space. Although in most cases these functions commingle, in examples like (i) they are separable. Thus, we would suggest that the nonmanual markings in boldface correspond to the direct expressions of syntactic agreement features in this possessive construction, whereas the italicized marking is, in fact, a co-expression of the manual pointing sign POSS.

Note that the eye gaze associated with POSS cannot spread, as shown in (ii), supporting the notion that this eye gaze is not like other nonmanual expressions of syntactic features.

$$\overline{\text{head tilt}_i}$$

$$\overline{\text{eye gaze}_i}$$

(ii) *[JOHN$_i$ POSS$_i$ FRIEND$_j$]$_{DP}$ HAVE CANDY

27. Interestingly, the agreement features of a possessor DP inside a possessive construction cannot be expressed nonmanually. When asked to articulate a head tilt associated with the possessor DP, signers inevitably produce a structure where the possessor DP is external to the possessive construction (e.g., in a topic position).

28. Prenominal and postnominal adjectives differ in other respects as well. For example, prenominal adjectives exhibit strict ordering constraints; postnominal adjectives do not.

29. There are many different analyses of DP-internal adjectives (see e.g., Abney 1987; Bernstein 1993; Cinque 1994; Holmberg 1993; Kayne 1994; Longobardi 1994; Valois 1991). The precise analysis of adjectives is not crucial to the current discussion. The result presented below that postnominal adjectives fall within the c-command domain of the DP's agreement features could be readily accommodated into most, if not all, of these proposals.

30. Nonmanual agreement markings spread over DP-internal postnominal adjectives, not DP-external ones (e.g., appositives).

$$\overline{}\text{t1-mv}$$

(i) [IX$_{det_i}$ CAR]$_{DP}$, BLUE, SUE BUY
   'That car, the blue one, Sue is buying.'

The appositive DP containing the adjective BLUE may also have an expression of nonmanual agreement, however, as in (ii). In such cases, the nonmanual agreement marking generally perseverates between the two sources, such that the eye gaze does not return to neutral position between the two DPs.

$$\overline{}\text{t1-mv}$$

(ii) [IX$_{det_i}$ CAR]$_{DP}$, BLUE, SUE BUY
    'That car, the blue one, Sue is buying.'

Chapter 7

1. Generally speaking, our rightward-movement proposal is in keeping with descriptive accounts of ASL (e.g., Baker and Cokely 1980d) and with Perlmutter's (1991) summary of the syntactic properties of ASL. However, Fischer, Lillo-Martin, and Petronio, and others building upon their work, have assumed leftward *wh*-movement. We return to the specific claims of Petronio and Lillo-Martin (1997) in section 7.4.1.

2. Variants of the sentence glossed in (4), which are grammatical, will be discussed later.

3. Although there have been claims in the literature that sentences such as (4) are grammatical, even proponents of a leftward-movement analysis such as Petronio and Lillo-Martin (1997, 50) have acknowledged that these sentences are less than fully acceptable. Conversely, sentences such as (2) are sometimes recognized as grammatical by proponents of leftward movement and sometimes claimed to be less than fully grammatical. These issues will be discussed in section 7.3.

4. Within the Minimalist Program, one would not expect to find optional overt movement. Cheng (1991) notes several languages that appear to exhibit optional *wh*-movement, including Egyptian Arabic and Bahasa Indonesia. She claims that these languages are really in-situ languages (e.g., like Chinese); instances of apparent overt fronting of a *wh*-phrase do not involve *wh*-movement, but instead are analyzed as reduced clefts or topicalization structures. ASL differs in significant respects from the types of languages that Cheng analyzes as in-situ languages. The process that we analyze as *wh*-movement cannot be accounted for in terms of topicalization, since topics occur sentence-initially but moved *wh*-phrases occur sentence-finally. (As we will discuss, ASL does have base-generated *wh*-topics, occurring sentence-initially.) There is also no evidence in ASL for the type of cleft construction proposed by Cheng.

One question that naturally arises is whether cases where the *wh*-phrase has moved overtly might differ semantically from those where this has not occurred.

Indeed, there do seem to be semantic differences, which warrant further investigation. Cases that involve overt movement seem to convey a presupposition of the TP proposition and (additional) focus on the *wh*-phrase. In this respect, the distinction between overt and covert movement appears to be analogous to the use of stress on the *wh*-phrase in languages like French, Norwegian, and English. For example, compare the following two English sentences:

(i) Who *arrived*?

(ii) *Who* arrived?

In the latter case, there is a presupposition that somebody arrived. Thus, the readings of (i) and (ii) correlate with those of the ASL sentences shown in (iii) and (iv).

$$\overline{\hspace{2.5cm}\text{wh}\hspace{1.5cm}}$$
(iii) WHO ARRIVE

$$\overline{\hspace{2.5cm}\text{wh}\hspace{1.5cm}}$$
(iv) ARRIVE WHO

(See Lambrecht 1994 for discussion of the relation between intonational stress and semantic focus; see also Rochemont 1986 for discussion of *wh*-constructions specifically in this regard.) The proper syntactic analysis of such distinctions is a question for further research.

5. Petronio (1991) also proposes that nonmanual *wh*-marking is associated with the +wh feature. She later retracts this suggestion (Petronio 1993, 54) because *wh*-marking does not occur in what she analyzes to be +wh indirect questions (clauses that we believe are not true +wh clauses). To extend their account to such constructions, Petronio and Lillo-Martin (1997) suggest that nonmanual *wh*-marking is associated with the combination of features +WH and +F(ocus), and further, that the +F feature cannot occur in +wh indirect questions.

6. Such signs may, however, have other readings that do not involve a +wh feature. In those cases, we assume a different lexical feature specification, not including the +wh feature. For example, there are situations in which signs that normally function as *wh*-signs may be used without the +wh-feature (and associated *wh*-marking), such as when the sign WHO serves to name a musical group or a baseball player, as in the 1945 Abbott and Costello routine, "Who's on First."

7. Notice that, even though the +wh feature resides in C, the manual *wh*-phrase in [Spec, CP] satisfies the locality requirement for lexical material to bear the +wh feature. This may be attributable to the fact that the +wh feature in C is shared by the Spec through specifier-head agreement (Rizzi 1991).

8. The position of C relative to TP remains to be justified, as will be discussed later in this chapter. Suffice it to say for the moment that constructions equivalent to those illustrated here but with C, and therefore the +wh feature, to the left of TP would also not be grammatical.

9. The intensity of *wh*-marking with in-situ *wh*-phrases will be addressed in section 7.2.2.3.

10. Multiple *wh*-questions in English such as *Who likes what?* do not have direct counterparts in ASL. This kind of restriction against multiple *wh*-questions has been noted in other languages as well (e.g., Adams 1984, Calabrese 1984, and Rizzi 1982b for Italian; McCloskey 1979 for Irish). An apparent exception to this restriction in ASL involves *wh*-phrases that are strongly D-linked (in Pesetsky's (1987) sense); these can occur in ASL questions of the kind 'Which of these men read which of those books?', although even in these cases, multiple *wh*-questions are somewhat marginal. Samek-Lodovici (1993) makes a similar observation for Italian.

11. Although a slight head shake occurs normally as part of the cluster of properties associated with nonmanual *wh*-marking, a more pronounced head shake occurs over the tag in this construction. The notation is not intended to indicate that there is not a head shake associated with the *wh*-marking that extends over the whole sentence.

12. Having two identical signs adjacent to each other is dispreferred. For example, (iii), with a right-dislocated pronominal intervening between the *wh*-object and the tag, is preferred to (i). Alternatively, as shown in (ii), a generic *wh*-sign (which will be discussed later) may occur in the tag following WHO.

$$\frac{\overline{\quad\quad\quad\quad\quad\quad\quad\quad\quad} \; \overline{\text{hs}}}{\text{wh}}$$

(i) *JOHN SEE WHO, WHO

$$\frac{\overline{\quad\quad\quad\quad\quad\quad\quad\quad\quad} \; \overline{\text{hs}}}{\text{wh}}$$

(ii) JOHN SEE WHO, "WHAT"
'Who did John see, who?'

$$\frac{\overline{\quad\quad\quad\quad\quad\quad\quad\quad\quad} \; \overline{\text{hs}}}{\text{wh}}$$

(iii) JOHN$_i$ SEE WHO, IX$_i$, WHO
'Who did John$_i$ see, him$_i$, who?'

13. Note that the sign order in (15) may also occur as part of another construction, but with different prosody and nonmanual marking, as shown in (i). Such constructions, involving an initial base-generated topic plus a *wh*-question, are discussed in the next subsection.

$$\frac{\overline{\text{top/wh} \quad\quad\quad\quad\quad\quad} \; \overline{\text{wh}}}{}$$

(i) WHO, LIKE JOHN WHO
'Who, who likes John?'

14. The sign glossed here as "WHAT" is a two-handed sign produced with open palms, facing upward, and is distinguished from another lexical item, usually glossed as WHAT (without quotation marks), which is articulated with the index finger of the dominant hand sweeping down the open nondominant hand. These two signs have different distributions, as briefly discussed in NKBAM 1997. The use of "WHAT" will be discussed further shortly.

15. Although it requires some effort to create a plausible context, a sentence like (i) is possible.

Context: You are discussing a group of finicky eaters who will be coming to a party. Someone has just told you that Bob won't eat meat and Sally won't eat vegetables. So, you ask about the third guest:

$$\text{t1-mv}$$

(i) "WHAT", MARY, WON'T EAT "WHAT"
   'What is it that *Mary* won't eat?'

If the first two signs were reversed, the topic marking on MARY would be that associated with a base-generated topic (and the interpretation of the sentence would differ accordingly).

16. Lillo-Martin (1990, 219–220) claims that a *wh*-phrase cannot precede a topic and thus appears to be disputing the grammaticality of examples like (17).

17. Although some of our informants strongly prefer (i) to (ii), this preference is not as strong as the contrast between (iii) and (iv). Sentences such as (ii) have been reported as acceptable in the literature.

(i)   WHO, JOHN LOVE "WHAT"
       'Who, who does John love?'

(ii)   (?)WHO, JOHN LOVE WHO
       'Who, who does John love?'

(iii)   JOHN$_i$, MARY LOVE IX$_i$
       'As for John, Mary loves him.'

(iv) * JOHN, MARY LOVE JOHN
       'As for John, Mary loves John.'

18. It has been suggested (e.g., Epstein 1992) that *wh*-phrases may not be topicalized. Note, however, that we are analyzing *wh*-topics as base-generated topics. *Wh*-phrases have been attested in topic position in other languages, such as Chinese; indeed, Xu and Langendoen (1985, 16, fn. 20) state explicitly that "a WH-phrase can appear in TOP position in Chinese." *Wh*-topics in Chinese, Japanese, and German are also discussed in Wu 1996, Miyagawa 1987, and Grohmann 1997, 1998, respectively (as well as in papers cited in those works).

19. The notation here is meant to highlight perseveration in the manual and nonmanual channels. In the glossing of the nonmanual markings, the labels indicate the underlying source of the marking and the dashed line indicates perseveration of the marking between those sources. The nonmanual *wh*-marking is maintained throughout. In the manual channel, it is the nondominant hand that perseverates in this example; there may or may not be a distinct onset for the

second occurrence of the "WHAT" sign. In subsequent sections, a single *wh*-marking will be indicated.

20. Similar effects are found with WHICH and *wh*-MANY, as reported in NKB 1994.

21. There is another way in which a sentence like (25) may become acceptable. If the final manual *wh*-sign is not present, it may be replaced by an intense nonmanual realization of *wh*-marking that occurs in the same position where the manual *wh*-sign would otherwise have appeared, as in (i); the final manual sign must be held in such cases.

```
       wh- - - - - - - - - - - - - [intense wh-marking]
(i)  "WHAT", JOHN LIKE- - - - - - - - - - - -
     'What is it that John likes?'
```

It appears that the nonmanual expression in (i) is substituting for the manual expression of the *wh*-sign (comparable with the example given in chapter 3 of the sign NOT-YET, which can be signed with only the characteristic nonmanual markings that normally accompany the manual sign). It is possible that when constructions like (25) have been reported to be grammatical, the sentence produced was in fact equivalent to (i), but again this can be no more than speculation in the absence of video exemplars of constructions reported to be grammatical.

22. NKBAM (1997) further show that such perseveration can even mask topic marking in a sentence like (i), which may alternatively be realized with *wh*-marking extending across the entire utterance, as in (ii).

```
       wh           t2-bg                              wh
(i)  WHO, VEGETABLE, PREFER POTATO "WHAT"
     'Who, as for vegetables, who prefers potatoes?'

                                                       wh
(ii) WHO, VEGETABLE, PREFER POTATO "WHAT"
     'Who, as for vegetables, who prefers potatoes?'
```

23. Perseveration of intensity is manifested somewhat differently for the brow furrow and head shake components of the nonmanual expression of *wh*-marking. This difference is more general and involves the articulatory characteristics of those two expressions. With respect to brow furrow, the maximally lowered position is maintained throughout the signing. However, since the head shake intrinsically involves movement (rather than maintenance of a position), it continues between the two occurrences of the +wh feature, but two separate peaks of intensity are nonetheless identifiable at the locations of the relevant features. This is true as well for the intensity of head nods when there is more than one source for the head nod; this effect was illustrated in figure 4.4.

24. The proper account of indirect questions and semiquestions (in the sense of Suñer (1993), who argues for significant linguistic distinctions between the two) is more puzzling. In a semiquestion like *John wonders what Mary likes*, the embedded clause is a +wh complement that corresponds semantically to a question. The ASL equivalent of this construction also involves a +wh complement clause

that exhibits the same characteristics as direct questions (in terms of word order and nonmanual marking). In contrast, the ASL version of sentences like *John knows what Mary likes* differs significantly from ASL semiquestions. Embedded complement clauses of verbs like KNOW in ASL do not exhibit nonmanual *wh*-marking, nor do they exhibit the word order typical of *wh*-questions. Thus, the embedded clause in such constructions in ASL does not appear to be a normal +wh clause. This bears further investigation, but see NMLBK 1998b for discussion.

25. Whereas *wh*-marking involves lowered eyebrows, yes-no marking involves raised eyebrows, as well as a forward head tilt; the last sign is normally held (Baker and Cokely 1980d; Baker-Shenk 1983).

26. QMwg might be either in C or in [Spec, CP]. We have not found evidence to determine more precisely where it occurs. The resolution of this issue is peripheral to the current discussion, however.

27. This is consistent with the facts of nonmanual question marking generally. It is otherwise hard to determine the position of C, since ASL does not seem to have lexical complementizers, although several candidates have been proposed in the literature (including the sign glossed as "THATc" by Liddell (1980), proposed to be a complementizer that occurs to the right of relative clauses by Petronio (1993); Fischer (1990) has suggested that THAT, INDEX, and SELF may occur as complementizers, all in postclausal position).

There is, incidentally, general agreement in the recent ASL literature that C is to the right of TP (even by those who assume that [Spec, CP] is to the left of TP). It is worth noting, however, that this conclusion is based on analyses that are independently highly problematic (e.g., Matsuoka 1997; Petronio 1993; Petronio and Lillo-Martin 1997; Romano 1991).

28. The nonmanual marking associated with rhetorical *wh*-questions (labeled "rh/wh") differs from the marking for information-seeking *wh*-questions ("wh") in the position of the eyebrows (raised rather than lowered). Nonetheless, the same head shake that frequently co-occurs with information-seeking *wh*-questions is found with rhetorical *wh*-questions, as well. Often in the ASL literature, the markings that we have labeled "rh/wh" and "rh/y-n" are not differentiated, but are uniformly marked as "rhq." Although the differences between the two are subtle, the markings are distinguishable (see Baker-Shenk 1983, 1986; HNMKB 1997).

29. Some researchers report different data for rhetorical question constructions. For example, Petronio (1991) and Wilbur (1994a) suggest that the preferred position for a *wh*-phrase in a rhetorical question is the right periphery of the question clause. According to Wilbur (1994a, 231), "[O]ur subjects have strong, and in some cases, absolute, preference for the wh-sign as the last sign in the rhetorical question ..." In Wilbur 1996, 216, she again says, "[T]he wh-sign is uniformly preferred on the right of the Wh-clause"; subsequently, though, she modifies this: "A situation in which the preference for the Wh-sign on the right of the Wh-clause may be overridden occurs when the Wh-word appears in situ in the Wh-clause ..." (p. 216). We (closest to the position taken in Petronio 1991) find that the basic word order possibilities in information-seeking and rhetorical questions are essentially the same (see HNMKB 1997).

30. Rhetorical yes-no questions with the QMwg sign are rare. Thus, in yes-no rhetorical questions, nonmanual rh/y-n marking normally spreads over the entire question.

31. Fischer (1990), for example, analyzes rhetorical questions as free relatives, occurring within the same matrix clause as the answer that follows. Wilbur (1994a,b) analyzes the *wh*-question and its answer as constituting a "pseudocleft." She claims that a *wh*-rhetorical question-answer sequence differs significantly in structure from a yes-no rhetorical question-answer sequence. Only in the latter case does she consider that the question and answer are *not* contained in a single matrix clause.

32. HNMKB (1997) demonstrate that rhetorical questions have essentially the same syntactic characteristics and distribution of nonmanual marking as information-seeking questions. This is true for both *wh*-questions and yes-no questions. Moreover, the answers to rhetorical questions and information-seeking questions have the same syntactic properties. In particular, they can consist of anything from a single word to an entire stretch of discourse. Potentially, then, the answer alone can contain more material than can be accommodated within a single clause. HNMKB (1997) also consider the consequences of several single-clause proposals for rhetorical *wh*-questions and show that such analyses cannot account for the data. Even those who have proposed single-clause analyses for *wh*-rhetorical questions have proposed that yes-no rhetorical question-answer sequences do consist syntactically of a question followed by an answer. HNMKB (1997) argue for unifying *wh*- and yes-no rhetorical question constructions.

33. Petronio (1991) discusses in greatest detail grammaticality judgments on rhetorical questions, but she clearly states that *wh*-questions are comparable with respect to word order and scope of nonmanual marking: "The patterns found with the non-manual whq marker and the wh-terms in wh-questions are the same patterns found with the rhq marker and the wh-terms in the question segment of the rhq sentences" (p. 214). Petronio (1991, 212) reports that "signers who came from Deaf families where their parents used ASL" usually reported sentences with an initial *wh*-object to be ungrammatical, whereas "signers who came from hearing families (i.e. their parents did not use ASL)" sometimes concurred with the native signers' judgments and sometimes did not.

34. Petronio and Lillo-Martin (1997) use their observation that such sentences are considered more acceptable when presented in context than when presented in isolation to support their analysis of these constructions as involving a null *wh*-element (rather than a *wh*-trace) in subject position plus a "double" *wh*-word base-generated in a $+F$ C. Petronio and Lillo-Martin's use of claims that grammaticality judgments are sensitive to the availability of contextual information as evidence to support their analysis will be addressed shortly.

35. The same is true for any other grammatical construction as well, of course.

36. Lillo-Martin (1990, 216–218) explains the impossibility of extraction in terms of a parameterization of the notion of barrierhood. In Lillo-Martin 1990 and 1992, she explores the consequences of the supposed impossibility of extraction from embedded clauses in ASL for learnability and acquisition.

37. Example (55) is taken from Petronio and Lillo-Martin 1997, although the authors themselves do not mark the sentence with an asterisk or any other notation indicating that it is less than fully grammatical. However, sentences comparable to this one are marked with an asterisk in, for example, Lillo-Martin 1990, ex. (16) and Lillo-Martin 1992, ex. (12a).

$$\overline{\text{whq}}$$
(i) *WHO BILL FEEL JOHN 'LIKE'

38. Petronio and Lillo-Martin's (1997, 25) attribution of work to "ABKN" requires explanation: "Recent works (Aarons, Bahan, Kegl, & Neidle 1992; Aarons 1994; Neidle, Kegl, & Bahan 1994; and Neidle, Kegl, Bahan, Aarons, & McLaughlin [sic] 1994) challenge this generalization. (Henceforth, when discussing claims that are common to all these works, we will use the acronym ABKN.)" There is a further problem with attribution. As discussed in NMLBK 1998b, when Petronio and Lillo-Martin refer to Neidle, Kegl, Bahan, Aarons, and MacLaughlin 1994, cited as a "talk," they are (albeit selectively) referring to the in-press manuscript for NKBAM 1997 (based only in part on the 1994 talk presented by Neidle, Kegl, Bahan, and Aarons).

39. Lillo-Martin and Fischer (1992) formulate a descriptive statement about the cases where spread is optional versus obligatory, but they do not propose an explanation, leaving details of the mechanism and domain of the spread to be worked out.

40. Note that varying judgments of this kind differ from Petronio's (1991) reported "mixed judgments," which characterized a mixed pool of native and nonnative judgments (see section 7.3.2).

41. The importance of such scrutiny will be particularly apparent in section 7.4.1.1, where we discuss Petronio and Lillo-Martin's representation of data from commercially available videotapes.

42. Petronio and Lillo-Martin (1997, 18) state, "It is quite possible that no language uses rightward WH-movement (although WH-elements may occur on the right edge of a sentence through a different process). This phenomenon remains unexplained, yet its statistical strength is such as to lead an investigator to expect that WH-movement will be leftward in the next language studied."

43. Petronio and Lillo-Martin do not address the licensing of null "twins" (which may be modals, verbs, wh-phrases, etc.).

44. Petronio and Lillo-Martin (1997, 34) draw a distinction between wh and non-wh "twins" (erroneously referred to as "doubles" in the following quotation): "One difference between the WH-doubles and the non-WH-doubles is that while the latter have only a [+F] feature, the former have both [+F, +WH]. We have observed independently that [+WH] elements can move to spec-CP either at the surface level or at LF. Hence, while non-WH-double operators do not move until LF, WH-doubles can move at the surface." Note, however, that this movement, whether at or prior to LF, involves not only wh-phrases, but also lexical heads, such as modals. Recognizing head movement of a modal to [Spec, CP] as a po-

tential problem, Petronio and Lillo-Martin (1997, 32, fn. 15) suggest only that "an alternative analysis employing a null OP [operator] phrase is possible."

45. As illustrated, this null "twin" of a lexical "double" is claimed to raise to a leftward (phrasal) operator position, leaving behind a trace (of some kind), in any event.

46. This differs from Lillo-Martin 1990, 214, where right-peripheral *wh*-signs were not considered to be in C: "I believe that the wh-words found at the right are best analyzed as a copy of the left wh-word, rather than a right COMP, though I will not provide any arguments for this hypothesis here."

47. Among the questions that come to mind are these:

• What is the theoretical status of "twins" and "doubles" as proposed by Petronio and Lillo-Martin?
• What is the nature of the movement process by which a lexical "twin" ("doubled" by the element in C) raises to [Spec, CP] (a phrasal position)?
• How are restrictions concerning what may be "doubled" explained?
• To what extent is this "focus via doubling" mechanism, involving "twins," "doubles," and the Final Double Filter (see (76)), peculiar to ASL? Is there any crosslinguistic support for such an analysis?

48. Petronio and Lillo-Martin (1997) suggest that those WHICH-phrases involve heavy NP shift rather than *wh*-movement. NMLBK (1998b) present arguments against this suggestion.

49. In fact, Petronio and Lillo-Martin attempt to use similar examples to demonstrate the opposite. They claim that the ungrammaticality of sentences like (i) shows that phrasal material cannot occur in sentence-final position. However, the source of the ungrammaticality in their examples is the form of the possessive phrase they use. See discussion in chapter 6 and MacLaughlin 1997.

$$\overline{}^{\text{whq}}$$
(i) *DIE WHO MOTHER
'Whose mother died?'
(Petronio and Lillo-Martin 1997, ex. (65))

50. The occurrence of the head nod over anything less than the entire sentence, as in (64), would be contested by Petronio and Lillo-Martin, who claim that head nods and negative head shakes necessarily occur over clausal domains (and who analyze the final sign in examples like (64) as occurring in C). Petronio and Lillo-Martin cannot account for the distribution of the head nod in (64) and the negative head shake in (65). Their differing claims about the scope of negative marking have been addressed in chapter 3.

51. Petronio and Lillo-Martin attempt to rule out the alternative analysis that such constructions involve tags by stipulating that they are only considering sentences without a prosodic break (although, in fact, tags need not display a discernible prosodic break).

52. It is interesting that in Petronio and Lillo-Martin 1997, the examples cited from commercially available videotapes include no *wh*-questions, although the

primary source of their examples, Baker and Cokely 1980e, includes many such questions. In fact, the corresponding textbook (Baker and Cokely 1980a, 15) provides a generalization about their distribution; see the quotation at the beginning of this section. In any event, Petronio and Lillo-Martin's representation of the examples they do cite is problematic, as we will discuss (see also NMLBK 1998b).

53. The examples from Baker and Cokely 1980e under discussion here are available in digitized format at our Web site, along with the other video examples discussed in this book. (We thank Dennis Cokely for allowing us to make the digitized video available.)

54. Petronio and Lillo-Martin suggest that such an element is independently motivated by the existence of "covert" *wh*-questions in ASL. As first observed by Baker-Shenk (1983), *wh*-questions do not always require an overt *wh*-sign, as illustrated in (i).

    <u>   wh</u>
(i) NAME
   'Name?'

We agree that such sentence fragments exist. Their usage is comparable to that of sentence fragments in other languages and does not require postulation of new null *wh*-elements.

55. Moreover, when this null *wh*-element moves to [Spec, CP], as they claim it must, it presumably leaves a *wh*-trace behind, in any event.

56. Although sentences that contain solely a *wh*-phrase analyzed to be in a sentence-initial [Spec, CP] position and a *wh*-trace internal to TP are not represented by Petronio and Lillo-Martin (1997, 51) as unequivocally acceptable to native signers (those who reject them "accept an initial WH-object if there is also a final double"), apparently contextual information does not result in improved acceptability ratings. Instead, Petronio and Lillo-Martin speculate that "for stylistic reasons some consultants require a [+F +WH] C^0 to be associated with overt lexical material."

57. Prosody in such sentences suggests exactly the opposite, in fact. See figure 2.1 for a detailed transcription of a comparable sentence.

                <u>   wh</u>
(i) JOHN BUY YESTERDAY "WHAT"
   'What did John buy yesterday?'

Petronio and Lillo-Martin also offer no explanation for changing the analysis of constructions they had previously presented as single sentences involving optional spread of nonmanual marking, such as (50) from Petronio 1991 or examples presented in Lillo-Martin and Fischer 1992.

58. To account for cases where spread occurs over the entire CP, Petronio (1993) suggests that whq marking is associated with C and obligatorily spreads over the entire CP. This is the same explanation she offers for the distribution of negative marking and the head nod ("hn") that is marked on many of her examples.

Therefore, she does not predict, and cannot explain, the differences in distribution we find for these markings (and goes so far as to deny that there are differences, claiming that they all occur obligatorily over the entire CP). Furthermore, she cannot account for the diminishing versus increasing intensity of these different markings that we have explained in terms of the differing locations of the features with which the markings are associated (on our analysis).

59. Under this analysis, spread of *wh*-marking would no longer be optional; in each structural *wh*-question configuration (including in-situ questions), *wh*-marking would spread obligatorily over its c-command domain. However, there are still other cases in which a nonmanual marking spreads optionally (e.g., negative marking, nonmanual agreement markings within DP), so the optional spread of nonmanual markings could not be completely eliminated.

References

Aarons, Debra. 1994. Aspects of the syntax of American Sign Language. Doctoral dissertation, Boston University.

Aarons, Debra, Benjamin Bahan, Judy Kegl, and Carol Neidle [ABKN]. 1992. Clausal structure and a tier for grammatical marking in American Sign Language. *Nordic Journal of Linguistics* 15, 103–142.

Aarons, Debra, Benjamin Bahan, Judy Kegl, and Carol Neidle [ABKN]. 1994. Subjects and agreement in American Sign Language. In *Perspectives on sign language structure: Papers from the Fifth International Symposium on Sign Language Research*, eds. Inger Ahlgren, Brita Bergman, and Mary Brennan, 13–28. Durham: International Sign Language Linguistics Association.

Aarons, Debra, Benjamin Bahan, Judy Kegl, and Carol Neidle [ABKN]. 1995. Lexical tense markers in American Sign Language. In *Language, gesture, and space*, eds. Karen Emmorey and Judy S. Reilly, 225–253. Hillsdale, NJ: Lawrence Erlbaum.

Abney, Steven P. 1987. The English noun phrase in its sentential aspect. Doctoral dissertation, MIT.

Abraham, Werner, Samuel David Epstein, Höskuldur Thráinsson, and C. Jan-Wouter Zwart, eds. 1996. *Minimal ideas: Syntactic studies in the minimalist framework*. Philadelphia: John Benjamins.

Adams, Marianne. 1984. Multiple interrogation in Italian. *The Linguistic Review* 4, 1–27.

Aikhenvald, Alexandra Y., and Robert M. Dixon. 1998. Dependencies between grammatical systems. *Language* 74, 56–80.

Allan, Keith. 1977. Classifiers. *Language* 53, 285–311.

Ann, Jean. 1993. A linguistic investigation of the relationship between physiology and handshape. Doctoral dissertation, University of Arizona.

Arnaudova, Olga. 1996. The Bulgarian noun (adjective) movement to D. In *University of Trondheim working papers in linguistics 28*, eds. Mila D. Vulchanova and Lars Hellan, 1–28. Trondheim: University of Trondheim, Department of Linguistics.

Bahan, Benjamin. 1996. Non-manual realization of agreement in American Sign Language. Doctoral dissertation, Boston University.

Bahan, Benjamin, Judy Kegl, Robert G. Lee, Dawn MacLaughlin, and Carol Neidle [BKLMN]. In press. The licensing of null arguments in American Sign Language. *Linguistic Inquiry.*

Bahan, Benjamin, Judy Kegl, Dawn MacLaughlin, and Carol Neidle [BKMN]. 1995. Convergent evidence for the structure of determiner phrases in American Sign Language. In *FLSM VI: Proceedings of the Sixth Annual Meeting of the Formal Linguistics Society of Mid-America*, eds. Leslie Gabriele, Debra Hardison, and Robert Westmoreland, 1–12. Bloomington: Indiana University Linguistics Club.

Bahan, Benjamin, and Laura Petitto. 1980. Aspects of rules for character establishment and reference in ASL storytelling. Unpublished manuscript, The Salk Institute for Biological Studies.

Baker, Charlotte. 1976a. Eye-openers in ASL. Paper presented at the California Linguistic Association Conference, San Diego State University.

Baker, Charlotte. 1976b. What's not on the other hand in American Sign Language. In *Papers from the Twelfth Regional Meeting, Chicago Linguistic Society*, eds. Salikoko S. Mufwene, Carol A. Walker, and Sanford B. Steever, 24–32. Chicago: University of Chicago, Chicago Linguistic Society.

Baker, Charlotte. 1977. Regulators and turn-taking in American Sign Language discourse. In *On the other hand: New perspectives on American Sign Language*, ed. Lynn Friedman, 215–236. New York: Academic Press.

Baker, Charlotte. 1980. Sentences in ASL. In *Sign language and the deaf community: Essays in honor of William C. Stokoe*, eds. Charlotte Baker and Robbin Battison, 75–86. Silver Spring, MD: National Association of the Deaf.

Baker, Charlotte, and Dennis Cokely. 1980a. *American Sign Language: A student text. Units 1–9.* Silver Spring, MD: T.J. Publishers.

Baker, Charlotte, and Dennis Cokely. 1980b. *American Sign Language: A student text. Units 10–18.* Silver Spring, MD: T.J. Publishers.

Baker, Charlotte, and Dennis Cokely. 1980c. *American Sign Language: A student text. Units 19–27.* Silver Spring, MD: T.J. Publishers.

Baker, Charlotte, and Dennis Cokely. 1980d. *American Sign Language: A teacher's resource text on grammar and culture.* Silver Spring, MD: T.J. Publishers.

Baker, Charlotte, and Dennis Cokely. 1980e. Videotapes that accompany *American Sign Language: A student text.* Silver Spring, MD: T.J. Publishers.

Baker, Charlotte, and Carol A. Padden. 1978. Focusing on the nonmanual components of American Sign Language. In *Understanding language through sign language research*, ed. Patricia Siple, 27–57. New York: Academic Press.

Baker, Mark C. 1988. *Incorporation: A theory of grammatical function changing.* Chicago: University of Chicago Press.

Baker, Mark C. 1996. *The polysynthesis parameter*. New York: Oxford University Press.

Baker-Shenk, Charlotte. 1983. A micro-analysis of the nonmanual components of questions in American Sign Language. Doctoral dissertation, University of California, Berkeley.

Baker-Shenk, Charlotte. 1985. The facial behavior of deaf signers: Evidence of a complex language. *American Annals of the Deaf* 130, 297–304.

Baker-Shenk, Charlotte. 1986. Factors affecting the form of question signals in American Sign Language. In *Diversity and diachrony*, ed. David Sankoff, 407–414. Amsterdam: John Benjamins.

Barker, Chris. 1995. *Possessive descriptions*. Stanford, CA: CSLI Publications. [Distributed by Cambridge University Press.]

Battison, Robbin. 1978. *Lexical borrowing in American Sign Language*. Silver Spring, MD: Linstok Press.

Belletti, Adriana. 1990. *Generalized verb movement*. Turin: Rosenberg & Sellier.

Bellugi, Ursula. 1980. How signs express complex meanings. In *Sign language and the deaf community*, eds. Charlotte Baker and Robbin Battison, 53–74. Silver Spring, MD: National Association of the Deaf.

Bellugi, Ursula, David Corina, Freda Norman, Edward Klima, and Judy Reilly. 1989. Differential specialization for linguistic facial expression in left and right lesioned deaf signers. Santa Fe, NM: Academy of Aphasia.

Bellugi, Ursula, and Susan D. Fischer. 1972. A comparison of sign language and spoken language: Rate and grammatical mechanisms. *Cognition* 1, 173–200.

Bergsland, Knut, and Moses Dirks. 1981. *Atkan Aleut school grammar*. Anchorage: University of Alaska, National Bilingual Materials Center.

Bernstein, Judy B. 1993. Topics in the syntax of nominal structure across Romance. Doctoral dissertation, CUNY.

Bittner, Maria, and Ken Hale. 1996. The structural determination of Case and agreement. *Linguistic Inquiry* 27, 1–68.

Blees, Marja, Onno Crasborn, Harry van der Hulst, and Els van der Kooij. 1996. SignPhon: A database tool for phonological analysis of sign languages. Poster presented at TISLR (Theoretical Issues in Sign Language Research) 5, September 19–22, Montreal.

Bobaljik, Jonathan. 1995. Morphosyntax: The syntax of verbal inflection. Doctoral dissertation, MIT.

Borer, Hagit. 1984. *Parametric syntax*. Dordrecht: Foris.

Boster, Carole Tenny. 1996. On the quantifier–noun phrase split in American Sign Language and the structure of quantified noun phrases. In *International review of sign linguistics*, eds. William H. Edmondson and Ronnie B. Wilbur, 159–208. Mahwah, NJ: Lawrence Erlbaum.

Bouchard, Denis. 1997. Sign languages and language universals: The status of order and position in grammar. *Sign Language Studies* 91, 101–160.

Bouchard, Denis, and Colette Dubuisson. 1995. Grammar, order and position of *wh*-signs in Quebec Sign Language. *Sign Language Studies* 87, 99–139.

Boyes Braem, Penny. 1981. Features of the handshape in American Sign Language. Doctoral dissertation, University of California, Berkeley.

Braze, Dave. 1997. Objects, adverbs, and aspect in ASL. In *"Is the Logic Clear?" Papers in honor of Howard Lasnik*, eds. Jeong-Seok Kim, Satoshi Oku, and Sandra Stjepanović, 21–54. (University of Connecticut Working Papers in Linguistics 8.) Storrs, CT: University of Connecticut, Department of Linguistics. [Distributed by MITWPL, Department of Linguistics and Philosophy, MIT.]

Brentari, Diane. 1988. Backward verbs in ASL: Agreement re-opened. In *CLS 24*. Part 2, *Parasession on Agreement in Grammatical Theory*, eds. Diane Brentari, Gary Larson, and Lynn MacLeod, 16–27. Chicago: University of Chicago, Chicago Linguistic Society.

Brentari, Diane. 1990. Theoretical foundations of American Sign Language phonology. Doctoral dissertation, University of Chicago.

Brentari, Diane. 1998. *A prosodic model of sign language phonology*. Cambridge, MA: MIT Press.

Bresnan, Joan. 1976. On the form and functioning of transformations. *Linguistic Inquiry* 7, 3–40.

Bresnan, Joan. 1977. Transformations and categories in syntax. In *Basic problems in methodology and linguistics*, eds. Robert E. Butts and Jaakko Hintikka, 261–282. Dordrecht: D. Reidel.

Brody, Michael. 1995. *Lexico-Logical Form: A radically minimalist theory*. Cambridge, MA: MIT Press.

Cahana-Amitay, Dalia. 1997. Syntactic aspects of the production of verbal inflection in aphasia. Doctoral dissertation, Boston University.

Calabrese, Andrea. 1984. Multiple questions and focus in Italian. In *Sentential complementation: Proceedings of the International Conference held at UFSAL*, eds. Wim de Geest and Yvan Putseys, 67–74. Brussels: Foris.

Campbell, Richard. 1991. Tense and agreement in different tenses. *The Linguistic Review* 8, 159–183.

Campbell, Richard. 1994. Specificity operators in SpecDP. Unpublished manuscript, Oakland University.

Cardinaletti, Anna. 1994. On the internal structure of pronominal DPs. *The Linguistic Review* 11, 195–219.

Carroll, John M., Thomas G. Bever, and Chava R. Pollack. 1981. The non-uniqueness of linguistic intuitions. *Language* 57, 368–383.

Carstens, Vicki. 1991. Morphology and syntax of determiner phrases in Kiswahili. Doctoral dissertation, UCLA.

Charrow, Veda R. 1974. Deaf English: An investigation into the written English competence of deaf adolescents. Doctoral dissertation, Stanford University.

Charrow, Veda R., and Ronnie B. Wilbur. 1975. The deaf child as a linguistic minority. *Theory into Practice* 14, 353–359.

Cheng, Lisa Lai-Shen. 1991. On the typology of *wh*-questions. Doctoral dissertation, MIT.

Chinchor, Nancy. 1978. The structure of the NP in ASL: Arguments from research on numerals. Unpublished manuscript, Brown University.

Chinchor, Nancy. 1981. Numeral incorporation in American Sign Language. Doctoral dissertation, Brown University.

Chinchor, Nancy, Joan Forman, François Grosjean, Michael Hajjar, Judy Kegl, Ella Lentz, Marie Philip, and Ronnie Wilbur. 1976. Sign language research and linguistic universals. In *University of Massachusetts occasional papers in linguistics 2*, ed. Justine Stillings, 70–94. Amherst: University of Massachusetts, GLSA.

Chomsky, Noam. 1970. Remarks on nominalization. In *Readings in English transformational grammar*, eds. Roderick Jacobs and Peter Rosenbaum, 184–221. Waltham, MA: Ginn.

Chomsky, Noam. 1981. *Lectures on government and binding*. Dordrecht: Foris.

Chomsky, Noam. 1982. *Some concepts and consequences of the theory of government and binding*. Cambridge, MA: MIT Press.

Chomsky, Noam. 1986. *Barriers*. Cambridge, MA: MIT Press.

Chomsky, Noam. 1991. Some notes on economy of derivation and representation. In *Principles and parameters in comparative grammar*, ed. Robert Freidin, 417–454. Cambridge, MA: MIT Press.

Chomsky, Noam. 1993. A minimalist program for linguistic theory. In *The view from Building 20*, eds. Kenneth Hale and Samuel Jay Keyser, 1–52. Cambridge, MA: MIT Press.

Chomsky, Noam. 1994. Bare phrase structure. (MIT Occasional Papers in Linguistics 5.) MITWPL, Department of Linguistics and Philosophy, MIT, Cambridge, MA. [Published in *Evolution and revolution in linguistic theory: Essays in honor of Carlos Otero*, eds. Héctor Campos and Paula Kempchinsky, 51–109. Washington, DC: Georgetown University Press, 1995. Also published in *Government and Binding Theory and the Minimalist Program*, ed. Gert Webelhuth, 383–439. Oxford: Blackwell, 1995.]

Chomsky, Noam. 1995a. Categories and transformations. In *The Minimalist Program*, 219–394. Cambridge, MA: MIT Press.

Chomsky, Noam. 1995b. *The Minimalist Program*. Cambridge, MA: MIT Press.

Cinque, Guglielmo. 1994. On the evidence for partial N-movement in the Romance DP. In *Paths towards Universal Grammar: Studies in honor of Richard S. Kayne*, eds. Guglielmo Cinque, Jan Koster, Jean-Yves Pollock, Luigi Rizzi, and Raffaella Zanuttini, 85–110. Washington, DC: Georgetown University Press.

Cinque, Guglielmo. 1999. *Adverbs and functional heads: A cross-linguistic perspective*. New York: Oxford University Press.

Cogen, Cathy. 1977. On three aspects of time expression in ASL. In *On the other hand: New perspectives on American Sign Language*, ed. Lynn Friedman, 197–214. New York: Academic Press.

Cokely, Dennis, and Charlotte Baker-Shenk. 1980. *American Sign Language: A teacher's resource text on curriculum, methods, and evaluation*. Washington, DC: Gallaudet University Press.

Comrie, Bernard. 1976. *Aspect*. Cambridge: Cambridge University Press.

Cooper, William E., and Jeanne Paccia-Cooper. 1980. *Syntax and Speech*. Cambridge, MA: Harvard University Press.

Corina, David P. 1989. Recognition of affective and non-canonical linguistic facial expressions in deaf and hearing subjects. *Brain and Cognition* 9, 227-237.

Cormier, Kearsy. 1998. Grammatical and anaphoric agreement in American Sign Language. Master's thesis, University of Texas at Austin.

Cormier, Kearsy, Stephen Wechsler, and Richard P. Meier. 1999. Locus agreement in American Sign Language. In *Lexical and constructional aspects of linguistic explanation*, eds. Gert Webelhuth, Jean-Pierre Koenig, and Andreas Kathol, 215–229. Stanford, CA: CSLI Publications. [Distributed by Cambridge University Press.]

Corver, Norbert, and Henk van Riemsdijk, eds. 1991. *Studies on scrambling: Movement and nonmovement approaches to free word-order phenomena*. Berlin: Mouton de Gruyter.

Coulter, Geoffrey R. 1979. American Sign Language typology. Doctoral dissertation, University of California, San Diego.

Coulter, Geoffrey R. 1990. Emphatic stress in ASL. In *Theoretical issues in sign language research*. Vol. 1, *Linguistics*, eds. Susan Fischer and Patricia Siple, 109–125. Chicago: University of Chicago Press.

Coulter, Geoffrey R., ed. 1993. *Phonetics and phonology: Current issues in ASL phonology*. Vol. 3. New York: Academic Press.

Cowart, Wayne. 1997. *Experimental syntax: Applying objective methods to sentence judgments*. London: SAGE Publications.

Delsing, Lars-Olof. 1993. The internal structure of noun phrases in the Scandinavian languages. Doctoral dissertation, University of Lund.

De Vriendt, Sera, and Max Rasquinet. 1989. The expression of genericity in sign language. In *Current trends in European sign language research: Proceedings of the 3rd European Congress on Sign Language Research*, eds. Siegmund Prillwitz and Tomas Vollhaber, 249–255. Hamburg: Signum-Verlag.

Dubuisson, Colette. 1996. La collaboration entre linguistes et informateurs sourds: Une question de confiance (Collaboration between linguists and deaf informants: A question of confidence). In *Spécificités de la recherche linguistique sur les langues signées* (Specificities of linguistic research on signed languages), eds. Colette Dubuisson and Denis Bouchard, 205–211. Montréal: Association canadienne-française pour l'avancement des sciences.

Eastman, Carol M., ed. 1992. *Codeswitching.* Philadelphia: Multilingual Matters Ltd.

Ekman, Paul 1992. Facial expression of emotion: An old controversy and new findings. In *Processing the facial image,* ed. Vicki Bruce, 63–69. Oxford: Clarendon Press.

Ekman, Paul and Wallace V. Friesen. 1978. *Facial action coding system.* Palo Alto, CA: Consulting Psychologists Press.

Emmorey, Karen. In press. Space on hand: The exploration of signing space to illustrate abstract thought. In *Spatial schemas and abstract thought,* ed. Meredith Gattis. Cambridge, MA: MIT Press.

Emmorey, Karen, Ursula Bellugi, Angela Friederici, and Petra Horn. 1995. Effects of age of acquisition on grammatical sensitivity: Evidence from on-line and off-line tasks. *Applied Psycholinguistics* 16, 1–23.

Enç, Mürvet. 1991. The semantics of specificity. *Linguistic Inquiry* 22, 1–25. .

Epstein, Samuel David. 1992. Derivational constraints on Ā-chain formation. *Linguistic Inquiry* 23, 235–259.

Fischer, Susan. 1974. Sign language and linguistic universals. In *Actes du Colloque franco-allemand de grammaire transformationnelle: II. Etudes de sémantique et autres* (Acts of the Franco-Germanic Colloquium on Transformational Grammar: II. Semantic and other studies), eds. Christian Rohrer and Nicolas Ruwet, 187–204. Tübingen: Niemeyer.

Fischer, Susan. 1975. Influences on word order change in American Sign Language. In *Word order and word order change,* ed. Charles Li, 1–25. Austin: University of Texas Press.

Fischer, Susan. 1990. The head parameter in ASL. In *SLR '87: Papers from the Fourth International Symposium on Sign Language Research,* eds. William H. Edmondson and Fred Karlsson, 75–85. Hamburg: Signum-Verlag.

Fischer, Susan, and Bonnie Gough. 1978. Verbs in American Sign Language. *Sign Language Studies* 18, 17–48.

Fischer, Susan, and Wynne Janis. 1989. Verb sandwiches in American Sign Language. In *Current trends in European sign language research: Proceedings of the 3rd European Congress on Sign Language Research,* eds. Siegmund Prillwitz and Tomas Vollhaber, 279–293. Hamburg: Signum-Verlag.

Fischer, Susan, and Wynne Janis. 1992. License to derive: Resolving conflicts between syntax and morphology in ASL. Paper presented at the annual meeting of the Linguistic Society of America, Philadelphia, PA.

Fishman, Joshua A. 1971. *Sociolinguistics: A brief introduction.* Rowley, MA: Newbury House.

Fishman, Joshua A. 1972. The sociology of language. In *Language and social context: Selected readings*, ed. Pier Paulo Giglioli. Harmondsworth, England: Penguin Books.

Forman, Joan, and Betsy McDonald. 1978. Investigation into the structure of the NP and the VP. Paper presented at the Sign Language Symposium, MIT.

Fretheim, Thorstein. 1995. Why Norwegian right-dislocated phrases are not afterthoughts. *Nordic Journal of Linguistics* 18, 31–54.

Fretheim, Thorstein. 1996. Pragmatic functions of right dislocation: The Norwegian story. Handout from a talk presented at Boston University, October 1996.

Friedman, Lynn A. 1975. Space, time and person reference in ASL. *Language* 51, 940–961.

Friedman, Lynn A. 1976a. The manifestation of subject, object, and topic in the American Sign Language. In *Subject and topic*, ed. Charles N. Li, 125–148. New York: Academic Press.

Friedman, Lynn A. 1976b. Phonology of a soundless language: Phonological structure of the ASL. Doctoral dissertation, University of California, Berkeley.

Friedman, Lynn A. 1977. Formational properties of American Sign Language. In *On the other hand: New perspectives on American Sign Language*, ed. Lynn A. Friedman, 13–56. New York: Academic Press.

Frishberg, Nancy, and Bonnie Gough. 1973. Time on our hands. Paper presented at the 3rd Annual May California Linguistics Meeting, Stanford, CA.

Gee, James Paul, and Judy Kegl. 1982. Semantic perspicuity and the locative hypothesis: Implications for acquisition. *Journal of Education* 164, 185–209.

Giorgi, Alessandra, and Giuseppe Longobardi. 1991. *The syntax of noun phrases: Configuration, parameters, and empty categories*. Cambridge: Cambridge University Press.

Groat, Erich, and John O'Neil. 1996. Spell-Out at the LF interface. In *Minimal ideas*, eds. Werner Abraham, Samuel David Epstein, Höskuldur Thráinsson, and C. Jan-Wouter Zwart, 113–139. Amsterdam: John Benjamins.

Grohmann, Kleanthes K. 1997. German superiority. In *Groninger Arbeiten in Germanistischer Linguistik 40*, eds. Werner Abraham and Kleanthes K. Grohmann, 97–107. Groningen, The Netherlands: Rijksuniversiteit Groningen, Germanistisch Instituut.

Grohmann, Kleanthes K. 1998. Speculations on the syntax and semantics of German multiple interrogatives. In *University of Maryland working papers in linguistics 6*, eds. Elixabete Murguia, Acrisio Pires, and Lucia Quintana, 71–101. College Park: University of Maryland, Department of Linguistics.

Grosjean, François. 1979. A study of timing in a manual and a spoken language: American Sign Language and English. *Journal of Psycholinguistic Research* 8, 379–405.

Grosjean, François. 1982. *Life with two languages: An introduction to bilingualism*. Cambridge, MA: Harvard University Press.

Gumperz, John J. 1971. *Language in social groups*. Stanford, CA: Stanford University Press.

Gumperz, John J. 1982a. *Discourse strategies*. Cambridge: Cambridge University Press.

Gumperz, John J., ed. 1982b. *Language and social identity*. Cambridge: Cambridge University Press.

Haegeman, Liliane. 1995. *The syntax of negation*. Cambridge: Cambridge University Press.

Haegeman, Liliane. 1997. Elements of grammar. In *Elements of grammar: Handbook in generative syntax*, 1–71. Boston: Kluwer.

Hale, Kenneth, and Samuel Jay Keyser. 1991. On the syntax of argument structure. (Lexicon Project Working Paper 24.) Cambridge, MA: MIT, Center for Cognitive Science.

Hale, Kenneth, and Samuel Jay Keyser. 1993. On argument structure and the lexical expression of syntactic relations. In *The view from Building 20*, eds. Kenneth Hale and Samuel Jay Keyser, 53–109. Cambridge, MA: MIT Press.

Hanke, Thomas, and Siegmund Prillwitz. 1995. SyncWRITER: Integrating video into the transcription and analysis of sign language. In *Sign language research 1994: Proceedings of the Fourth European Congress on Sign Language Research, Munich, September 1–3, 1994*, eds. Heleen F. Bos and Gertrude M. Schermer, 303–312. (International Studies on Sign Language and Communication of the Deaf 29.) Hamburg: Signum.

Hasegawa, Nobuko. 1984–85. On the so-called "zero pronouns" in Japanese. *The Linguistic Review* 4, 289–341.

Haverkort, Marco. 1998. Feature checking and syntactic structure: Some evidence from language development and breakdown. In *Issues in the theory of language acquisition*, eds. Norbert Dittmar and Zvi Penner, 1–17. Bern: Peter Lang.

Heller, Monica, ed. 1988. *Codeswitching*. Berlin: Mouton de Gruyter.

Hoffmeister, Robert J. 1977. The influential point. In *Proceedings of the National Symposium on Sign Language Research and Teaching*, ed. William Stokoe, 177–191. Silver Spring, MD: National Association of the Deaf.

Hoffmeister, Robert J. 1978. The development of demonstrative pronouns, locatives, and personal pronouns in the acquisition of ASL by deaf children of deaf parents. Doctoral dissertation, University of Minnesota.

Hoffmeister, Robert J. 1982. The acquisition of language abilities by deaf children. In *Communication in two societies: Monographs in social aspects of deafness*, eds. Harry Hoemann and Ronnie Wilbur. Washington, DC: Gallaudet University Press.

Holmberg, Anders. 1986. Word order and syntactic features in the Scandinavian languages and English. Doctoral dissertation, University of Stockholm.

Holmberg, Anders. 1993. On the structure of predicate NP. *Studia Linguistica* 47, 126–138.

Hoza, Jack, Carol Neidle, Dawn MacLaughlin, Judy Kegl, and Benjamin Bahan [HNMKB]. 1997. A unified syntactic account of rhetorical questions in American Sign Language. In *Syntactic structure and discourse function: An examination of two constructions in ASL*, eds. Carol Neidle, Dawn MacLaughlin, and Robert G. Lee, 1–23. (Report No. 4.) Boston: Boston University, American Sign Language Linguistic Research Project.

Huang, C.-T. James. 1982. Logical relations in Chinese and the theory of grammar. Doctoral dissertation, MIT.

Huang, C.-T. James. 1984. On the distribution and reference of empty pronouns. *Linguistic Inquiry* 15, 531–574.

Izard, Carroll E. 1971. *The face of emotion*. New York: Appleton-Century-Crofts.

Jackendoff, Ray. 1977. $\bar{X}$ *syntax: A study of phrase structure*. Cambridge, MA: MIT Press.

Jacobowitz, E. Lynn, and William C. Stokoe. 1988. Signs of tense in ASL verbs. *Sign Language Studies* 60, 331–340.

Jaeggli, Osvaldo, and Kenneth J. Safir, eds. 1989. *The null subject parameter*. Dordrecht: Kluwer.

Janis, Wynne. 1995. A crosslinguistic perspective on ASL verb agreement. In *Language, gesture, and space*, eds. Karen Emmorey and Judy S. Reilly, 195–223. Hillsdale, NJ: Lawrence Erlbaum.

Jelinek, Eloise. 1983. Person marking in AUX in Egyptian Arabic. In *Linguistic categories: Auxiliaries and related puzzles*. vol. I, *Categories*, eds. Frank Heny and Barry Richards, 21–46. Dordrecht: Reidel.

Johnson, Robert E., and Scott K. Liddell. 1987. Agreement predicates in American Sign Language. Paper presented at the Fourth International Conference on Sign Language Linguistics, Lapeenranta, Finland.

Kayne, Richard S. 1994. *The antisymmetry of syntax*. Cambridge, MA: MIT Press.

Kegl, Judy. 1975. Some observations on bilingualism: A look at data from Slovene-English bilinguals. Master's thesis, Brown University.

Kegl, Judy. 1976a. Pronominalization in American Sign Language. Unpublished manuscript, MIT.

Kegl, Judy. 1976b. Relational Grammar and American Sign Language. Generals paper, MIT.

Kegl, Judy. 1977. ASL syntax: Research in progress and proposed research. Unpublished manuscript, MIT.

Kegl, Judy. 1981. Discontinuous morphemes in American Sign Language: Verb agreement and aspectual reduplication. Unpublished manuscript, Northeastern University.

Kegl, Judy. 1985a. Causative marking and the construal of agency in ASL. In *CLS 21*. Part 2, *Parasession on Causatives and Agentivity*, eds. William H. Eilfort, Paul D. Kroeber, and Karen L. Peterson, 120–137: Chicago: University of Chicago, Chicago Linguistic Society.

Kegl, Judy. 1985b. Locative relations in American Sign Language word formation, syntax, and discourse. Doctoral dissertation, MIT.

Kegl, Judy, Ella Mae Lentz, and Marie Philip. 1976. ASL pronouns and conditions on their use. Paper presented at the summer meeting of the Linguistic Society of America, Oswego, NY.

Kegl, Judy, Carol Neidle, Dawn MacLaughlin, Jack Hoza, and Benjamin Bahan [KNMHB]. 1996. The case for grammar, order and position in ASL: A reply to Bouchard and Dubuisson. *Sign Language Studies* 90, 1–23.

Kegl, Judy, and Howard Poizner. 1991. The interplay between linguistic and spatial processing in a right lesioned signer. *Journal of Clinical and Experimental Neuropsychology* 13, 38–39.

Kegl, Judy, and Howard Poizner. 1997. Crosslinguistic/Crossmodal syntactic consequences of left-hemisphere damage: Evidence from an aphasic signer and his identical twin. *Aphasiology* 11, 1–37.

Kegl, Judy, and Howard Poizner. 1998. Shifting the burden to the interlocutor: Compensation for pragmatic deficits in signers with Parkinson's disease. *Journal of Neurolinguistics* 11, 137–152.

Kegl, Judy, and Ronnie B. Wilbur. 1976. When does structure stop and style begin? Syntax, morphology, and phonology vs. stylistic variation in American Sign Language. In *Papers from the Twelfth Regional Meeting, Chicago Linguistic Society*, eds. Salikoko S. Mufwene, Carol A. Walker, and Sanford B. Steever, 376–396. Chicago: University of Chicago, Chicago Linguistic Society.

Kitagawa, Yoshihisa. 1986. Subjects in Japanese and English. Doctoral dissertation, University of Massachusetts, Amherst.

Klima, Edward S. 1964. Negation in English. In *The structure of language*, eds. Jerry Fodor and Jerrold Katz, 246–323. Englewood Cliffs, NJ: Prentice-Hall.

Klima, Edward S., and Ursula Bellugi. 1979. *The signs of language*. Cambridge, MA: Harvard University Press.

Koopman, Hilda, and Dominique Sportiche. 1991. The position of subjects. *Lingua* 85, 211–258.

Kuroda, S.-Y. 1988. Whether we agree or not: A comparative syntax of English and Japanese. *Lingvisticæ Investigationes* 12, 1–47.

Labov, William. 1972. *Sociolinguistic patterns*. Philadelphia: University of Pennsylvania Press.

Labov, William. 1975. Empirical foundations of linguistic theory. In *The scope of American linguistics: Papers from the First Golden Anniversary Symposium of the Linguistic Society of America, held at the University of Massachusetts, Amherst on July 24 and 25th*, ed. Robert P. Austerlitz, 77–133. Lisse: Peter de Ridder.

Labov, William. 1989. The exact description of the speech community: Short **a** in Philadelphia. In *Language change and variation*, eds. Ralph Fasold and Deborah Schiffrin, 1–57. Amsterdam: John Benjamins.

Lacy, Rick. 1974. Putting some of the syntax back into semantics. Paper presented at the annual meeting of the Linguistic Society of America, New York, NY.

Lambrecht, Knud. 1994. *Information structure and sentence form: Topic, focus, and the mental representation of discourse referents*. Cambridge: Cambridge University Press.

Lane, Harlan. 1992. *The mask of benevolence: Disabling the deaf community*. New York: Alfred Knopf.

Lane, Harlan, Penny Boyes Braem, and Ursula Bellugi. 1976. Preliminaries to a distinctive feature analysis of American Sign Language. *Cognitive Psychology* 8, 263–289.

Lane, Harlan, Robert J. Hoffmeister, and Benjamin Bahan. 1996. *A journey into the deaf-world*. San Diego, CA: DawnSign Press.

Langacker, Ronald W. 1969. On pronominalization and the chain of command. In *Modern studies in English: Readings in transformational grammar*, eds. David A. Reibel and Sanford A. Schane, 189–215. Englewood Cliffs, NJ: Prentice-Hall.

Lee, Robert G., Carol Neidle, Dawn MacLaughlin, Benjamin Bahan, and Judy Kegl [LNMBK]. 1997. Role shift in ASL: A syntactic look at direct speech. In *Syntactic structure and discourse function: An examination of two constructions in ASL*, eds. Carol Neidle, Dawn MacLaughlin, and Robert G. Lee, 24–45. (Report No. 4.) Boston: Boston University, American Sign Language Linguistic Research Project.

Lelièvre, Linda [*sic*]. 1996. Points de vue d'une assistante de recherche sourde (Perspectives of a deaf research assistant). In *Spécificités de la recherche linguistique sur les langues signées* (Specificities of linguistic research on signed languages), eds. Colette Dubuisson and Denis Bouchard, 197–204. Montréal: Association canadienne-française pour l'avancement des sciences.

Liddell, Scott K. 1977. An investigation into the syntax of American Sign Language. Doctoral dissertation, University of California, San Diego.

Liddell, Scott K. 1980. *American Sign Language syntax*. The Hague: Mouton.

Liddell, Scott K. 1986. Head thrust in ASL conditional marking. *Sign Language Studies* 52, 243–262.

Liddell, Scott K. 1995. Real, surrogate, and token space: Grammatical consequences in ASL. In *Language, gesture, and space*, eds. Karen Emmorey and Judy S. Reilly, 19–41. Hillsdale, NJ: Lawrence Erlbaum.

Liddell, Scott K. 1996. Spatial representations in discourse: Comparing spoken and signed languages. *Lingua* 98, 145–167.

Liddell, Scott K. In press. Blended spaces and deixis in sign language discourse. In *Language and gesture: Window into thought and action*, ed. David McNeill. Cambridge: Cambridge University Press.

Lillo-Martin, Diane. 1986. Two kinds of null arguments in American Sign Language. *Natural Language and Linguistic Theory* 4, 415–444.

Lillo-Martin, Diane. 1990. Parameters for questions: Evidence from *wh*-movement in ASL. In *Sign language research: Theoretical issues*, ed. Ceil Lucas, 211–222. Washington, DC: Gallaudet University Press.

Lillo-Martin, Diane. 1991. *Universal Grammar and American Sign Language.* Dordrecht: Kluwer.

Lillo-Martin, Diane. 1992. Sentences as islands: On the boundedness of Ā-movement in American Sign Language. In *Island constraints*, eds. Helen Goodluck and Michael Rochemont, 259–274. Dordrecht: Kluwer.

Lillo-Martin, Diane. 1995. The point of view predicate in American Sign Language. In *Language, gesture, and space*, eds. Karen Emmorey and Judy S. Reilly, 155–170. Hillsdale, NJ: Lawrence Erlbaum.

Lillo-Martin, Diane, Carole T. Boster, Kazumi Matsuoka, and Michiko Nohara. 1996. Early and late in language acquisition: Aspects of *wh*-questions in American Sign Language. In *Papers in honor of Stephen Crain: Language acquisition and processing*, eds. Kazumi Matsuoka and Anne Halbert, 13–24. (University of Connecticut Working Papers in Linguistics 6.) Storrs: University of Connecticut, Department of Linguistics. [Distributed by MITWPL, Department of Linguistics and Philosophy, MIT.]

Lillo-Martin, Diane, and Susan Fischer. 1992. Overt and covert *wh*-questions in American Sign Language. Paper presented at the 5th International Symposium on Sign Language Research, May 26, Salamanca, Spain.

Lillo-Martin, Diane, and Edward S. Klima. 1990. Pointing out differences: ASL pronouns in syntactic theory. In *Theoretical issues in sign language research.* Vol. 1, *Linguistics*, eds. Susan D. Fischer and Patricia Siple, 191–210. Chicago: University of Chicago Press.

Loew, Ruth C. 1984. Roles and reference in American Sign Language: A developmental perspective. Doctoral dissertation, University of Minnesota.

Loew, Ruth C., Judy Kegl, and Howard Poizner. 1997. Fractionation of the components of role play in a right-hemispheric lesioned signer. *Aphasiology* 11, 263–281.

Longobardi, Giuseppe. 1994. Reference and proper names: A theory of N-movement in syntax and Logical Form. *Linguistic Inquiry* 22, 609–665.

Lucas, Ceil, and Clayton Valli. 1989. Language contact in the American deaf community. In *The sociolinguistics of the deaf community*, ed. Ceil Lucas, 11–40. San Diego, CA: Academic Press.

Lucas, Ceil, and Clayton Valli. 1990a. ASL, English and contact signing. In *Sign language research: Theoretical issues*, ed. Ceil Lucas, 288–307. Washington, DC: Gallaudet University Press.

Lucas, Ceil, and Clayton Valli. 1990b. *Language contact in the American deaf community.* New York: Academic Press.

Lucas, Ceil, and Clayton Valli. 1990c. Predicates of perceived motion in ASL. In *Theoretical issues in sign language research.* Vol. 1, *Linguistics*, eds. Susan D. Fischer and Patricia Siple, 153–166. Chicago: University of Chicago Press.

MacLaughlin, Dawn. 1997. The structure of determiner phrases: Evidence from American Sign Language. Doctoral dissertation, Boston University.

MacLaughlin, Dawn, Carol Neidle, and Robert G. Lee [MNL]. 1996. Design specifications for SignStream™, a multimedia database tool for language research. (Report No. 3.) Boston: Boston University, American Sign Language Linguistic Research Project.

MacLaughlin, Dawn, Carol Neidle, Robert G. Lee, and David Greenfield [MNLG]. 1998. SignStream user's guide, version 1.0. (Report No. 7.) Boston: Boston University, American Sign Language Linguistic Research Project.

MacWhinney, Brian. 1995. *The CHILDES project: Tools for analyzing talk.* Hillsdale, NJ: Lawrence Erlbaum.

Mahajan, Anoop. 1991. Operator movement, agreement and referentiality. In *More papers on wh-movement*, eds. Lisa L. S. Cheng and Hamida Demirdache, 77–96. (MIT Working Papers in Linguistics 15.) Cambridge, MA: MIT, Department of Linguistics and Philosophy, MITWPL.

Matsuoka, Kazumi. 1997. Verb raising in American Sign Language. *Lingua* 103, 127–149.

Mayberry, Rachel. 1993. First-language acquisition after childhood differs from second-language acquisition: The case of American Sign Language. *Journal of Speech and Hearing* 36, 1258–1270.

Mayberry, Rachel. 1994. The importance of childhood to language acquisition: Insights from American Sign Language. In *The development of speech perception: The transition from speech sounds to spoken words*, eds. Judith Goodman and Howard Nusbaum, 57–90. Cambridge, MA: MIT Press.

Mayberry, Rachel, and Ellen B. Eichen. 1991. The long-lasting advantage of learning sign language in childhood: Another look at the critical period for language acquisition. *Journal of Memory and Language* 30, 486–512.

Mayberry, Rachel, and Susan Fischer. 1989. Looking through phonological shape to lexical meaning: The bottleneck of non-native sign language processing. *Memory and Cognition* 17, 750–754.

McCloskey, James. 1979. *Transformational syntax and model-theoretic semantics: A case study in Modern Irish.* Dordrecht: Reidel.

McCloskey, James. 1997. Subjecthood and subject positions. In *Elements of grammar: Handbook in generative syntax*, ed. Liliane Haegeman, 197–235. Boston: Kluwer.

McCloskey, James, and Ken Hale. 1983. The syntax of inflection in Modern Irish. In *Proceedings of NELS 13*, eds. Peter Sells and Charles Jones, 173–190. Amherst: University of Massachusetts, GLSA.

McDonald, Betsy. 1982. Aspects of the American Sign Language predicate system. Doctoral dissertation, State University of New York at Buffalo.

McIntire, Marina L., Don Newkirk, Sandra Hutchins, and Howard Poizner. 1987. Hands and faces: A preliminary inventory for written ASL. *Sign Language Studies* 56, 197–241.

McIntire, Marina L., and Judy Snitzer Reilly. 1988. Nonmanual behaviors in L1 and L2 learners of American Sign Language. *Sign Language Studies* 61, 351–375.

McIntire, Marina L., Judy S. Reilly, and Diane Anderson. 1994. Two forms of negation—or NOT. Paper presented at the 18th Boston University Conference on Language Development, Boston, MA.

Meier, Richard P. 1981. Icons and morphemes: Models of the acquisition of verb agreement in ASL. *Papers and Reports on Child Language Development* 20, 92–99.

Meier, Richard P. 1982. Icons, analogues, and morphemes: The acquisition of verb agreement in ASL. Doctoral dissertation, University of California, San Diego.

Meier, Richard P. 1990. Person deixis in American Sign Language. In *Theoretical issues in sign language research*. Vol. 1, *Linguistics*, eds. Susan D. Fischer and Patricia Siple, 175–190. Chicago: University of Chicago Press.

Meier, Richard P. 1993. A psycholinguistic perspective on phonological segmentation in sign and speech. In *Phonetics and phonology: current issues in ASL phonology*, ed. Geoffrey R. Coulter, 169–188. New York: Academic Press.

Meier, Richard P., and Elissa Newport. 1990. Out of the hands of babes: On a possible sign advantage in language acquisition. *Language* 66, 1–23.

Metlay, Donald S., and Ted Supalla. 1995. Morpho-syntactic structure of aspect and number inflections in ASL. In *Language, gesture, and space*, eds. Karen Emmorey and Judy S. Reilly, 255–284. Hillsdale, NJ: Lawrence Erlbaum.

Milroy, Lesley, and Pieter Muysken, eds. 1995. *One speaker, two languages: Cross-disciplinary perspectives on code-switching*. Cambridge: Cambridge University Press.

Miyagawa, Shigeru. 1987. *Wa* and the *wh* phrase. In *Perspectives on topicalization: The case of Japanese wa*, eds. John Hinds, Senko K. Maynard, and Shoichi Iwasaki, 185–217. Amsterdam: John Benjamins.

Moores, Donald. 1987. *Educating the deaf: Psychology, principles, and practices*. Boston: Houghton Mifflin.

Mougeon, Raymond, and Terry Nadasdi. 1998. Sociolinguistic discontinuity in minority language communities. *Language* 74, 40–55.

Neidle, Carol, Benjamin Bahan, Dawn MacLaughlin, Robert G. Lee, and Judy Kegl [NBMLK]. 1998. Realizations of syntactic agreement in American Sign Language: Similarities between the clause and the noun phrase. *Studia Linguistica* 52, 191–226.

Neidle, Carol, Judy Kegl, and Benjamin Bahan [NKB]. 1994. The architecture of functional categories in American Sign Language. Talk presented at Harvard University, Cambridge, MA, May 1994.

Neidle, Carol, Judy Kegl, Benjamin Bahan, and Debra Aarons [NKBA]. 1994. Rightward *wh*-Movement in American Sign Language. Paper presented at the Tilburg Conference on Rightward Movement, Tilburg, The Netherlands.

Neidle, Carol, Judy Kegl, Benjamin Bahan, Debra Aarons, and Dawn MacLaughlin [NKBAM]. 1997. Rightward *wh*-movement in American Sign Language. In *Rightward movement*, eds. Dorothee Beerman [*sic*], David LeBlanc, and Henk van Riemsdijk, 247–278. Philadelphia: John Benjamins.

Neidle, Carol, and Dawn MacLaughlin [NM]. 1998. SignStream™: A tool for linguistic research on signed languages. *Sign Language & Linguistics* 1, 111–114.

Neidle, Carol, Dawn MacLaughlin, Robert G. Lee, Benjamin Bahan, and Judy Kegl [NMLBK]. 1997. The SignStream™ project. (Report No. 5.) Boston: Boston University, American Sign Language Linguistic Research Project.

Neidle, Carol, Dawn MacLaughlin, Robert G. Lee, Benjamin Bahan, and Judy Kegl [NMLBK]. 1998a. The right(ward) analysis of *wh*-movement in ASL. *Language* 74, 819–831.

Neidle, Carol, Dawn MacLaughlin, Robert G. Lee, Benjamin Bahan, and Judy Kegl [NMLBK]. 1998b. *Wh*-questions in ASL: A case for rightward movement. (Report No. 6.) Boston: Boston University, American Sign Language Linguistic Research Project.

Newkirk, Don. 1976. Outline for a proposed orthography for American Sign Language. Unpublished manuscript, The Salk Institute for Biological Studies.

Newkirk, Don. 1979. The form of the continuative aspect on ASL verbs. Unpublished manuscript, The Salk Institute for Biological Studies.

Newkirk, Don. 1981. *SignFont handbook*. San Diego, CA: Emerson and Stern Associates.

Newport, Elissa. 1988. Constraints on learning and their role in language acquisition: Studies of the acquisition of American Sign Language. *Language Sciences* 10, 147–172.

Newport, Elissa. 1990. Maturational constraints on language learning. *Cognitive Science* 14, 11–28.

Newport, Elissa, and Richard P. Meier. 1985. The acquisition of American Sign Language. In *The crosslinguistic study of language acquisition*. Vol. 1, *The data*, ed. Dan Isaac Slobin, 881–938. Hillsdale, NJ: Lawrence Erlbaum.

Newport, Elissa, and Ted Supalla. 1980. The structuring of language: Clues from the acquisition of signed and spoken language. In *Signed and spoken language: Biological constraints on linguistic form*, eds. Ursula Bellugi and Michael Studdert-Kennedy, 187–212. Dahlem Konferenzen. Weinheim: Verlag Chemie.

Nover, Stephen. 1993. Who will shape the future of deaf education. *Deaf American* 43, 117–123.

Ouhalla, Jamal. 1991a. *Functional categories and parametric variation*. London: Routledge.

Ouhalla, Jamal. 1991b. Functional categories and the head parameter. Paper presented at the 14th GLOW Colloquium, Leiden.

Padden, Carol A. 1983. Interaction of morphology and syntax in American Sign Language. Doctoral dissertation, University of California, San Diego.

Padden, Carol A. 1988. *Interaction of morphology and syntax in American Sign Language*. New York: Garland.

Padden, Carol A. 1990. The relation between space and grammar in ASL verb morphology. In *Sign language research: Theoretical issues*, ed. Ceil Lucas, 118–132. Washington, DC: Gallaudet University Press.

Padden, Carol A., and Tom Humphries. 1988. *Deaf in America: Voices from a culture*. Cambridge, MA: Harvard University Press.

Padden, Carol A., and David M. Perlmutter. 1987. American Sign Language and the architecture of phonological theory. *Natural Language and Linguistic Theory* 5, 335–375.

Patrie, Carol. 1994. Educational interpreting: Who leads the way? *Registry of Interpreters for the Deaf Views* 11(2), 1, 19–20.

Perlmutter, David. 1991. The language of the deaf. *New York Review of Books*, March 28, 65–72.

Perlmutter, David. 1992. Sonority and syllable structure in American Sign Language. *Linguistic Inquiry* 23, 407–442.

Pesetsky, David. 1987. *Wh*-in-situ: Movement and unselective binding. In *The representation of (in)definiteness*, eds. Eric Reuland and Alice ter Meulen, 98–129. Cambridge, MA: MIT Press.

Pesetsky, David. 1997. Optimality Theory and syntax: Movement and pronunciation. In *Optimality Theory: An overview*, eds. Diana Archangeli and D. Terence Langendoen, 134–170. Malden, MA: Blackwell.

Petitto, Laura. 1983. From gesture to symbol: The acquisition of personal pronouns in American Sign Language. Doctoral dissertation, Harvard University.

Petitto, Laura, and Paula Marentette. 1991. Babbling in the manual mode: Evidence for the ontogeny of language. *Science* 251, 1493–1496.

Petronio, Karen. 1991. A focus position in ASL. In *Papers from the Third Student Conference in Linguistics*, eds. Jonathan Bobaljik and Tony Bures, 211–225. (MIT Working Papers in Linguistics 14.) Cambridge, MA: MIT, Department of Linguistics and Philosophy, MITWPL.

Petronio, Karen. 1993. Clause structure in American Sign Language. Doctoral dissertation, University of Washington, Seattle.

Petronio, Karen, and Diane Lillo-Martin. 1995. The direction of *wh*-movement in ASL. Paper presented at the annual meeting of the Linguistic Society of America, New Orleans.

Petronio, Karen, and Diane Lillo-Martin. 1997. WH-movement and the position of spec-CP: Evidence from American Sign Language. *Language* 73, 18–57.

Poizner, Howard, and Judy Kegl. 1992. The neural basis of language and motor behaviour: Perspectives from American Sign Language. *Aphasiology* 6, 219–256.

Pollock, Jean-Yves. 1989. Verb movement, Universal Grammar, and the structure of IP. *Linguistic Inquiry* 20, 365–424.

Pollock, Jean-Yves. 1997. Notes on clause structure. In *Elements of grammar*, ed. Liliane Haegeman, 237–279. Dordrecht: Kluwer.

Postal, Paul M. 1969. On so-called "pronouns" in English. In *Modern studies in English: Readings in transformational grammar*, eds. David A. Reibel and Sanford A. Schane, 201–224. Englewood Cliffs, NJ: Prentice-Hall.

Poulin, Christine. 1994. Null arguments and referential shift in American Sign Language. In *SCIL VI: Proceedings of the Sixth Annual Student Conference in Linguistics*, eds. Chris Giordano and Daniel Ardron, 267–281. (MIT Working Papers in Linguistics 23.) Cambridge, MA: MIT, Department of Linguistics and Philosophy, MITWPL.

Prillwitz, Siegmund, Regina Leven, Heiko Zienert, Thomas Hanke, and Jan Henning. 1989. HamNoSys. Version 2.0; Hamburg Notation System for Sign Languages: An introductory guide. (International Studies on Sign Language and Communication of the Deaf 5.) Hamburg: Signum.

Radford, Andrew. 1993. Head-hunting: On the trail of the nominal Janus. In *Heads in grammatical theory*, eds. Greville G. Corbett, Norman M. Fraser, and Scott McGlashan, 73–113. Cambridge: Cambridge University Press.

Reilly, Judy Snitzer, and Ursula Bellugi. 1996. Competition on the face: Affect and language in ASL Motherese. *Journal of Child Language* 23, 219–239.

Reilly, Judy Snitzer, Marina L. McIntire, and Ursula Bellugi. 1990. Faces: The relationship between language and affect. In *From gesture to language in hearing and deaf children*, eds. Virginia Volterra and Carol J. Erting, 128–141. New York: Springer-Verlag.

Reinhart, Tanya. 1976. The syntactic domain of anaphora. Doctoral dissertation, MIT.

Ritter, Elizabeth. 1991. Two functional categories in noun phrases: Evidence from Modern Hebrew. In *Perspectives on phrase structure: Heads and licensing*, ed. Susan D. Rothstein, 37–62. (Syntax and Semantics 25.) New York: Academic Press.

Rizzi, Luigi. 1982a. *Issues in Italian syntax*. Dordrecht: Foris.

Rizzi, Luigi. 1982b. Violations of the *Wh* Island Constraint and the Subjacency Condition. In *Issues in Italian syntax*, 49–76. Dordrecht: Foris.

Rizzi, Luigi. 1986. Null objects in Italian and the theory of *pro*. *Linguistic Inquiry* 17, 501–557.

Rizzi, Luigi. 1991. Residual verb second and the *Wh*-Criterion. (Technical Reports in Formal and Computational Linguistics.) Geneva: Université de Genève.

Rizzi, Luigi. 1997. The fine structure of the left periphery. In *Elements of grammar: Handbook in generative syntax*, ed. Liliane Haegeman, 281–337. Dordrecht: Kluwer.

Rochemont, Michael S. 1986. *Focus in generative grammar*. Philadelphia: John Benjamins.

Romano, Christine. 1991. Mixed headedness in American Sign Language: Evidence from functional categories. In *Papers from the Third Student Conference in Linguistics*, eds. Jonathan Bobaljik and Tony Bures, 241–254. (MIT Working Papers in Linguistics 14.) Cambridge, MA: MIT, Department of Linguistics and Philosophy, MITWPL.

Rosen, Sarah. 1989. Argument structure and complex predicates. Doctoral dissertation, Brandeis University. [Published by Garland, New York, 1990.]

Ross, Danielle, and Elissa Newport. 1996. The development of language from non-native linguistic input. In *Proceedings of the 20th Annual Boston University Conference on Language Development*, eds. Andy Stringfellow, Dalia Cahana-Amitay, Elizabeth Hughes, and Andrea Zukowski, 634–645. Somerville, MA: Cascadilla Press.

Samek-Lodovici, Vieri. 1993. Italian's postverbal focus position and its role in postverbal *wh*-extraction. Unpublished manuscript, Rutgers University.

Sandler, Wendy. 1987. Sequentiality and simultaneity in American Sign Language phonology. Doctoral dissertation, University of Texas.

Sandler, Wendy. 1989. *Phonological representation of the sign: Linearity and non-linearity in American Sign Language*. Dordrecht: Foris.

Schein, Jerome D. and Marcus T. Delk. 1974. *The deaf population of the United States*. Silver Spring, MD: National Association of the Deaf.

Schick, Brenda S. 1987. The acquisition of classifier predicates in American Sign Language. Doctoral dissertation, Purdue University.

Schick, Brenda S. 1990. The effects of morphosyntactic structure on the acquisition of classifier predicates in ASL. In *Sign language research: Theoretical issues*, ed. Ceil Lucas, 358–374. Washington, DC: Gallaudet University Press.

Schick, Brenda S., and Mary Pat Moeller. 1992. What is learnable in manually coded English sign systems. *Applied Psycholinguistics* 13, 313–340.

Schütze, Carson T. 1996. *The empirical base of linguistics: Grammaticality judgments and linguistic methodology*. Chicago: University of Chicago Press.

Selkirk, Elisabeth O. 1984. *Phonology and syntax: The relation between sound and structure*. Cambridge, MA: MIT Press.

Shepard-Kegl, James, Carol Neidle, and Judy Kegl. 1995. Legal ramifications of an incorrect analysis of tense in ASL. *Journal of Interpretation* 7, 53–70.

Simpson, J. M. Y. 1981. The challenge of minority languages. In *Minority languages today*, eds. Einar Haugen, J. Derrick McClure, and Derick Thomson, 235–241. Edinburgh: Edinburgh University Press.

Singleton, Jenny. 1989. Restructuring of language from impoverished input. Doctoral dissertation, University of Illinois, Urbana-Champaign.

Singleton, Jenny, and Elissa Newport. 1987. Constraints on learning: Studies in the acquisition of American Sign Language. *Papers and Reports on Child Language Development* 23, 1–22.

Singleton, Jenny, and Elissa Newport. 1994. When learners surpass their models: The acquisition of American Sign Language from impoverished input. Unpublished manuscript, University of Illinois, Urbana-Champaign.

Siple, Patricia. 1978. Visual Constraints for sign language communication. *Sign language studies* 19:7, 95–110.

Speas, Margaret. 1986. Adjunctions and projections in syntax. Doctoral dissertation, MIT.

Stokoe, William C. 1960. Sign language structure: An outline of the visual communication systems of the American deaf. (Studies in Linguistics Occasional Papers 8.) Buffalo, NY: University of Buffalo, Department of Anthropology and Linguistics.

Stokoe, William C., Dorothy C. Casterline, and Carl G. Croneberg. 1965. *A dictionary of American Sign Language on linguistic principles.* Silver Spring, MD: Linstok Press.

Stowell, Timothy A. 1991. Determiners in NP and DP. In *Views on phrase structure*, eds. Katherine Leffel and Denis Bouchard, 37–56. Dordrecht: Kluwer.

Suñer, Margarita. 1993. About indirect questions and semi-questions. *Linguistics and Philosophy* 16, 45–77.

Supalla, Samuel J. 1986. The classifier system in American Sign Language. In *Noun classes and categorization*, ed. Colette Craig, 181–214. Amsterdam: John Benjamins.

Supalla, Samuel J. 1991. Manually coded English: The modality question in signed language development. In *Theoretical issues in sign language research.* Vol. 2, *Psychology*, eds. Patricia Siple and Susan D. Fischer, 85–109. Chicago: University of Chicago Press.

Supalla, Ted. 1982. Structure and acquisition of verbs of motion and location in ASL. Doctoral dissertation, University of California, San Diego.

Supalla, Ted. 1990. Serial verbs of motion in ASL. In *Theoretical issues in sign language research.* Vol. 1, *Linguistics*, eds. Susan D. Fischer and Patricia Siple, 127–152. Chicago: University of Chicago Press.

Supalla, Ted. 1996. An implicational hierarchy in verb agreement in American Sign Language. Unpublished manuscript, University of Rochester.

Supalla, Ted, and Elissa L. Newport. 1978. How many seats in a chair? The derivation of nouns and verbs in ASL. In *Understanding language through sign language research*, ed. Patricia Siple, 91–132. New York: Academic Press.

Sutton, Valerie. 1981. *Signwriting for everyday use.* Boston: The Sutton Movement Writing Press.

Szabolcsi, Anna. 1987. Functional categories in the noun phrase. In *Approaches to Hungarian.* Vol. II, *Theories and analyses*, ed. István Kenesei, 167–189. Szeged: JATE.

Taraldsen, Knut Tarald. 1980. On the Nominative Island Condition, vacuous application, and the *That*-Trace Filter. Bloomington: Indiana University Linguistics Club.

Taraldsen, Knut Tarald. 1990. D-projections and N-projections in Norwegian. In *Grammar in progress: GLOW essays for Henk van Riemsdijk*, eds. Joan Mascaró and Marina Nespor, 419–431. Dordrecht: Foris.

Tervoort, Bernard T. 1968. You me downtown movie fun? *Lingua* 21, 455–465.

Thráinsson, Höskuldur. 1996. On the (non-)universality of functional categories. In *Minimal ideas*, eds. Werner Abraham, Samuel David Epstein, Höskuldur Thráinsson, and C. Jan-Wouter Zwart, 253–281. Amsterdam: John Benjamins.

Travis, Lisa. 1984. Parameters and effects of word order variation. Doctoral dissertation, MIT.

Uyechi, Linda. 1996. *The geometry of visual phonology*. Cambridge: Cambridge University Press.

Valois, Daniel. 1991. The internal syntax of DP. Doctoral dissertation, UCLA.

Veinberg, Silvana C., and Ronnie B. Wilbur. 1990. A linguistic analysis of negative headshake in American Sign Language. *Sign Language Studies* 68, 217–244.

Vikner, Sten. 1991. Verb movement and the licensing of NP positions in the Germanic languages. Doctoral dissertation, Université Genève.

Webelhuth, Gert, ed. 1995. *Government and Binding Theory and the Minimalist Program*. Oxford: Blackwell.

Wilbur, Ronnie B. 1979. *American Sign Language and sign systems: Research and application*. Baltimore, MD: University Park Press.

Wilbur, Ronnie B. 1990. An experimental investigation of stressed sign production. *International Journal of Sign Linguistics* 1, 41–59.

Wilbur, Ronnie B. 1994a. Arguments for sentential subjects in ASL. In *Perspectives on sign language structure: Papers from the Fifth International Symposium on Sign Language Research*, eds. Inger Ahlgren, Brita Bergman, and Mary Brennan, 215–235. Durham: International Sign Language Linguistics Association.

Wilbur, Ronnie B. 1994b. Foregrounding structures in American Sign Language. *Journal of Pragmatics* 22, 647–672.

Wilbur, Ronnie B. 1995. What the morphology of operators looks like: A formal analysis of ASL brow raise. In *FLSM VI: Proceedings of the Sixth Annual Meeting of the Formal Linguistics Society of Mid-America*, eds. Leslie Gabriele, Debra Hardison, and Robert Westmoreland, 67–78. Bloomington: Indiana University Linguistics Club.

Wilbur, Ronnie B. 1996. Evidence for the function and structure of *wh*-clefts in American Sign Language. In *International review of sign linguistics*, eds. William H. Edmondson and Ronnie B. Wilbur, 209–256. Mahwah, NJ: Lawrence Erlbaum.

Wilbur, Ronnie B., and Cynthia G. Patschke. 1998. Body leans and the marking of contrast in American Sign Language. *Journal of Pragmatics* 30, 275–303.

Wilbur, Ronnie B., and Brenda Schick. 1987. The effects of linguistic stress on ASL signs. *Language and Speech* 4, 301–323.

Winston, Elizabeth A. 1991. Spatial referencing and cohesion in an American Sign Language text. *Sign Language Studies* 73, 397–409.

Woodward, James. 1973. Deaf awareness. *Sign Language Studies* 2, 57–60.

Woodward, James. 1974. Implicational variation in American Sign Language: Negative incorporation. *Sign Language Studies* 5, 20–30.

Woodward, James. 1976. Black southern signing. *Language in Society* 5, 211–218.

Woodward, James, and Carol Erting. 1975. Synchronic variation and historical change in American Sign Language. *Language Science* 37, 9–12.

Woolford, Ellen. 1991. VP-internal subjects in VSO and nonconfigurational languages. *Linguistic Inquiry* 22, 503–540.

Wu, Jianxin. 1996. *Wh*-topic, *wh*-focus, and *wh*-in-situ. In *University of Maryland working papers in linguistics 4*, eds. Juan Carlos Castillo, Viola Miglio, and Julien Musolino, 173–192. College Park: University of Maryland, Linguistics Department.

Xu, Liejiong and D. T. Langendoen. 1985. Topic structures in Chinese. *Language* 61, 1–27.

Zagona, Karen. 1982. Government and proper government of verbal projections. Doctoral dissertation, University of Washington, Seattle.

Zamparelli, Roberto. 1995. Layers in the determiner phrase. Doctoral dissertation, University of Rochester.

Zimmer, June, and Cynthia Patschke. 1990. A class of determiners in ASL. In *Sign language research: Theoretical issues*, ed. Ceil Lucas, 201–210. Washington, DC: Gallaudet University Press.

Index of ASL Glosses

Subject Index

Object agreement, 34
  definite form, 34, 69
  indefinite form, 34, 69
  inflection, 33, 35
  nonmanual expression of, 65, 69
Object shift
  in ASL, 173n.17, 175n.5
  in Germanic, 35
Oralism. *See* Education of the deaf

Padden, C., 11, 29, 33, 111, 171n.8
Patschke, C., 18, 181n.6
Perlmutter, D., 111, 133
Perseveration, 45–47
  of agreement marking in DP, 46–47
  of classifier handshapes, 45
  of intensity, 118–121, 123–124, 170n.41, 189n.23
  manual, 45, 118
  of nondominant handshape, 118, 189n.20
  nonmanual, 46–47, 119, 170n.41
  of rh/wh marking, 125–126
  of *wh*-marking, 118–121, 189n.22
  of y-n marking, 123–124
Person distinctions, 36, 166–167n.14
  first person as unmarked form, 167n.21
Person features. *See* Features, agreement, person
Pesetsky, D., 187n.10
Petitto, L., 9
Petronio, K.
  distribution of nonmanual markings, 132, 138–139, 144, 169n.39, 169n.40, 173n.13, 193n.50, 194n.57, 194–195n.58
  focus position (*see* C, as clause-final position for focused elements)
  null elements (*see* Null elements posited by Petronio and Lillo-Martin)
  pooling of judgments, 164n.22
  rhetorical questions, 126, 190n.29, 191n.33
  wh-constructions, 114, 128–144, 193n.49
Phi-features. *See* Features, agreement
Phonemes, 27–29
Poizner, H., 40
Pollock, J.-Y., 63, 76, 83
Possession, inalienable, 95
Possessive DPs, 93–96, 100, 102, 182n.14
  compared with transitive clauses, 104–106
  as definite DPs, 96–97, 99–100, 102
  with definite vs. indefinite possessor, 94–95, 102
  structure of, 95
  wh-possessives, 94–95, 136, 183n.17, 193n.49
Possessive marker, 32, 101–102, 184n.17
  agreement with possessor, 97

articulation of, 32, 94–95, 182n.15
  in D, 96
  neutral form, 94–95, 101
  omission of, 95, 183n.17
Postal, P., 91
pro. See Null arguments
Projections
  agreement (*see* Agreement projections)
  aspect (*see* Aspect, position of projection in clause)
  determiner (*see* Determiner phrases)
  lexical vs. functional, 161n.1
  tense (*see* Tense)
Pronouns, 31, 91–92
  articulation of, 31, 33
  numeral incorporation, 167n.16
Proximity, 42–43

Questions. *See* Indirect questions; Rhetorical questions; Semiquestions; *Wh*-questions; Yes-no questions

Radford, A., 87
Reference
  indefinite, 90
  pronominal, 36
  unambiguous character of, 36, 168n.26
  use of space for (*see* Space, referential use of)
Reflexives, articulation of, 32
Register, 15
  formal, 12, 16
  "whisper," 183n.21
Reilly, J., 40
Residential schools. *See* Education of the deaf
Rhetorical question answer sequences, 124–126
  differing analyses of, 126, 191n.31, 191n.32
Rhetorical questions, 124–126
  compared with *wh*-questions, 126, 129, 190n.29, 191n.33
  extraction from embedded clauses, 125–126
  structure of, 125, 190n.29, 191n.31, 191n.32
Right dislocation, 55–56, 58, 59, 171–172n.8, 172n.10
  distinguished from tags, 57–58, 172n.9
  on nonexistence of in ASL, 56
Rizzi, L., 71, 111
"Role prominence," 161n.4, 174n.1, 180n.31
Role shift, 174n.4, 176n.10
Romano, C., 174n.5

Breinigsville, PA USA
20 May 2010
238434BV00005B/25/P